NEW
ENGLISH DRAMATISTS
8

INTRODUCED BY JOHN RUSSELL TAYLOR

COCKADE
Charles Wood

THE TRIGON
James Broom Lynne

ENTERTAINING MR SLOANE
Joe Orton

PENGUIN BOOKS

Penguin Books Ltd, Harmondsworth, Middlesex, England

—

Cockade
Published in Penguin Books 1965
Copyright © Charles Wood, 1965

—

The Trigon
First published by Jonathan Cape 1964
Published in Penguin Books 1965
Copyright © James Broom Lynne, 1964

—

Entertaining Mr Sloane
First published by Hamish Hamilton 1964
Published in Penguin Books 1965
Copyright © Joe Orton, 1964

—

Made and printed in Great Britain by
Hazell Watson & Viney Ltd
Aylesbury, Bucks
Set in Monotype Bembo

CONTENTS

INTRODUCTION

THE main problem in appreciating what modern artists are doing is as often as not knowing where to start. What does the artist bring to the creation of his work of art, in the way of received ideas, mental furniture, moral assumptions? What does he expect us to bring? How far are we in danger of radically misunderstanding what he is saying because we obstinately persist in going into the theatre, the cinema, or the art gallery expecting him to be saying something different, and then get puzzled and irritable because he does not live up to our misplaced expectations; or, worse, come out convinced whatever he may do or say that he has after all been doing precisely what we expected him to do from the first?

Easy enough to be superior about such mistakes, but when a work of art is successful enough in abstracting itself from preaching and message-mongering a word of guidance can often be invaluable to put us in the right frame of mind. It is helpful to know, for instance, that whatever we the viewers may think of 'clinical' modern architecture and the stark, industrial landscapes of the modern city, Antonioni likes them and finds them exciting, so that if we assume from the outset in his films that such settings must be intended to reflect the sterility of the characters' lives, we shall be wrong. In the same way, it is important to know from the outset when watching or reading plays by Charles Wood, the first dramatist represented in this volume, that he loves the army; he may go along with the attitudes which we would expect of a dramatist of his age (he was born in 1932) so far as to be anti-war, but anti-army, not at all – it is for him a subject of nostalgia rather than ridicule or righteous indignation.

Of the three one-act plays which make up Charles Wood's triple bill *Cockade*, two, *Prisoner and Escort* and *Spare*, are directly about the army and its way of life, while the third, *John Thomas*, is in a way about the military experience, the effect of uniform, the importance of authority and attitudes towards it, even though the subject is placed in an entirely civilian context. Of the three, *Prisoner and Escort* is much the most direct in its style, though if we look for any easy, direct message to go with the style we shall be disappointed. It concerns a prisoner being taken by train to a military prison, the two soldiers escorting him there, and a girl who gets involved with them along the way. The escort are respectively a leering, juvenile sadist and a parrot-like idiot trying constantly to live up to his company and surroundings in both knowingness and brutality. The prisoner is a born victim, edgy, difficult and ineffectual, too muddled to explain his actions even to himself, let alone anyone else. His main crime, it seems, though not by any means his only one, has been urinating on a German officer's boots during some combined Anglo-German parade in Germany. Why did he do it; what was he trying to prove? He insists that he is not anti-German; that had nothing to do with it. Was it, perhaps, a rebellion against the whole business of war, the idea of constantly, senselessly reshuffling, for ever lining up with yesterday's enemies to fight yesterday's allies in ghastly, pointless repetition? Maybe, but if so the unfortunate Jupp is quite unable to tell us; we understand him, if at all, in spite of rather than because of what he says, and in spite too of the full equipment of uncritical prejudices he carries with him, like his revulsion at the thought that the girl has had a coloured lover.

In other words, even in this apparently straightforward play we soon discover that the naturalism is only skin-deep. What appears to be almost a tape-recorder rendering of army speech proves on inspection to be a meticulously worked out, highly patterned verbal fantasia on military themes, which permits all sorts of things to emerge without ever directly stating them or forcing a simple, clear-cut judgement upon us; even the eminently dislikeable Corporal Blake is presented straight, as a phenomenon, neither heroic nor villainous, but just there. Seen in this light *Prisoner and Escort* is not so different after all from the other two plays, but they carry the method still further, or at least make it more obvious what Mr Wood is up to. *John Thomas* develops rather in the direction of Theatre of the Absurd, *Spare* in that of Theatre of Cruelty, but they are both unmistakably products of the same mind as *Prisoner and Escort*.

John Thomas is a light-weight piece, the lightest and easiest of the three, developing without complication its little parable about playing with fire, the timid bourgeois's dreams of power and uniformed glamour that make him a pushover, when it comes to the point, for anyone with even a little real power, a little real willingness to use force. *Spare* is altogether more substantial, and on first acquaintance considerably more mystifying. The action takes place, or appears to take place, in some sort of military museum, with the tattered regimental colours fluttering from the roof, three highly irreverent soldiers cleaning up down below, and someone stamping round up above constantly showering them all with dust. But little by little we get the idea that the museum is not really a museum at all, but a dramatic metaphor for the army as a whole, for military life with its mixture of garbled, rather cynically observed tradition, its slacking and skiving, and above all its terrible boredom, from which the only release is war itself.

Thus far at least we can go in explanation; and perhaps a step further, to suggest that the play shows two turns of a slowly revolving wheel – things change little by little, some get killed to be replaced by others almost identical, old soldiers grow older and fade away, but above and beyond the details military life, the army itself, flows on unchanging and unstoppable. That may be roughly what the play is about, but to try to pin down the dramatist any more exactly than that would be a mistake. He has not constructed, or attempted to construct, a reasoned intellectual argument; he has built instead a mysterious and compelling theatrical experience, made of rhythms and lights and colour and noise and silence, which on stage, in Patrick Dromgoole's memorable production, managed to rivet the attention even of those who really had not the faintest idea what it was all about. For Charles Wood is first and foremost a poet, and a master of theatrical effect. His plays depend no more on their susceptibility to ready prose paraphrase than do Shakespeare's sonnets or Edward Lear's *Nonsense Songs*; they simply choose their own manner of getting at us, and in that manner they work. The result may not be to everybody's taste, but at least it is positive enough, and personal enough, to make violent enemies or passionate partisans, and anyway to leave no one entirely indifferent.

The Trigon is altogether a milder and more traditional sort of play. Its author, James Broom Lynne, is a late developer as a writer, taking to drama only after some years as a professional designer and illustrator. Where Charles Wood's plays impress first of all by their extraordinary sharpness and sureness of effect, *The Trigon* impresses and entertains – for it should be said at once that it is very entertaining – mainly by its bright individual ideas and by two really excellent pieces of character-drawing; the play as a whole still has about it a certain, rather likeable, tentativeness which labels it clearly as the work of a beginner, though a beginner of more than a little promise.

The situation at the outset of the play could hardly be simpler or, in its admittedly rather limited terms, more satisfactory for those involved. Arthur and Basil live together in a relationship which, although it has its stormy passages, is really a nearly ideal balance, Basil being slightly sadistic and priding himself on his masterfulness, except that he gets fed up sometimes, while Arthur is a big soft baby, a self-made doormat who loves to be trampled on but believes deep down that he sees what should be done and often enough gets his own way about doing it. For outside interest – since their relationship, if suspiciously close to the outside eye, does not seem in any way compromising to them – there is Mabel, a jolly suburban miss who likes them both about equally, in different ways, and has no desire to get too closely, dangerously involved with either, preferring her simple dreams of a prince on a white charger who may one day come and carry her off.

Into this comfortable, well-insulated dream-factory comes Charles, in answer to an advertisement. He seems to be the answer to all their dreams, but before long he has upset everything. He gets Basil and Arthur really quarrelling, instead of merely playing at it; he unsettles Mabel, assuming for the time being the appearance of a prince on a white charger, but then briskly drops her in the mud when he has finished with her; and in the end he is left alone, in solitary possession of the flat, perhaps the unhappiest of them all. In fact, though, I think that Charles's role is the weakest link in the play; he is there as a catalyst, but he is not presented simply as such, in such a way that we are not tempted to ask why he is doing what he is doing; instead, Mr Broom Lynne starts us asking awkward questions and does not always provide enough answers to keep us happy.

However, this is a relatively small point. The play as a whole depends rather on the credibility of the relations among the three other characters, and their gradual break-up under the ruthless impact of

Charles. And here it is almost totally successful: the two completely suburbanized characters, Arthur and Mabel, are observed with devastating accuracy, both in the way they talk and in the way they think. They take on a sufficiently rounded, independent life of their own for us to be able to see them from several points of view, to appreciate how they look to themselves, and at the same time to judge them by the standards that other people in the play apply to them. Basil too is credible as written, and the ambiguity about how much we should believe of what he himself says about his 'good war', whether intentional or not, works perfectly well in context. Apart from which, the play is often very funny; not in any modish black-humour sort of way, but just funny about the way people are and the way they react to each other. *The Trigon* suggests that James Broom Lynne's *forte* may well prove to be a quiet, unshowy, essentially traditional sort of play about ordinary people in situations only just a little out of the ordinary. The Esther McCracken or Dodie Smith *de nos jours*? Well, I can think of many worse things to be.

Joe Orton is a 25-year-old labourer, actor and inmate of Wormwood Scrubs (in that order). The comedy of *Entertaining Mr Sloane*, his first play, is undeniably of the type known as 'black', though whether the term is very happily applied in this case remains arguable. For what emanates from the play above all is a vast and all-embracing amiability; far from being meant really to shock us out of our lethargy, our normal, routine, uncritical responses to life, it works insidiously round our prejudices and preconceptions, building its comedy so easily and agreeably out of materials which we would usually think disagreeable and quite unsuited to comic treatment that by the time we escape from the dramatist's influence and start examining more coolly what we have been seeing we are likely to be amazed at what we have accepted with hardly a second thought.

Despite this odd ability to freeze for the time being an audience's normal moral responses – something which usually upsets the British theatre-goer no end – the play has been very successful: in terms of commercial success the most successful of the three works in this book, but also critically successful, in that the London critics voted it the best new play of the year in *Variety*'s poll and Terence Rattigan, of all people, was widely quoted as saying that it was the best British play of the last twenty-five years. The play, then, as well as being of interest for its own inherent merits, is clearly a straw in the wind, indicating with some precision what will and what will not go in the commercial theatre today. And considered in this light it really is rather surprising.

It may perhaps best be considered as an *Arsenic and Old Lace*, 1964 model. I think that all Mr Orton has set out to do is to provide an evening's light comic entertainment; I don't imagine that behind his play there is any vision of the world and its ways fighting for expression, as there certainly is behind *Cockade* and probably is behind *The Trigon*. So, like Charles Wood in *Prisoner and Escort* and James Broom Lynne in *The Trigon*, he gives us three characters in an established relationship with each other and then brings in a fourth as a catalyst. But both his given characters and his newcomer are weirder than in either of the other plays. The Kemp family, with their solitary house in the middle of a rubbish dump, consists of Kath, a superannuated Baby Doll whose often expressed desire to be motherly demonstrates itself chiefly in her habit of wandering round 'in the rude' under her flimsy dress, and virtually raping her lodger on his first night there; Ed, a stolid businessman homosexual with a taste for body-builders who drops in from time to time; and Dadda, a nasty-tempered old man who has not spoken to Ed for twenty years, ever since he found him 'committing some kind of felony in the bedroom'. Into this cosy little den of suburban iniquity wanders the smooth-skinned, fair-haired Mr Sloane, whom we gather before long to be a murderer, possibly psychopathic but anyway on the loose and more than a little sinister.

Perhaps we are in for another *Night Must Fall*, with the family welcoming into their bosom decidedly more than they bargained for. But not a bit of it; in the event it proves to be the murderer who is no match for them; he is pettish, childish, and does not know what he wants beyond the immediate requisites of a life of comfort, inactivity, and as far as possible luxury; Kath and Ed, on the other hand, know exactly what they want, and know well enough how to get it. In a word, they want him. They are ready to make his cage reasonably gilded, to treat their pet well, but they will not stand any signs of independence from him, and regard his murder of their old father quite blandly ('Well, it's been a pleasant morning', remarks Ed casually when it's all over) as a good weapon to use against him in keeping him under control. What looked like being a story of a cuckoo in the nest has turned, almost before we know what is happening, into another tale of the spider and the fly.

Entertaining? Undoubtedly. Mr Orton knows how to put a play together in the manner of the moment without going too far and worrying Aunt Edna; Aunt Edna may be pushed to a sharp intake of breath or a mildly outraged giggle at hearing rough, adult words like 'arse' or 'titties' spoken on the West End stage, but she will enjoy feeling with-it, and stay to the end. The New Drama has done its work well in conditioning audiences so that if they are not quite ready to accept, say, Arden or Livings straight, they are at least prepared for a good commercial substitute. That, it seems to me, is what *Entertaining Mr Sloane* offers, and it is none the worse for that. Theatre, living theatre, needs the good commercial dramatist just as much as the original artist, for without the one the other is unlikely to get his chance in the first place. Joe Orton is the first dramatist to write a solid, well-managed commercial play which belongs specifically and unmistakably to the 1960s; and that in itself entitles him to quite a sizeable salute.

JOHN RUSSELL TAYLOR

CHARLES WOOD

Cockade

First presented at the New Arts Theatre Club on 16 October 1963 by Michael Codron with the following cast:

PRISONER AND ESCORT

JUPP	Alfred Lynch
BLAKE	Norman Rossington
HOSKINSON	Tim Preece
GIRL	June Barry

JOHN THOMAS

JOHN THOMAS	Norman Rossington
MAN FROM UPSTAIRS	Alfred Lynch

SPARE

HARRY	Alfred Lynch
DICKIE BIRD	Norman Rossington
GARIBALDI	Tim Preece
SPRATT	Bryan Pringle
FREDDIE	Alfred Lynch
DRUMMER	Martin Jarvis

Directed by Patrick Dromgoole
Designed by Alan Barrett

CHARACTERS

A PORTER
BLAKE *Corporal 17/21st Lancers*
HOSKINSON *Trooper*
HARRY JUPP *Trooper/Ex-Corporal 17/21st Lancers*
A GIRL

SETTING

A modern railway carriage of a steam train or diesel operating on the route to Edinburgh through Birmingham and Darlington.

And the platform of a station.

The carriage is framework only with a corridor and luggage rack that is net or some other string-like rope for the bars of a cage-like effect.

Across the stage from left to right is station platform, or black night when the train is moving.

At the back pasted on walls a huge pastiche of recruiting poster that stays for all three plays. Or any evocative graphic decoration that can be constant.

SCENE ONE

The Platform

[*Three* SOLDIERS *clip across the platform and straggle to a stop at one end.* BLAKE *stops nearer the middle and swings hands on hips fully in command, never mind the Stationmaster, to check it's the right platform. It is.*]

BLAKE: Right. Right then. [*The station echoes to the iron-vaulted roof with station noises but not many trains. A steady steam hiss from one at the back ... which we can't see properly.*] Can't trust the bastards – had me before today they have ... the bastards. [*A whistling* PORTER. *He whistles across with his trolley.* CORPORAL BLAKE *and* TROOPER HOSKINSON *are dressed for escort duty.* JUPP *is without a hat, and in shoes.* HOSKINSON *stands with* JUPP *and close to him, a greatcoat between them.* HOSKINSON *stamps his feet to pouch his trousers properly over his gaiters.*] Right. Should be in.

HOSKINSON: British Railways.

BLAKE: They do it out of pure bastardry. They've had me on the wrong bastard train before today. Jack? Darlington? [*This to the whistling* PORTER.]

PORTER: Catterick?

BLAKE: This it?

PORTER: Should be. Catterick? 'k your horrible luck.

HOSKINSON: Get some in.

BLAKE: Belt up Hoskinson – you shame me.

PORTER: Before you come up son. I was in the Andrew. [*The* PORTER *is a cocky sprightly youth unabashed by superiors, life, or the bastards grinding him down. Very much a matelot. Stoker of course.*]

BLAKE: Stoker.

PORTER: Of course. Killick's delight.

[*A little hornpipe, and off with the trolley.*]

BLAKE: You do shame me with your nig nog phrases Hoskinson.

HOSKINSON: Well. [*A nervous bray from* HOSKINSON *who is not sure*

19

how to behave … Whether to be mucko chummo or very regimental …
He manages a tremble in between, but now and then slips.]

BLAKE: I almost feel sorry for old Jupp – forced to associate cheek to
cheek with you …

JUPP: Don't bother.

BLAKE: No – I won't.

[*They stand.* HOSKINSON *quiet while he tries hard to think of some
merry quip for the Corporal. The* PORTER *heel toes across looking
hard at Hoskinson and Jupp. He grins.*]

PORTER: Brown jobs.

BLAKE: Jack – when's it in?

A VOICE: That Brummagem bike.

[*The* PORTER *sticks his two fingers up the voice. The* STATION
ANNOUNCER *coughs into his Tannoy. A train is heard approach-
ing.*]

PORTER: My foreman.

BLAKE: This it?

PORTER: All he can do is sack me.

[BLAKE *stands with the other two as the train approaches. The* PORTER
nips off for the bike and a nearby train weak throat whistles.]

STATION ANNOUNCER: The next train at platform twelve will
be the nine forty-five for Darlington – and the north. Calling
at …

[*Lighted windows flash past the faces of the three soldiers and the
train slows down as the* PORTER *dances past with a wrapped up and
labelled bike. He rings the bell and says to Hoskinson and Jupp …
thrusting his head between them and pushing off the greatcoat…*]

PORTER: Never again – not even a Christmas Club. [*Then sees the
handcuffs as* BLAKE *sees the reserved compartment and makes for it –
after him* HOSKINSON *and* JUPP. PORTER *left.*]

A VOICE: That Brummagem bike.

PORTER: And you. [*Another two fingers up his Foreman's Jacksy almost
absent mindedly as he looks after the Three Soldiers.*] Too bloody
true.

SCENE TWO

The compartment.

> [HOSKINSON *and* JUPP *enter, followed by* BLAKE *who slides the door shut.*]

BLAKE: 'Oskinson – get those blinds down your end. [*He pulls them down himself at his end.*]

HOSKINSON: Right Corporal.

JUPP: My leash the blinds – what about these?

BLAKE: They rubbing? They'll rub you raw before we get back Jupp – I promise you. Sit down 'Oskinson. I got to tell you everything? Sit down and sit him down with you.

JUPP: Let's have them off then.

BLAKE: You want to take your kit off 'Oskie?

HOSKINSON: I'm all right, corporal.

BLAKE: Are you? Please yourself – I'm not proud myself. I'd as soon wear jock strap and anklets. Comfort see. Please yourself – it's a long way to Catterick. Don't know why we have to wear all this rubbish ... [BLAKE *takes off his equipment. Rolls it up carefully so he won't have to clean it again before putting it back on his locker – rolls it in his belt. The lanyard dangles.*] All very appropriate in it? What's this for – lassoo him should he do a bunk?

HOSKINSON: That's a laugh. Lassoo him – that's a giggle Corporal Blake.

BLAKE: Only you won't do a bunk this time Jupp – this time Jim Blake's got you taped.

HOSKINSON: Yes.

> [BLAKE *throws his kit up into the luggage rack above* JUPP's *head – the pistol lanyard drops and jerks into swing as the train pulls away. The* PORTER *runs alongside.*]

BLAKE: We're off.

PORTER: Get your hair cut Pongo.

BLAKE: About time.

PORTER: Get some in.

BLAKE: And you. [*An 'Up you' to the Porter and a grin as* BLAKE *sits down. The* PORTER *falls back (running backwards) as the train gathers speed in sound.*]

PORTER: Time ex Stripey – fireside flotilla and never again.

[*And he is gone. As* JUPP *puts his feet up.*]

BLAKE: Feet up! Get those feet down Jupp.

[BLAKE *throws the feet off –* HOSKINSON *pulls viciously on the handcuffs.*]

HOSKINSON: People got to sit there.

BLAKE: Corporals got to sit there in their best slacks ...

JUPP: A fussy man – fastidious.

BLAKE: I'll tell you. Smiler Lewis is a mucker of mine ... we broke in our first pair of boots ...

JUPP: Old boots.

BLAKE: When Smiler heard you'd been picked up ...

JUPP: He was no doubt highly chuffed.

BLAKE: And when he heard I'd been warned off for escort – his joy knew no bounds.

JUPP: As they say on the pictures.

BLAKE: We've been muckers a long time – like I said – Smiler and me. Our minds are in accord. We think the same way about the same things. About you – mate are we in accord about you.

JUPP: When are you going to strike off me shackles?

BLAKE: How do you feel about it 'Oskie – about being tied to this thing?

HOSKINSON: Somebody has to do it. Somebody has to do the job ... you know I always do my job to the best of my ability ...

JUPP: Turn me on – you toe rag. You beautiful little toe rag. Here – now stand on your head and whistle 'God save the Queen'! You toe rag.

BLAKE: All spice and cookhouse curry in he? Not for long though.

HOSKINSON: Not when we gets him to the nick.

BLAKE: Salt his tail a bit before then – it's a long way to Catterick. A fag 'Oskie – have a fag.

HOSKINSON: Yes – but you have one of mine corp.

BLAKE: In full – corporal in full 'Oskie my old. You have one of mine ... not gasping then Jupp? Thought you was – thought you was bound to be gasping for a fag ... You'll go short in the nick I promise you.

JUPP [*leans back his eyes closed*]: Don't use them – corp.

BLAKE: Never did like the looks of you Jupp – bit too big headed ...

HOSKINSON: That's what I thought.

BLAKE: ... that day you first poked your head in the Corporals' Mess ... I said to Smiler you were a nit.

HOSKINSON: I think he's a nit.

BLAKE: A first class prima nit – a cootie. Watch him I said – round and round he'll go scratching up things he shouldn't. Round and round digging into things with them sharp little stabbers – till some bastard combs him out and cracks him on a thumb nail. Yes. Picking and niggling – yes.

HOSKINSON: We got a nit in our room ...

BLAKE: Open 'em.

HOSKINSON: He's a nit – always dropping the room in the shit.

BLAKE: Open your eyes – your bleeding nit's eyes. You're dealing with Jim Blake now – not his poxy ina ... what you think you're on? Your father's yacht?

JUPP: Strategic Reserve – what you on?

HOSKINSON: Cheeking.

BLAKE: On your feet – up. Move him 'Oskie – on your feet imshi.
    [HOSKINSON *pulls Jupp to his feet.*]

JUPP: Games?

BLAKE: Give us your wrist 'Oskie – cheeking is it?

JUPP: Games is it?
    [BLAKE *unlocks* HOSKINSON'S *half of the cuffs.*]
    Time you took these off – Q.R.R.'s do not ...

BLAKE: ... do not cover you. Q.R.R.'s was made for soldiers – Q.R.R.'s was made for men ...

JUPP: Q.R.R.'s ...

BLAKE: ... was not made for twats. Queen's Rules and Regulations do not protect you. Not twats like you, shagged? Want to get your head down. Had a rare old time on the run – beat yourself up on your little holiday I'll bet. Fancy a quiet kip do you whilst the train jogs on? Hard ship. It's not going to be a bit like that – whilst 'Oskie and me hark to your snores of sweet stinky finger – not a bit of it. What do twats do? They hang. They hang hairy below bellies. So – you hang Jupp like all the other twats. [*Clips the hand-*

cuffs to the luggage rack – high.] One hand high the Chinese voter. Standing room only all the way, Jupp. Little trick I learned from a Yank Provost – never thought I'd hate anyone enough to use it … you are the very first.

HOSKINSON: Saving it special like – that right corp? Corporal.

BLAKE: Well I'll tell you …

HOSKINSON: Yes.

BLAKE: You can do it high …

HOSKINSON: Yes.

BLAKE: You can do it low … if you do it low – he can sit …

HOSKINSON: You've done it high.

JUPP: All coppers are …

HOSKINSON: I must remember it corporal.

BLAKE: What was that you said Jupp?

JUPP: What?

HOSKINSON: That … what you said.

JUPP: Oh that – what I said. I said all coppers are …

BLAKE: You know I'm not a copper Jupp. Why did you say that?

HOSKINSON: All coppers are what?

BLAKE: You know I'm not a copper …

JUPP: You're not?

BLAKE: I'm just an ordinary swaddie – doing an ordinary job in an ordinary way.

JUPP: What are you then?

HOSKINSON: And me.

JUPP: And you – give over.

HOSKINSON: Our duty.

BLAKE: You did it …

JUPP: What are you then?

BLAKE: Many's the time you did it.

HOSKINSON: I remember – he did it.

JUPP: Oh yes.

BLAKE: Many many's the time …

HOSKINSON: Only doing our duty – what we're told to do.

JUPP: Hardly.

BLAKE: On your own – no prompting – no 'hardly's about it … you did the very same thing Jupp.

JUPP: No no – I didn't …

BLAKE: No no and you did.

HOSKINSON: That's it.

BLAKE: Final.

HOSKINSON: No come backs.

JUPP: All coppers …

BLAKE: We had that out.

HOSKINSON: We're not …

BLAKE: Never were.

JUPP: … bastards.

BLAKE: I can't deny it – I have my name on the shithouse wall.

JUPP: It's …

BLAKE: Yes?

HOSKINSON: Hullo?

JUPP: It's a long way to Catterick.

BLAKE: Too true. [*Lies back feet up and pulls his beret over his eyes – arms folded.* HOSKINSON *does exactly the same. A train whistles cold.*]

BLAKE: Lights – 'Oskie.

[HOSKINSON *switches off the lights.*]

HOSKINSON: Want the bulb out Corporal? That's what we do …

BLAKE [*looks from under his beret at Hoskinson all eager in his seat*]: Nig nog games – don't shame me 'Oskie.

[HOSKINSON *looks at the grinning Jupp and lies back – beret over eyes just like master.*]

BLAKE [*lifts his beret again*]: Here Jupp – they tell me the great speckled sloth kips upside down arse to the kissing sun … try it Jupp.

[*A neigh from* HOSKINSON. *The train wails for Jupp as he shifts about to get near to comfort. He shivers.*
Fade out. Noise of rushing train.]

SCENE THREE

The compartment.

[*Dark with just the centre light dim.* BLAKE *and* HOSKINSON *kip while the train jogs on.*]

JUPP: Yip yip yip – abandon ship – yip yip yip. [*He screams very loud and laughs as he shouts it out.* BLAKE *leaps to his feet and turns and*

25

turns like an idiot. HOSKINSON *grips the edge of his seat very frightened. The train stops. Jerks still. It is a station.*]

JUPP: To the guard – guard turn out yip yip yip.

BLAKE: 'kin 'll – 'kin 'll. Shut it.

HOSKINSON: Hey hey.

JUPP: Hey hey Cathusalem Cathusalem Cathusalem – hey hey Cathusalem ...

BLAKE: Pack it in – shut it.

JUPP: ... Harlot of Jerusalem.

HOSKINSON [*flicks the lights on*]: Lights.

BLAKE: Shut it – 'fore I stuff something in it. I promise you.

HOSKINSON: I thought we'd piled up.

JUPP: Promise me – not your socks – for fuck's sake if not for my sake not your stiff grey socks.

HOSKINSON: I honestly thought we'd crapped it.

JUPP: Your boot – your old boots' knickers ... your bloody great schonk ... but not your socks I beg of you ...

BLAKE: Belt up. Now. Jack it.

HOSKINSON: Shouting.

BLAKE: Asking.

JUPP: Waiting. Waiting on you to have a go. Have a go Blake – thump me you bastard.

HOSKINSON: Wrap up.

BLAKE: I'm tempted. The temptation's there Jupp.

JUPP: I should – I shan't let you kip.

BLAKE: You'll chew on this – should I have any more ... now jag it in.

JUPP: Rattled.

HOSKINSON: I was just getting started. Just got me head down serious ...

BLAKE: There is accidents.

JUPP: Threats of red violence.

HOSKINSON: On a moving train.

BLAKE: Jammy.

HOSKINSON: With all that's moving.

BLAKE: Piece of cake.

HOSKINSON: Getting off – he slips getting off.

BLAKE: Nicht hinauslehen ...

HOSKINSON: What's that?

BLAKE: ... bevor der zug halt.

HOSKINSON: Oh.

BLAKE: Open door.

HOSKINSON: Alighting – train still moving.

BLAKE: He knows it – deutsche sprechen for watch it the zug's not still moving.

HOSKINSON: They swing open – can't trust them.

BLAKE: Tried to save him sir – best we could.

HOSKINSON: Caught his feet sir ...

BLAKE: Dragged along on his mush.

HOSKINSON: Lots of things ...

BLAKE: Caught his fingers in the door – slam – crack 'orrible.

HOSKINSON: ... could happen.

BLAKE: Caught his nose with my boot heel – steel sharp as a clicker ...

JUPP: What does your chicko think of her daddy. He's shown me pictures.

[*The train starts again with a jerk as* BLAKE *gets hold of* JUPP'S *collar.*]

BLAKE: Rag up now Jupp – clever lad.

GIRL [*opens the door and shuts it just as quickly*]: Sorry.

[BLAKE *turns as the door shuts.*]

BLAKE: Oh yes ...

HOSKINSON: You've got his rag up now Jupp.

BLAKE: Tart.

HOSKINSON: Talking about his children.

BLAKE: Skirt. You see that 'Oskie?

HOSKINSON: I wouldn't stand for that.

BLAKE: See that – lovely little chick – a princess.

HOSKINSON: Oh yes?

JUPP: Like your missus – got hairs on her chest.

BLAKE: I see you. I perceive your drift Jupp. You *want* to be thumped ... you want me to thump holy joy out of you don't you. That's it – you are a proper little machonist ... it's all sexual.

HOSKINSON: Was she coming in?

BLAKE: Don't care if you do go blind do you? Wouldn't want to mark you lad – one's enough with Smiler Lewis busted ... you're a very shrewd ... Anyway – thumpo's is out with your lot – lick the lathi you do ... you and Gandhi ... You want to go and draw a dhoti. Met your kind before – thumped holy tit and tears out of them I have ... they don't get the message. Sticks and stones ... where you sloping off to?

HOSKINSON: Down the ...

BLAKE: Back ... sticks and stones may break your bones but that's not what will finish you – know what will?

JUPP: You tell me.

BLAKE: The calling – names are what will hurt you.

HOSKINSON: Can't I go?

BLAKE: What you on 'Oskinson?

HOSKINSON: Going to have a look that's all.

BLAKE: You randy Hardon. That princess – back. You're not going nowhere – you stay here.

HOSKINSON: Lats.

BLAKE: Leave the loving to young Blake here – you can be two's up.

JUPP: Give over.

HOSKINSON: You going?

BLAKE: Watch him.

HOSKINSON: On my own.

BLAKE: Your tod.

HOSKINSON: And him?

BLAKE: Observation.

HOSKINSON: On my own – after Smiler.

BLAKE: Lesson one – now we know.

HOSKINSON: Not to trust him?

BLAKE: Watch him all the time.

HOSKINSON: Watch him all the time.

BLAKE: Everywhere – the slash house even.

HOSKINSON: Peeking?

BLAKE: Through that little round peek hole ... they will Jupp ... for fear of self abuse.

JUPP: Snurge. Both of you – I've seen you with girls' bikes.

HOSKINSON: No knowing what he might do.

BLAKE: What's a snurge?

HOSKINSON: Capers.

JUPP: It's worse for men ...

HOSKINSON: And me here – Jack Jones.

BLAKE: A snurge.

JUPP: Five years first offence.

HOSKINSON: I'm not sure it's not against regulations.

JUPP: That's right 'Oskie – five years.

BLAKE: What?

JUPP: Snurging.

HOSKINSON: Leaving me here on my jack with him – I'm not sure
it's not against regulations.

JUPP: I've seen you both with girls' bikes.

HOSKINSON: I mean – look what happened to Smiler.

BLAKE: Were you there?

HOSKINSON: No – I wasn't there.

BLAKE: With Smiler on that train?

HOSKINSON: No – I wasn't there Corporal.

BLAKE: So you don't know.

HOSKINSON: No I don't know.

JUPP: Ask me – I was there. I know.

[*A pause and* BLAKE *looks at Jupp.*]

BLAKE: And you do. The len of your comb 'Oskie.

HOSKINSON: And Smiler was a corporal.

BLAKE: Your comb 'Oskie ...

[*Comb to Blake.*]

HOSKINSON: Yes – but should I need you. I got to know where you
are corporal in case I need you.

BLAKE: Ooooooooooh ... chatty.

HOSKINSON: The tickets and everything – I haven't got the tickets.

JUPP: Give him the tickets.

BLAKE: You don't need them – I'll be back.

JUPP: Too bloody true.

HOSKINSON: Only along the corridor eh?

JUPP: You'll be back.

HOSKINSON: That's where you'll be eh?

BLAKE: I'm going for a slash – on the way I'm thinking of chatting
up the princess – I promise you ... two's up.

JUPP: No chance.

BLAKE: Bets.

JUPP: No chance.

BLAKE: More chance than you Jupp.

HOSKINSON: More chance than you Jupp.

BLAKE: Never known the fatal charm to fail myself. I'll give you a demonstration – followed by a demonstration with an explanation. Purely for the education and you should have some recent to fret over; long sex-starved hours to come in the Mallet ... when you've done scraping and shining your Kiwi tin ... buffed up the night pail – arranged your kit for the thirty thousandth time – squared off your bed boards and doubled round-round-round-round in full pack and double-double, here, there, and everywhere on G.M.T. Watch the demo and think of Jim Blake satisfied, adjusted, and laughing little cobs. Get frantic – I'd like to think of you frantic and doing your nut. Poke your head round the door and cop another twenty-eight for attempt at escape – because they won't like you. They're all like me. Only I'm just a bastard. They're professional with careers to think of.

JUPP: No chance.

BLAKE: You're tired. So he knows I'm bound to – tell him about the crumpet I've buttered ... tell him some of the stories I told you coming down ... go on 'Oskie.

HOSKINSON: Yes. More chance than you Jupp.

BLAKE: Tell him 'Oskie ... that tart in Devizes ... you must remember the tart in Devizes ... and there was the Irish bint – you know – the one as kept her drawers in her handbag ...

HOSKINSON: Last bus to West Lavington?

BLAKE: Last bus to West Lavington – no it was a real ...

HOSKINSON: Well – this girl she was at the Town Hall – at the dance.

BLAKE: That's it. Tell him – let me hear you start ...

HOSKINSON: Dancing.

BLAKE: Princess.

HOSKINSON: At this dance ...

BLAKE: Every Thursday night they ran 'em – you know pay night – you know rake it in.

HOSKINSON: Well – she was ...

BLAKE: A princess ... I promise you.

JUPP: Princess! You know what? One day some years to come when she's ripe – some hairy-arsed squaddie will steer your little apple – your little chicko ... round the sweaty floor by power of his grin and he'll take her outside and he'll pluck her! Daddy.

BLAKE: That's it. I try to talk to you like you were a human being ... an adult and what do you do ... I'll show you Jupp ... try to treat you like you were a decent – and what do you do? Now jack it in. Now jack it in. Now you watch it. Watch him 'Oskie – if he gives you any ... I promise you I'll make him pay ... [*Furious but tamping it down he slams out.*]

JUPP: Pay! You couldn't make pussy pay.

HOSKINSON: You heard what he said?

JUPP: You heard what I said?

HOSKINSON: Why don't you take it easy?

JUPP: Why don't you take a day off?

HOSKINSON: He tried to treat you decent.

JUPP: I'm sure – you call this decent?

HOSKINSON: More decent – such as you deserve – more decent than what you did.

JUPP: What did I do?

HOSKINSON: If you don't know Jack.

JUPP: I know – do you?

HOSKINSON: I was there.

JUPP: Were you?

HOSKINSON: Yes.

JUPP: So was I.

HOSKINSON: He only did that because he can't trust you to turn his back.

JUPP: Go on.

HOSKINSON: If you behaved yourself ...

JUPP: Go on.

HOSKINSON: All you had to do ..

JUPP: Yes corporal – no corporal ... kiss my old boot's fat arse corporal – is that it?

HOSKINSON: Well he is an N.C.O.

JUPP: Is that what he is? I thought he was a piddle on the carpet. N.C.O. – he don't know the meaning of the word.

HOSKINSON: And you do?

JUPP: No – I don't.

HOSKINSON: There you are then.

JUPP: Where?

HOSKINSON: Eh?

JUPP: Where am I?

HOSKINSON: Hanging from that rack like a don't know what.

JUPP: You don't know what?

HOSKINSON: Wrap up will you – do us all a favour and give your other end a chance.

JUPP: Big stroppy soldier aren't you – where'd you learn to be a big stroppy squaddie like daddy?

HOSKINSON: Wrap up – you.

JUPP: Where was it ...? [*Sings to the tune of 'Candy Kisses'.*]

> Little nig nogs wrapped in denims
> Mean more to me than Naafi tea.

HOSKINSON: Nig nog – I may be ...

JUPP:
> They didn't mean it.
> So they tell me ...

HOSKINSON: Least I've not messed about like you.

JUPP:
> As I whispered sweet nothings
> In their little pig ears
> In the games room
> Playing ping pong
> They'll be our soldiers
> Some of the time.

HOSKINSON: Filthy.

JUPP: Ping pong?

HOSKINSON: What you did.

JUPP: Did the trick though eh?

HOSKINSON: Filthy.

JUPP: What do you laugh at?

HOSKINSON: I don't laugh at that.

JUPP: Then you've no sense of humour.

HOSKINSON: I hope I have – I laugh at wit.

JUPP: No you don't – you laugh at others.

HOSKINSON: If that was funny – I don't think much of your sense of humour.

JUPP: It lets me down actually. It flops out when I least expect it and there I am – let down. My grandfather was gassed.

HOSKINSON: I certainly don't think it's funny.

JUPP: No? Well – must be the way I say it ... my grandfather was gassed?

HOSKINSON: Honestly I don't dig you at all.

JUPP: I thought you'd enjoy that. Here's another one for you ... my uncle who I'm told was a nice bloke and I just remember him as a smile on the far end of a piece of chocolate ... so I can't argue. My uncle sits at home and he dribbles. And he looks a nice bloke with all the set of a nice bloke – it's only his eyes and his wet mouth look comical ... No. I thought I told that one better. Everybody laughs. You've heard it before.

HOSKINSON: I think you're off your rocker – I thought that all along ... you flipped.

JUPP: I did indeed. But it was a royal flip – specially for the Queen's Birthday.

HOSKINSON: I saw it – rank behind. I was in the rank behind.

JUPP: You hardly thought it was funny.

HOSKINSON: Hardly.

JUPP: Hardly did I Jack. I thought you were funny. I thought all of us were funny with what we were. Rank on rank of wet khaki papheads – best boots sunbursts all along the cobbles. Beezed up and buffed up like a camp of thick as shit guardsmen. Medals out also – that's what got me off ...

HOSKINSON: It was only another parade – had them all the time.

JUPP: Too true – only another. Just one more parade. Here – here's another story to add to your collection of wit. Now I told you about my grandfather ... I had a father too ...

HOSKINSON: Look a bit daft without one wouldn't you?

JUPP: Well I've been without one ... no don't laugh yet ... and I had a brother but he's not funny because I can remember throwing stones at him ... well to cut a long story short my father was lucky – he lived to see them all carved on the wall ... then a D.P. climb-

ing out of Celle camp one night after a bit of nooky slit his throat
for being on stag ... No? It was a bit near the knuckle ... Just try
paphead ... just try to put yourself under the weight of history ...
not the sort that gets crowned and marries commoners ... but the
sort that scrubs steps after telegrams and thinks there was a reason
for it ... And you still can't see why I did it?

[*The door slides open and* BLAKE *stands back to let the girl in.*]

GIRL: Honestly, I thought I'd never get ...

BLAKE: Sit down.

GIRL: ... a seat. The whole train's packed.

BLAKE: The train's packed in it?

GIRL: And don't they push and shove?

BLAKE: Reserved that's why.

GIRL: Always the same. I tried to get up and down the train twice ...
I did.

BLAKE: We had it reserved for us.

GIRL: You ought to have. I wish I'd taken the trouble.

BLAKE: Out of that corridor.

GIRL: I must say it's nice to get out of that corridor – don't they push
and shove?

BLAKE: Sit down then.

HOSKINSON: She can sit over here – you can sit over here.

BLAKE: Pack it in 'Oskie.

GIRL: Never any thought of giving up their seats to a lady.

BLAKE: Sit down then – get the weight off your feet.

GIRL: Nice to take the weight off your feet if nothing else.

BLAKE: You going far?

GIRL: You going to Catterick?

BLAKE: Oh yes – we're stationed there.

GIRL: Oh yes – that's nice. I know ...

BLAKE: Well – you know – there's good and there's bad ...

GIRL: I know. I know somebody who was there – George?

BLAKE: George?

HOSKINSON: George?

GIRL: That's right – he didn't like it though – not Catterick.

BLAKE: Well – you know ... there's good and there's bad ... [*Sits
next to the girl.*]

34

GIRL: That's right.

BLAKE: Fags out 'Oskie.

HOSKINSON: Have one of mine.

BLAKE: You smoke a lot do you? Heavy like?

GIRL: Oh yes – I started young.

BLAKE: Hear that 'Oskie – she started young.

HOSKINSON: That's right – she started young.

BLAKE: Heavy. You smoke cigars?

GIRL: Eh?

BLAKE: Nice big brown cigars?

GIRL: Don't be silly – who ever saw a girl smoking a cigar?

BLAKE: Lovely.

GIRL: Too big for me ...

BLAKE: Hear that 'Oskie – too big for her.

HOSKINSON: That's right - too big for her?

BLAKE: Light 'Oskie.

HOSKINSON: She want lighting up? [*Leans over to give the Girl a light.*]

BLAKE: She don't need lighting up.

GIRL: I'm bright enough.

BLAKE: Hear that 'Oskie – she's bright enough.

HOSKINSON: That's right – she's bright enough.

BLAKE: He's bright.

GIRL: He looks bright.

BLAKE: Not as bright as you though.

GIRL: What's he got that gun for?

BLAKE: I've got one too ...

GIRL: Let's see it.

BLAKE: Hear that 'Oskie – she wants to see it.

HOSKINSON: That right – she wants to see it.

BLAKE: He's the one to watch though.

GIRL: Who?

HOSKINSON: Who me?

GIRL: He says you're the one to watch – that right?

HOSKINSON: Who me?

GIRL: He looks nice.

HOSKINSON: Certainly.

BLAKE: He is nice – but not as nice as you though.
[JUPP *yawns – long and loaded.*]
GIRL: What's he standing up there for?
HOSKINSON: No – the corporal's the bloke to watch.
GIRL: What's he doing? Up there ...
[BLAKE *whispers to her. She giggles.*]
GIRL: Oh – aren't you awful ...
BLAKE: Go on it's true – you ask him.
GIRL: Shall I?
BLAKE: Yes – go on – ask him. His name's Jupp.
GIRL: Shall I?
BLAKE: Go on.
GIRL: I daren't – go on.
BLAKE: Tell her Jupp – tell my little bright princess why you're
hanging from the rack like that.
GIRL: I daren't – is it because you've messed your breeches? That's
what he said ... he said it ... [*She giggles.*] Oh – it's not right is it?
What's the matter with – not speaking?
BLAKE: We've had him doctored – he can't speak. We only keep
him for his coat and his big brown eyes ...
GIRL: Ooooooooh can I stroke him?
BLAKE: Hear that 'Oskie – she said can I stroke him?
HOSKINSON: That right – can she stroke him?
[*The train stops suddenly and the greatcoat falls off the luggage rack.
The* GIRL *was standing and she falls back on Blake who has a hand-
ful.* HOSKINSON *puts his head out of the window.*]
GIRL: He's got handcuffs on.
BLAKE: That's right – wish you had.
GIRL: Well I haven't – Handy.
BLAKE: Wish you had.
GIRL: What's he done – leave off.
BLAKE: Kiss if I do.
JUPP: Kiss if I do.
GIRL: Don't be so damned childish. Look – jack it in ... I want to
know what he's done.
JUPP: Rape.
GIRL: Oh.

HOSKINSON: No he didn't.

BLAKE: He said so.

GIRL: Oh.

BLAKE: The colonel's daughter.

HOSKINSON: He didn't did he?

JUPP: Oh my God – give us a chance – you seen her?

BLAKE: Oh yes.

JUPP: Rather the bloody colonel.

BLAKE: Only I know the full story. He crept up on her one dark and stormy Wuthering Heights night ... no moon see ... black as the ace ... cold, wet underfoot – no night to get down to being raped I can tell you. I know the full story ... down the stables she was saying goodnight to her favourite steed – a stallion very hands high, one by name Marmaduke ... I know the full story – straight from the horse's mouth. Guarded only by her trusty brown retriever – when he came – out of the night came this hot panting nutter ... he stabbed the poor faithful dog dead – jodhpurs over the moon and he took his wicked will ... like this – like this like this ...

[BLAKE *grabs the girl and tries to suck her neck. She struggles and wins. The train starts up again.* BLAKE *sits back grinning fast and guffing breath.*]

BLAKE: Now. Now see – I promise you I know the full story ... now the colonel's gone spare naturally being as his daughter's in the family way – he was saving her for a chinless ... and he gives us marching orders – bring him back dead, alive, or hanging like a wrinkled old rolled old pull through ... and I'll chop him off regimentally.

GIRL: More likely you. Look at that – you've torn my coat and my hair all over ...

BLAKE: I was only demonstrating his foul crime ...

HOSKINSON: I didn't know that you know – wouldn't put it past him.

GIRL: I don't mind a bit of fun. You didn't do all that did you ...

HOSKINSON: No – he didn't.

BLAKE: No – he didn't.

GIRL: Well – I mean.

37

BLAKE: It was the padre's daughter.

HOSKINSON: The padre's daughter ... that's it – well done.

GIRL: You soldiers and your dirty talk. Mauling a girl around just because she's friendly. I thought you weren't like that – you with the moustache ... him – he's disgusting but I thought you were bit different to him.

HOSKINSON: Only a joke.

BLAKE: Can't take a joke.

GIRL: I can take a joke.

HOSKINSON: Can't a bloke make a joke?

BLAKE: Who's she think she is?

GIRL: They going to keep you up here all the way? [*Talks close to Jupp.* BLAKE *and* HOSKINSON *sling words at each other as a back ground.*]

BLAKE: Fanny from Larkhill.

GIRL: All the way to Catterick?

HOSKINSON: The Bulford Belle – Silk Hill leaves in her hair ...

GIRL: It's ever such a long way ...

BLAKE: That's it 'Oskie – you was there.

HOSKINSON: Most likely Big Tits from where was it?

BLAKE: Everywhere. The Richmond Belle.

HOSKINSON: Eskimo Nell.

BLAKE: That's it – you was there 'Oskie.

GIRL: I know about these M.P.s – they're real cruel – you know what I mean?

BLAKE: I know about these tarts – teasers. Most of them still with the nappy rash ...

GIRL: M.P.s came for my brother once. He was in the army – Fred? Fred Canning? No? No – well he was in the Fusiliers of course.

BLAKE: Fusilier Fred of the 'Skin Backs'.

GIRL: It was because he stayed at home.

HOSKINSON: That all?

BLAKE: I know this tart – I've seen her kind in every back shanty cafe from here to Warcop.

GIRL: I mean our mum was ill. He had to didn't he? I was still schooling ... and our dad's been gone since the war.

BLAKE: I know you. Silly little tarts painted up to look like women ... rubbish I promise you.

38

GIRL: And the baby. Well she dies. The baby. These two in red
hats? Redcaps? They came for Fred. He liked the army you know
– he did ... he liked the army – thought it was a good life – and he
wouldn't hurt a fly – he was really happy. He was going to go back
– he told them – only they wouldn't listen ...

BLAKE: 'They didn't mean it
                      So they tell me.' I bet.

GIRL: He was going back – honest he was ... he did like the army ...
he was a good brother and he wasn't given to lying ... they
wouldn't listen though – just laughed and told him to get his
jacket on. Not even his breakfast.

BLAKE: Hard lines.

HOSKINSON: What a ding dong shame.

JUPP: Bastards.

GIRL: Yes.

BLAKE: She hasn't got the message 'Oskie.

GIRL: They gave us some money.

BLAKE: Here Fanny – you think this lark's a Butlin's?

GIRL: This major. He'd been a major in the army I think and you
had to keep calling him major – everybody did – he did. Didn't
stop him interfering with me. Yes.

BLAKE: You don't know the times I've heard this lot.

GIRL: I went to see our Fred when our mum died – he was still in
prison and his face was all in bruises. Where they'd hit him? He
said they hadn't – but how else? He had to say that – with them
listening.

BLAKE: Did it himself.

GIRL: He did not.

BLAKE: Did it himself.

GIRL: He did not do it himself.

BLAKE: They do.

GIRL: He did not do it himself.

JUPP: I don't suppose he did.

GIRL: No – he didn't.

BLAKE: He did. They do 'Oskie ... well known fact – bang their
heads against the door – scream and shout and push their heads
against the wall ... some of them.

GIRL: He did not do it himself.

BLAKE: The right nutters.

HOSKINSON: Brother Fred.

BLAKE: Doolally tap. It's the strain see – and it gets the doolally lads first.

GIRL: It was them.

BLAKE: I doubt it.

GIRL: You see – they'll beat you up ... just you cheek them and they'll do what they did to Fred. He told me all about what these redcaps was like – how they got lads into trouble with hands in their pockets ... just for having their hands in their pockets.

BLAKE: Let's put you right on one thing darling ...

GIRL: That sort of thing.

BLAKE: ... we're not redcaps. I hate redcaps. We are not even Regimental Police are we?

HOSKINSON: Redcaps ... we're not redcaps.

GIRL: I've been told they're the worst.

BLAKE: Eh?

GIRL: The regimentals – them as were dead regimental.

HOSKINSON: We're not ...

BLAKE: Never were ...

HOSKINSON: ... on the police.

BLAKE: ... on the provost.

HOSKINSON: I'm a tradesman.

GIRL: That makes it worse. You – his own mates. What was it you did?

BLAKE: I'll tell you what he did.

GIRL: Can't I talk to him?

BLAKE: Come to think of it – I can't allow you to talk to the prisoner.

JUPP: More than your job's worth.

BLAKE: That's it. Yes. How very understanding. Come and sit down here with me princess and I'll tell you the story of my life ... a demonstration by numbers followed by an explanation ...

GIRL: Thanks all the same – it's the demonstrating I don't like.

BLAKE: Out. Now we know where we stand I'll have to turf you out ... what you let her in for 'Oskie?

HOSKINSON: Not me.

BLAKE: You must have done.

HOSKINSON: Hey.

BLAKE: Out.

HOSKINSON: Course if she's lively ...

BLAKE: Strips off.

HOSKINSON: One man leg show.

BLAKE: You fancy Jupp do you? This is a reserved compartment – military personnel, royal family and tarts about to pup should they ask ... breathe deep my darling and push your majesty. But you do fancy Jupp don't you?

GIRL: Why don't you give them a mouthful – why don't you?

BLAKE: Can't do you much good though can he – strung up there ... hanging from that rack like a kosher chicken.

JUPP: Why a kosher chicken?

BLAKE: Want me to let him down?

GIRL: Keeps his hands to himself – more than I can say ...

HOSKINSON: ... for some – hardly got much option has he?

BLAKE: Do you come here often?

HOSKINSON: No – only when I'm breathing heavy.

BLAKE: Tell us all about your life darling. The story of my life ... How you came to ...

HOSKINSON: How did you come to?

BLAKE: They say first and last.

HOSKINSON: Sweeties – in the park?

BLAKE: It was the vicar.

HOSKINSON: The quack.

BLAKE: The butcher.

HOSKINSON: The baker.

BLAKE: The candle?

HOSKINSON: The landlord.

BLAKE: The landlord's missus – or even ...

HOSKINSON: Even?

BLAKE: Brother Fred?

HOSKINSON: Fred.

GIRL: Fred.

BLAKE: Fusilier Fred.

JUPP: Wrap up will you – give the girl some – wrap up ...

BLAKE: Droit dee elder brother ... all the best families have traditions. I respect tradition princess. My dearest wish is to have it off with tradition – prefer it royal of course but I can take it baron only. Was it Fred in the fine old tradition of warm in winter? And he did it himself.

GIRL: He did not.

BLAKE: He did.

HOSKINSON: I remember him telling me – he did it himself.

BLAKE: 'Course he was thick as shit and twice as nasty.

GIRL: He did not.

JUPP: Take no notice.

BLAKE: Oh yes. Fred was off his rails.

GIRL: He was not.

BLAKE: Fusilier Fred.

HOSKINSON: He was docile – wasn't he?

GIRL: Belt up you damned ... stinking bastards. [*She sits and cries – a mixture of rage and great forgotten sorrow which now floods in.*]

BLAKE [*crows with delight*]: She's got your number 'Oskie ... I always thought you was a stinking bastard.

HOSKINSON: Ooooooooh – doesn't take her long does it.

BLAKE: Soon changes her tune – stops putting it on.

HOSKINSON: Didn't take long to find her out did it ...?

BLAKE: Oooooooooh aren't you awful. I'll give her awful.

JUPP: You got a sister 'Oskie?

HOSKINSON: Don't get personal.

BLAKE: A lovely girl.

HOSKINSON: What about my sister?

JUPP: Goes with his chicko.

BLAKE: Now pack that in.

HOSKINSON: She's a decent girl.

BLAKE: A lovely girl.

JUPP: I can tell that.

BLAKE: You didn't tell me you'd got a sister 'Oskie.

JUPP: He's got a lovely sister.

BLAKE: She ... er ... she all right is she?

HOSKINSON: She's hardly a tart ... like that.

JUPP: She a teaser?

HOSKINSON: Do you mind if we change the subject?

BLAKE: She a bramah is she?

JUPP: Tell us about your sister 'Oskie. Youth club – round the club most evenings? Coffee bar?

HOSKINSON: No coffee barring ... I'll tell you that. In by ten or a belting. Our dad wouldn't stand for that.

JUPP: 'kin 'ell.

BLAKE: Dead right too.

HOSKINSON: What's wrong with that?

JUPP: Tell us more.

HOSKINSON: Jag it.

BLAKE: She live with you – always round – sitting with her knees up?

HOSKINSON: Till she gets married. Oh yes – she lives at home until she gets married.

JUPP: Any pictures?

HOSKINSON: Shut it.

JUPP: You haven't seen her have you corp – ask 'Oskie to show ouy pictures.

BLAKE: She a bramah then?

JUPP: Indeed.

BLAKE: Getting wed is she 'Oskie?

JUPP: I should go – go on – now [to the GIRL].

GIRL: It's not right – he wasn't mental.

BLAKE: He did do it himself – with his head hard.

HOSKINSON: He was like Jupp here ...

GIRL: No. He wasn't like you – he wasn't as clever as you ...

BLAKE: Stroll on.

HOSKINSON: Clever?

GIRL: But he liked the army – I don't know why.

BLAKE: And Jupp. Found a home he did.

HOSKINSON: Army don't like him – that's the only thing.

JUPP: Getting back to your sister.

HOSKINSON: Keep your filthy nose out of my family.

GIRL: I know about his sister.

HOSKINSON: I think that's highly in doubt – without a doubt ... I doubt it.

JUPP: I know about your sister.

HOSKINSON: I doubt if you'd know a decent girl if you saw one.

JUPP: Is she decent?

GIRL: I bet she's decent.

JUPP: Does she keep herself decent?

GIRL: I bet she's ever so big-headed.

JUPP: Is she decent?

GIRL: I bet she's a very good girl.

HOSKINSON: What's wrong with that?

GIRL: Stuck up ... thinks she's better than the rest.

HOSKINSON: And she is ... she's a decent girl.

JUPP: How do you know Jack – your Dad tell you ...?

GIRL: Yes. How do you know she's so decent? She might have free love.

HOSKINSON: Shut up will you – keep your decent noses out of a filthy family.

JUPP: Clanger, 'Oskie. Rattled.

GIRL: I bet she's smug – your sister.

BLAKE: Jupp's very respectable.

GIRL: Least he's not smug.

BLAKE: Before it gets out of hand I'll tell you how respectable Jupp is shall I?

HOSKINSON: Don't he think he's something. Big headed. Slip of the tongue that's all.

BLAKE: He slipped more than his tongue didn't he 'Oskie?

HOSKINSON: And if being respectable is being smug as you call it ...

JUPP: It is.

BLAKE: Follows then, that Jupp is highly smug then.

JUPP: What I think is right and what Her Majesty's Generals ...

BLAKE: Never.

HOSKINSON: Tell her how respectable he is then Corporal Blake.

GIRL: I don't want to know.

BLAKE: Her Tisswasses Generals have never even heard of you.

JUPP: There's one that has.

BLAKE: Just one?

JUPP: Very definitely.

BLAKE: Well – he wasn't was he?

JUPP: Herr von ... Kisswasti ... whatever his bleeding name was.

BLAKE: Well he wasn't was he – he was a deutscher kraut General wasn't he?

JUPP: And his face is still hot.

BLAKE: Never. You was marched off so fast your feet did not touch the virgin square.

JUPP: He saw enough.

BLAKE: Never in a million years – and if he did! ... it's always happening to these kraut Generals ...

JUPP: Christ – he was there ... where my hand is – that near.

BLAKE: ... they're misunderstood.

HOSKINSON: You see how respectable he is.

GIRL: I don't want to know.

BLAKE: Don't you know already? Didn't it get in the papers in Blighty? It didn't get in the papers Jupp.

JUPP: It got where I wanted it. He'll remember.

BLAKE: Oh well – let me fill you in then princess.

HOSKINSON: Two's up.

GIRL: I don't really want to know you know.

BLAKE: Be an education for you. Stop me if you've heard it Jupp; Admin. Parade in Germany – standing there tits all bare was Jupp and me.

HOSKINSON: And me.

BLAKE: And 'Oskie. Done a bit has 'Oskie.

JUPP: And it is a bit.

BLAKE: Be upstanding then Jupp – you want to tell it.

JUPP: Tell her who else then.

BLAKE: Who else? My old mate Smiler who you got stripped ...

JUPP: Who else? Standing there alongside of us.

BLAKE: Didn't notice.

HOSKINSON: Brigade H.Q.?

JUPP: And the others.

BLAKE: And the others? What others, Jupp?

JUPP: The other we was waiting for.

BLAKE: Who was – you was?

JUPP: You was waiting ... And didn't I see you in the haircut queue the night previous? Didn't I see you elbows bent, beezing and buffing, pressing and dressing stiff as a guardroom blanket?

BLAKE: Not me you didn't Jack. I'm a baron – you might have seen him ... I employ others to do my kit, and I'm never checked.

JUPP: Didn't I see you medals up then?

BLAKE: You might have seen that.

JUPP: A bright lot – standing there – thumbs down the seams of their slacks – rank on rank of smug faced one step from cretins ... beer bint and fag tickets ... swaying together – and the band played a jolly little tune while we waited ... This lot – my lot? In the history books – this is me ... this is how I'll be sorted out, classified, lumped together with this bunch? Standing there – on parade ... medals up ... all the lot of us with the badges of our period ... blue white yellow – Korea ... purple green – Malaya Palestine Cyprus ... black green yellow – Kenya. And the others who should have known better. France and Germany. Africa Star – Italy – Burma ... every Star. Not a flicker on their smug fat faces. Not a sign of emotion as they watched the ski caps slope past ...

BLAKE: What you expect – expect us to burst into tears?

GIRL: A few tears ...

BLAKE: You're the dab hand at tears ...

GIRL: ... wouldn't do you any harm.

BLAKE: ... give us a few more – I can't resist a wet eye.

HOSKINSON: He expects us to burst into tears because he lost his old man or something – grandad or something – gassed or something ...

BLAKE: No – was it the Jerries? You giving us the old down with the krauts? Goose step – whip in puddy – breeches and jackboots and quivering naked Jew girls ...

GIRL: You'd have liked that.

BLAKE: Lapped it up my girl.

GIRL: You look like a German officer.

BLAKE: You ever see one?

JUPP: I didn't say that.

GIRL: But he does.

BLAKE: Seen 'em – I've shot 'em.

GIRL: He does look like a German.

JUPP: I didn't say anything about barbed wire and the Jews and that.

46

BLAKE: No – but that's what you're on about – what's up ... you a Yiddel? Living in the past. That's your trouble – unless you're a Yiddel?

JUPP: I'm not saying that.

BLAKE: Good soldiers. Rather fight with 'em.

HOSKINSON: And they don't like the Russians.

BLAKE: Better if we'd kept going – joined up with the jerries and kept going ... we'd have knocked seven colours of shit out of old Joe ...

JUPP: And now we'd be starting on China ...

BLAKE: That's it – we got to sooner or later.

HOSKINSON: You can't blame the jerries for everything – what's a few Jews less?

JUPP: You can't say that.

HOSKINSON: I've said it.

GIRL: What did you do?

HOSKINSON: I've as much right as you to say it.

JUPP: Look it wasn't that they were jerries ... it was ... I don't know ... the two together – the two of us, khaki and wermacht green stood young ... and the smug look on the officers' faces ...

BLAKE: Officers.

JUPP: And on mine – I could see myself too ...

BLAKE: Bleeding acrobat.

JUPP: It didn't make sense – here we were limbering up for another go ... this time muckers ... I mean – one of those wars was a waste of time.

HOSKINSON: That's what we want – a good war.

JUPP: A few years ago we were saving mankind – right?

BLAKE: Who was – you was? I was saving Jim Blake.

JUPP: You've seen them. Did you see them march past – green uniforms shining brasses – real chuffed. No – you know what? They were taking the mick. A few years back they were being jumped on good and hard ... back. Deutschland deutschland. Oh very hilarious.

BLAKE: Jerries always was fond of uniforms.

JUPP: Military maniacs all of them. What about my old man – and lots of others as weren't there to have the mick taken out of them ...? Whilst this lot was playing a game of soldiers – pushing out their poxy chests – my old man was pushing up the daisies and his mates, full of spandau bullets and bits of Krupp tubing.

BLAKE: I know what you're full of.

JUPP: All of them chuffed to our house – and that medal clinking refugee from Stalingrad leading them on ... I had him. His face was nigh on scarlet. So red it nigh on melted his ritterkreuz. I pissed on his boots.

BLAKE: Down with the krauts.

JUPP: Don't get me wrong – It wasn't just the jerries. I wasn't just having a go at the jerries. I was shooting it up the kilt of every stupid bastard as braces up to the beat of a drum.

BLAKE: You was?

JUPP: Trumpet.

BLAKE: You was?

JUPP: Tin bleeding whistle.

BLAKE: You was?

JUPP: Up the kilt of every twat as thinks it's more than just a great carve up.

BLAKE: You did it. You braced – I saw you. You was one of the biggest bullshitters in the regiment.

JUPP: So I did. So I lapped up playing at soldiers.

BLAKE: Lapped it up – always said too much bullshit aggravated the brain.

JUPP: Well I changed didn't I? Saw the light.

HOSKINSON: Do you good if you had.

JUPP: I slashed on his boots. [*Smiles very happy at the thought. And the train stops suddenly. He is thrown across the carriage and jerks his hand in the handcuffs. Steam and a clanking noise from outside as* HOSKINSON *opens the window and puts his head out. A car horn.*]

GIRL: Did you hurt yourself?

JUPP: My wrist. These blasted handcuffs.

GIRL: He's hurt himself.

BLAKE: He's not hurt.

HOSKINSON: We've stopped.

BLAKE: Hoskinson's bright. We've stopped.

GIRL: It's all red.

BLAKE: Due to us stopping. 'Oskie says we've stopped.

JUPP: It's all right.

BLAKE: There.

GIRL: Let him down.

HOSKINSON: Can't see much.

BLAKE: You won't.

GIRL: He's hurt.

BLAKE: Tell him to go sick. [*Pokes his head out above Hoskinson's.*]

GIRL: Have you got a hankie?

JUPP: No. It's all right.

GIRL: Let me put a hankie wound round it – keep it from chapping.

HOSKINSON: I thought it might be Brum.

BLAKE: It's not.

HOSKINSON: It's not Brum – don't think so at any rate.

GIRL: I get out at Birmingham. [*She balances on the seat and ties a handkerchief round Jupp's wrist.*]

JUPP: You do.

GIRL: What happens?

JUPP: Am I like Fred? I feel helpless like Fred felt – do I look hopeless? It was so long ago ... and it was over so fast – I might never have done it.

GIRL: What happens?

JUPP: Shepton Mallet ... this to Catterick then the Mallet where they pound you – do they pound you, and then out. Roll on ... out.

GIRL: I've been living with a chap. I liked him and I've lived with him like we was married ... before that messed about – he stopped me ... you know? But I wasn't on the game properly – never took money ... I just messed about ... there.

JUPP: Well.

GIRL: When you get out.

JUPP: A long long time ... They got a list as long as your arm. Conduct prejudicial's the least of it ... there's wilful destruction of W.D. property... I burned it – arson – impersonating an officer ... I said I was a captain ... desertion, gunpowder treason and plot ... I wish they'd left me a day longer. I'd have done magnificent things.

GIRL: You do look like he looked – a bit.

JUPP: I know how I look. I look like a corporal I know looked when they got him for buggery and they didn't try him until they got evidence ... we all knew and they made him go to the cookhouse normally under escort ... because he was still a corporal until he was guilty. He used to grin tears at us and we all felt dirty – he felt dirty ... we used to look all at the roof rather than look at him grinning at us helpless ... If I'd not done it that way.

BLAKE: But you did Jupp. [*Still outside the window over Hoskinson.*]

HOSKINSON: Eh?

BLAKE: Is it Brum 'Oskie?

HOSKINSON: You're hurting corporal ... [*He giggles.* BLAKE *presses down on him.*]

GIRL: I did earn good money for a bit – in a shop. I'm not with him now. He went a long time back – he said he would. I expected him to really.

BLAKE: Keep looking for Brum 'Oskie.

GIRL: You married?

JUPP: Yes.

GIRL: No – not now.

JUPP: Her old man was an old time squaddie.

GIRL: I could help – anywhere else I could help.

BLAKE: Go on darling you help ... don't be put off ... I want to turn round quick and see you helping.

JUPP: No – they all tried to help at finger's length ... thumb and finger ... the Padre – a spiritual lack my dear boy. The Psychiatrist ... you ever wet the bed? The Provost Sergeant – get stuck in with that mop – soon forget your worries.

GIRL: I don't see why you did it.

BLAKE: Help him.

HOSKINSON: What?

BLAKE: Not you 'Oskie – sit still – I won't have your little cherry.

GIRL: I mean you was a corporal – you was getting on in the army ... not like our Fred.

BLAKE: He did it himself.

GIRL: That was a help.

JUPP: I don't need any help.

BLAKE: He's a right wet ... get helped.

GIRL: No – perhaps I need some … I've never been to Birmingham before – I'm starting again? All right.

JUPP: No.

[*A pause. Then* BLAKE *turns suddenly and is furious to see them just looking at each other.*]

HOSKINSON: Oooooh – that hurt.

BLAKE: Now then – a bucket of water for you.

HOSKINSON: My pistol sticking into me.

[*The train starts.* BLAKE *pulls the girl down.*]

BLAKE: I told you to watch these 'Oskie … Another minute and they'd have been well away. You have got some filthy habits Jupp.

GIRL: Don't pull me round.

BLAKE: He did it to himself didn't he – your Fred.

GIRL: He did not.

JUPP: Don't let him stir it up.

BLAKE: Because he was mentally hatchah …

GIRL: He did not.

BLAKE: Yes.

GIRL: No.

[BLAKE *stops her from swiping him with her handbag and takes it from her.*]

GIRL: Give it me.

BLAKE: What's in it? [*He opens it.*]

GIRL: Don't you open my handbag.

JUPP: Give it back to her.

BLAKE: Why – what you got to hide?

GIRL: You're not supposed to go round opening girls' handbags.

BLAKE: Yes I am. Rough old thing – where d'you whip it – Woolies?

GIRL: Please give it to me.

JUPP: Come on Blake.

HOSKINSON: Cheap old thing in it corporal – wouldn't be seen dead with a handbag like that – rough.

JUPP: What's your handbag like darling …?

BLAKE [*puts it behind his back*]: Breast round me to get it. To you 'Oskie.

[*She grabs it.* BLAKE *does too. The fastening goes. Some of the contents come out on to the floor.*]

51

GIRL: You've broken it now ... See – now the fastening's broke with your messing about ...

JUPP: You'd best go.

BLAKE: Go on – slope off.

GIRL: My things.

JUPP: It's nearly Brum.

GIRL: Give me my things.

HOSKINSON: Here.

BLAKE: Give us it.

[HOSKINSON *gives it to him and giggles.*]

BLAKE: Had you thought Jupp.

HOSKINSON: Here's a turn up.

GIRL: That's mine.

BLAKE: Your help – where she's been at?

HOSKINSON: Mawomba.

GIRL: That's my snap.

JUPP: Give it to her Blake – don't you ever take a day off?

BLAKE: No – you. I'm thinking of you.

HOSKINSON: Makes you think.

BLAKE: And old Jupp here – getting on fine he was.

HOSKINSON: You know what they say?

BLAKE: You think it's true?

HOSKINSON: What's wrong with her own kind?

BLAKE: Is it true? Just academic – is it true?

GIRL: I don't know what you're on about.

BLAKE: Here Jupp – shufti this my old.

GIRL: I told you about him. Yes yes – I told you. I did. I told you I'd left him – he'd left me ... that's why I'm going to Brum.

BLAKE: You didn't tell him your boy friend was as black as the ace of spades.

HOSKINSON: And most like a cannibal.

BLAKE: No wonder Fred went spare – brother to a Kuke ... I'd beat my own head in.

GIRL: He was kind – and he helped me out when I was desperate ... give it me.

BLAKE: Out – jeldi.

HOSKINSON: We know what you was desperate for.

BLAKE: Beat it.

HOSKINSON: Get a jildi on – bahdin ... that's what they say isn't it.

BLAKE: Isn't there enough of us? Down the train – here down the train.

GIRL: But you knew.

HOSKINSON: Disgusting. Imshi.

JUPP: Well – I didn't hear you say he was coloured.

BLAKE: Down the train – there's a couple of your mates down the train – you go and tap them up.

HOSKINSON: Jembo – that's what they say isn't it?

BLAKE: No 'Oskie. Go on – you can't miss them ... two sons of Africa scoffing Kit-e-Kat sandwiches. Tap 'em up – they'll be a help to you.

JUPP: There's good and there's bad you know.

GIRL: So? No – I thought so.

BLAKE: Out – raus.

GIRL: Yes. Filthy lot – your sly double filthy meanings – think you're the first to try it on. I've thrown out better than you before breakfast – and as for you ... you're as bad – you are as bad, high and mighty set the world to rights or whatever – messing in public. I reckon the doctor must have been right about you wetting the bed.

HOSKINSON: Get back to Ghana.

BLAKE: That's it – that's it. Get back to Ghana.

GIRL: And you can all go where it's a bleeding sight hotter. [*She goes, leaving the door open.* BLAKE *shuts it.*]

BLAKE: What a turn up eh? And old Jupp fancied her. That right Jupp – you fancied her?

HOSKINSON: You can't do anything with them once they've been with a black.

BLAKE: You'll be a good bloke now Jupp? That so. It's the calling that hurts in it? Sticks and stones?

HOSKINSON: In it funny – she was ever so pretty really.

BLAKE: Not a peep.

HOSKINSON: They can't find satisfaction you see.

BLAKE: Not a peep – all the way back. Bets?

HOSKINSON: She'll do anything – they get a hold.

BLAKE: It ain't true 'Oskie.

HOSKINSON: Voodoo.

BLAKE: No.

HOSKINSON: How do they get a white woman to flog her oggins for them then? You read it all the time.

BLAKE: It is not true 'Oskie.

HOSKINSON: And they hands her round – parties ... it's a tribal custom.

BLAKE: You been at those Sunday papers again.

HOSKINSON: It's not only what you hear ⌐ it's what you read. There was that woman down the road from us – wouldn't have it – she let her house to them – she wouldn't have it. Next to no time it was full of them, they was there, hanging out the windows all hours – and they grew that stuff in the back ...

BLAKE: You're discriminated. There's sod all wrong with the Spades and they stick to themselves ... I hate the bloody Kukes though ... taxi drivers. You've got a morbid interest. You ought to get posted to Nairobi – you fancy a bit yourself.

HOSKINSON: She was quite pretty, though, wasn't she?

BLAKE: Fair. Can't say I fancies her much now though. Funny in it? Even old Jupp cried off.

JUPP: Leave me out.

BLAKE: You cried off.

HOSKINSON: Well.

BLAKE: Very true 'Oskie. You're back then Jupp.

JUPP: It doesn't bother me.

BLAKE: Lies.

HOSKINSON: Creepy though in it?

BLAKE: Eyes.

JUPP: I didn't think anything of it.

BLAKE: Lies. She saw your eyes. She saw your eyes step to the rear two paces ... and I did.

HOSKINSON: It is creepy – exciting ...

JUPP: Surprise that's all.

BLAKE: Might let you down. Take those off – don't seem right for a white man – fancy a game of three-card brag?

JUPP: No. I'll stay here. I'll do a bunk. You'd best not take me down or I'll do a bunk and get you busted like I got Smiler Lewis ... stripped. I'll not come down.

BLAKE: No – I twigged that. What you on Jupp ...?

HOSKINSON: They put more into life don't they? Funny feeling in it?

BLAKE: What you on Jupp?

JUPP: What's Smiler on?

BLAKE: He'll get made up – there aren't many of us left ...

HOSKINSON: Sort of exciting ... funny feeling.

JUPP: There's more of us ...

BLAKE: I doubt it mate. What you on Jupp?

JUPP: Adventure training – what you on?

HOSKINSON: All right if I pays a visit corporal?

BLAKE: It didn't mean a thing.

JUPP: Maybe not – but it means a lot to me. And you. [*Rattles his handcuffs.*]

HOSKINSON: All right?

BLAKE: What?

HOSKINSON: Pay a visit?

BLAKE: Eh?

HOSKINSON: Take a leak.

BLAKE: What do you want me to do? Hold it for you?

HOSKINSON: No. [*He opens the door to the corridor and stands.*]

BLAKE: No it doesn't mean a thing.

HOSKINSON: All right?

BLAKE: You're not up there for slashing on parade – don't mean a thing to me. I see 'em in the parks all the time on leave ...
   [HOSKINSON *goes.*]
   You're up there simply because you dropped old Smiler in it. He carried the can. You wouldn't understand – you haven't got any mates ... We've forgotten all about 'down with the krauts' boy ...

JUPP: It wasn't down with the krauts.

BLAKE: Eyes again Jupp.

JUPP: It was – frightened ... it was ... just no.

BLAKE: What we put it down to is sheer lack of live and let live – prejudice. [*Sits on the seat and looks up at Jupp.*
   Black-out.]

SCENE FOUR

In the darkness the train pulls into B'ham station where they say 'Birmingham New Street' and we hear people getting off. Lights up on a platform.

> [*The* GIRL *stands looking at the blinds down and black carriage in which* JUPP *and* BLAKE *sit,* JUPP *biting the handkerchief.*]

HOSKINSON [*talks to the Girl*]: Brum – good dancing in Brum – some good places. I like dancing. Good band – you know. You staying in Brum? We get posted all over the shop you know – I might get posted to the T.A. – near Brum. You like dancing?

GIRL: Dance off.

HOSKINSON: I'm not like him you know. Nothing wrong with the Spades so long as they stick to themselves – I'm not discriminated. Do they …?

GIRL: Now go away filth …

HOSKINSON: What are you then? Having it off with Spades. No – look he asked me to come out and see you …

GIRL: Who?

HOSKINSON: The one you're looking at through that black. Jupp. He just wanted to say he was sorry about what occurred and could he have your address – you got an address? You got digs? Well. So he could write. And he said perhaps I could pop down and see you like on a forty-eight should I get one and tell you how he's getting on in the nick.

GIRL: Just clear off. I don't want to see your kind any more than I have to … [*The guard whistles. Doors slam shut and there's a hurry up puff from the train.*]

HOSKINSON: Now that's not being fair to yourself, is it? You've got to live haven't you? You're going to some address aren't you? Somewhere we can contact you – should any … only jildi … [*Gets into the train. Stands with the door open …*]

> [BLAKE *opens the door and looks out at* 'Oskie.]

HOSKINSON: Not even a kind word for poor old Harry Jupp then? [*The train starts to move and the* GIRL *runs alongside the door. She gives an envelope to Hoskinson.*]

BLAKE: 'Oskinson.

HOSKINSON: This it?

GIRL: Where I am – give it him if he wants it. [*She runs backwards as the train gains speed.*]

HOSKINSON: Try Aston – that's where your mates hang out.

BLAKE [*stands at the door as* HOSKINSON *comes back down the corridor*]: Where you been?

　[HOSKINSON *comes into the carriage.* BLAKE *lets him past.*
　HOSKINSON *stands looking out. The* GIRL *is gone in the black.*]

BLAKE: Where you been?

HOSKINSON: Been for a slash en I?

BLAKE: Long enough for a Barclay's en you? What you got there?

HOSKINSON [*close to Jupp puts the envelope in his left breast pocket and buttons it*]: Pay book corporal. That's all. [*And close to Jupp he says*] Don't bite on that handkerchief Jupp – you'll tear it.

CURTAIN

2. JOHN THOMAS

A Bed Sitter.

> [JOHN THOMAS *comes in and plugs in the kettle, then he hangs up his raincoat by the tape under its black grease piped collar.*
> *A badly packed parcel on the table. Brown paper made black by the rain and whipped round and round with string like a roped steer. Looks like a pair of boots under the paper and string.*
> *You'd think it was precious.*
> *A knock on the door.*]

JOHN THOMAS: Just hold on ... with you in a minute. [*He puts the boots under the table and covers them with a towel. Then he opens the door to the* MAN FROM UPSTAIRS.] Yes? They let you down then.

MAN FROM UPSTAIRS: What you expect? Selection? Should be bred to it – born not made.

JOHN THOMAS: They've picked up some bad habits. Very loose – every way but the right way.

MAN FROM UPSTAIRS: I'm having divers friends in tonight.

JOHN THOMAS: Upstairs?

MAN FROM UPSTAIRS: ... just so you don't wonder.

JOHN THOMAS: Certainly. Fellow colleagues from the Town Hall?

MAN FROM UPSTAIRS: Parks and Cleansing.

JOHN THOMAS: Now that is a coincidence ...

MAN FROM UPSTAIRS: In the event – I like to keep them sweet.

JOHN THOMAS: ... for my forefather was in lumberjacking.

MAN FROM UPSTAIRS: ... In Housing ...

JOHN THOMAS: Not here.

MAN FROM UPSTAIRS: ... we couldn't hardly survive without their co-operation.

JOHN THOMAS: Ontario.

MAN FROM UPSTAIRS: But it works both ways.

JOHN THOMAS: You scratch my back ...

MAN FROM UPSTAIRS: I tip Cleansing the wink.

JOHN THOMAS: ... I scratch yours.

MAN FROM UPSTAIRS: He gives me the wire.

JOHN THOMAS: They would have a lot in common.

MAN FROM UPSTAIRS: I pick up the mail for Parks.

JOHN THOMAS: I envy him the outdoor life.

MAN FROM UPSTAIRS: He sees me right for roller towels.

JOHN THOMAS: You've got to haven't you?

MAN FROM UPSTAIRS: Just so you know – that's all. Going out?

JOHN THOMAS: Just got in.

MAN FROM UPSTAIRS: Your kettle's boiling.

JOHN THOMAS: Shocking out.

MAN FROM UPSTAIRS: Got wet did you?

JOHN THOMAS: Just that bit from the tube. Wringing by the top of the street. I walk along thinking I ought to live the other way.

MAN FROM UPSTAIRS: Under the arcade all the absolute way – mind you'd have to live with all nations ... and not mind their ways.

JOHN THOMAS: Funny how it's just that end.

MAN FROM UPSTAIRS: Streets full of them now – fifty per cent of a bus queue grins like the back row of the nigger minstrels ...

JOHN THOMAS: They're clever you know – don't see them walking this way and getting soaked.

MAN FROM UPSTAIRS: So long as they don't.

JOHN THOMAS: You can't do anything about it. You're not stopping? I mean there's a cup for you.

MAN FROM UPSTAIRS: What you got under the board?

JOHN THOMAS: I don't follow you. I don't know where you mean ... which board is that?

MAN FROM UPSTAIRS: It's all right.

JOHN THOMAS: No – it's all right.

MAN FROM UPSTAIRS: No – it's just me being nosey.

JOHN THOMAS: Oh.

MAN FROM UPSTAIRS: I wondered if I could – well. Seem to have run out of sugar.

JOHN THOMAS: We ought to do something about it. It's a very real problem what you were saying a couple of days ago ... when jobs are affected it's not race any more – is it?

MAN FROM UPSTAIRS: They threatening you that way?

JOHN THOMAS: It could come to that, it's almost a statistical certainty ... what with the steady influx and the general shortage of teachers. It could come to that – when they reach the standard.

MAN FROM UPSTAIRS: Won't come to that. Not for me at any rate. Be a long time before the public will stand for coloured civic dignitaries. Can you see it?

JOHN THOMAS: The more that come in.

MAN FROM UPSTAIRS: Well it's not likely is it?

JOHN THOMAS: It's our children though.

MAN FROM UPSTAIRS: Never noticed – you don't though do you when they're well behaved?

JOHN THOMAS: They're like children in a lot of ways – bright colours is the way that comes to mind – their predilection for colours.

MAN FROM UPSTAIRS: Only if you can spare it.

JOHN THOMAS: I can – if we can't help each other?

MAN FROM UPSTAIRS: I've got a basin.

JOHN THOMAS: I bought a couple of pound yesterday.

MAN FROM UPSTAIRS: Put it in here – I brought it down.

JOHN THOMAS: Thanks.

MAN FROM UPSTAIRS: Only I thought I ought to warn you off.

JOHN THOMAS: Party is it?

MAN FROM UPSTAIRS: No.

JOHN THOMAS: Not being nosey ...

MAN FROM UPSTAIRS: The usual thing that's all.

JOHN THOMAS: That be enough?

MAN FROM UPSTAIRS: So don't go typing any more letters of complaint to the landlord saying I keep you awake half the night – all right? [He takes his sugar and goes upstairs slamming the door shut behind him.]

JOHN THOMAS: He's gone – who else? [Makes his tea and pours some into a pint mug.] Like Tottenham Court Road ... who else? Like Regent Street – what you think this is?
Paddington Main Line Station?
Like Paddington Main Line Station?
What do you think this is? The Watford By-pass?
Like Piccadilly Circus. [He sips his tea.]

Coloured civic dignitaries, he has got a point there. Is it likely? Turn again Little Black Sambo, Lord Mayor of London. Rombard of D Stream.

[*He reassures himself by touching the boots parcel, then goes to the wardrobe.*]

Or extend the hypothesis ... meet Captain Uncle Tom of the Blues.

They have brought a certain element of bingo all the fours droopy drawers to The Cricket.

Rastus. Bishop of Bath and Wells.

[*He looks inside the wardrobe, then goes to the washbasin in the corner.*]

Ought I to shave?

For the full effect?

What do you think this is? Paddington Main Line?

[*There is a large mirror over the washbasin. It hangs horizontally.* JOHN THOMAS *takes it down and props it vertically against his bed. He takes off his coat and then thinks about the window ... Draws the curtains. Knock on the door.*]

JOHN THOMAS [*panics. Puts his coat back on ... Dithers and opens the door*]: Yes?

MAN FROM UPSTAIRS: I'm sorry.

JOHN THOMAS: Can I help you?

MAN FROM UPSTAIRS: I wanted some tea as well. Have you got some tea?

JOHN THOMAS: I have – yes.

MAN FROM UPSTAIRS: Did you go then on Saturday?

JOHN THOMAS: No – were you up there?

MAN FROM UPSTAIRS: They won't see me up there until there's a vast improvement all round – not again.

JOHN THOMAS: It's heartbreaking on the whole.

MAN FROM UPSTAIRS: Taken the mirror down?

JOHN THOMAS: Yes – I just put it there.

MAN FROM UPSTAIRS: Yes – it wasn't there a brief moment ago.

JOHN THOMAS: Don't you take your mirror down?

MAN FROM UPSTAIRS: Quick.

JOHN THOMAS: I'm cleaning the wall behind it.

MAN FROM UPSTAIRS: No need for that.

JOHN THOMAS: Why not?

MAN FROM UPSTAIRS: We'll all have to do it won't we? You start that it's like somebody cleans his boot studs and bulls the instep ... a very good idea now everybody do it.

JOHN THOMAS: I'll put it back.

MAN FROM UPSTAIRS: Thank you.

JOHN THOMAS: Keep the packet. And let me have a packet back – the one and nine.

MAN FROM UPSTAIRS: You asking?

JOHN THOMAS: Eh?

MAN FROM UPSTAIRS: Or telling?

JOHN THOMAS: I'm going out.

MAN FROM UPSTAIRS: Not in those boots you're not.

JOHN THOMAS: When you come down again don't expect me to answer the door because I'm going out.

MAN FROM UPSTAIRS: Nobody would let you into their house or a restaurant in those boots. Can you picture it?

JOHN THOMAS: All right for motor biking.

MAN FROM UPSTAIRS: How much motor biking do you do? That's patently a lie ... you haven't got one.

JOHN THOMAS: I'm getting it gradual.

MAN FROM UPSTAIRS: I've got a typewriter you know – I can type letters to the landlord. Don't start revving late at night down here and fill my room full of smog.

No there's a reason for it.

JOHN THOMAS: So if I don't answer – you'll know why.

MAN FROM UPSTAIRS: Right.

That mirror.

JOHN THOMAS: What?

Manage to make yourself very clear will you?

MAN FROM UPSTAIRS: You know.

JOHN THOMAS: I'm a tenant same as you – aren't I?

MAN FROM UPSTAIRS: But before we're all cleaning behind ... fair warning?

JOHN THOMAS: And you.

MAN FROM UPSTAIRS: I'm telling you.

JOHN THOMAS: Oh dear – I have a lot of this.

MAN FROM UPSTAIRS: A friendly warning – fair enough? The poxy mirror back or I poxy well belt you.

JOHN THOMAS [*shuts the door in his face. The* MAN FROM UPSTAIRS *kicks the bottom panel just once and not hard.* JOHN THOMAS *listens to him going upstairs – hears the upstairs door shut and follows footsteps across the ceiling. He takes off his coat and waits*]: My attitude is too soft. I'm going out. I'm slack. Dead soft and soft as tit is soft. Yes.

I ought to be pick hard, ice incisive, plough in stones. Only I'm soft as milk. Yes.

Loathe it/like it. Well it's better out than in. Mary had a little lamb, she also had a lion. I've often seen her little lamb but never caught her lyin'. I've often seen myself sitting here being a lion. A lion of a lion ... a big wild, ear clipping, anti-heuristic, shaggy, larruping lion – roar.

All be lions.

Come on now – all together ... let's hear you roar ... when I roar, you roar. When I stamp, you stamp. Roar ... ROAR. Stamp ... STAMP.

Tell you what – all the teachers. All the teachers – when I say roar you roar ...

Right, little prelim ... they usually have a sheet, if I had a sheet it would help. I could write where you were to roar ... no let's see how loud can we roar ... no, no, first all the civic dignitaries – you stamp. All the civic dignitaries, when I say stamp ... you stamp but not until the teachers say roar, only not yet, I haven't said roar. And so on – pick it up ... pass it on when I say roar all the roars and when I say stamp all the stamps from the civics ... after the teachers say roar. Not at once, on the last exciting whooosh of the roar – let me get my stand up stamp in first or we will not know where we are ... will we? Lucid. And so on – pick it up. You'll soon pick it up.

Yes?

Roar ... didn't hear a thing ... you'll never make teachers ... roar. When I say roar ... you roar.

Roar ... ROAR.

It's coming. Now then civics — let's show the teachers some stamping.

Stamp ... STAMP.

Roar ... ROAR.

Come on ... come on ... bring me up. When I say roar every time I say roar ... strip tease ... roar ... ROAR. Little fluttery coat.

Stamp ... STAMP.

That's it ... now then now then.

Yes – yes.

[JOHN THOMAS *takes his trousers off and goes to the wardrobe —
then he reaches up into the wardrobe for something on a coat hanger.
A knock on the door.*

JOHN THOMAS *runs to the mirror — remembers his trousers ...
Another knock on the door and a* VOICE.]

VOICE: Open up – police.

JOHN THOMAS: I'm not decent.

VOICE: Put your trousers on – just put your trousers on.

JOHN THOMAS: I'm putting them on – fast as I can.

VOICE: You a brown hatter?

JOHN THOMAS: No.

VOICE: What's wrong with that?

JOHN THOMAS: I'm not that's all.

VOICE: Taking your trousers off – just put them back on that's all.

JOHN THOMAS: Yes. I'm sorry.

[JOHN THOMAS *has them on. He opens the door to the Man from
upstairs.*]

JOHN THOMAS: Come in – I'm sorry there's been this business over the trousers.

MAN FROM UPSTAIRS: Why?

JOHN THOMAS: Puts me on a bad footing.

MAN FROM UPSTAIRS: Knackers.

JOHN THOMAS: Sit down. Not up to last season's showing are they?

MAN FROM UPSTAIRS: Who?

JOHN THOMAS: You don't follow them then?

MAN FROM UPSTAIRS: Just routine arrest that's all – nothing to feel happy about.

JOHN THOMAS: Will it be in the papers?

MAN FROM UPSTAIRS: Are you in business?

JOHN THOMAS: I'm a teacher.

MAN FROM UPSTAIRS: You filthy thing – you disgusting knobby old randbag you.

JOHN THOMAS: No.

MAN FROM UPSTAIRS: Sex crimes have been reported.

JOHN THOMAS: Not me.

MAN FROM UPSTAIRS: I don't know.

JOHN THOMAS: You do.

MAN FROM UPSTAIRS: When you were just starting to read were you known at the library to be particularly drawn to the libidinous?

JOHN THOMAS: I'm not obliged to say anything.

MAN FROM UPSTAIRS: You're a young man.

JOHN THOMAS: I'm old enough to know my own mind.

MAN FROM UPSTAIRS: A young man should be out mating.

JOHN THOMAS: I do.

MAN FROM UPSTAIRS: You're not past it are you?

JOHN THOMAS: Yes – I'm too old for it now.

MAN FROM UPSTAIRS: This is just the sort of sex crime that would be committed by someone past it.

JOHN THOMAS: I was joking.

MAN FROM UPSTAIRS: Why?

JOHN THOMAS: I like a joke as much as anyone.

MAN FROM UPSTAIRS: Do you carry on in front of that mirror?

JOHN THOMAS: I shave if that's what you mean – and I look at my face ... when I'm washing.

MAN FROM UPSTAIRS: I don't look at my face.

JOHN THOMAS: No look – here's a good one. Listen here's a good one – do you know this one? Come over to the mirror ... [*They go over to the mirror*. JOHN THOMAS *looks in the mirror – screams and covers his face.*] Quick – help – arson – who was that?

MAN FROM UPSTAIRS: Who? [*He looks in the mirror.*]

JOHN THOMAS: Who's that?

MAN FROM UPSTAIRS: Adolf Hitler.

JOHN THOMAS: Thank goodness. I thought it was me.

MAN FROM UPSTAIRS: What do you do over by that mirror?

JOHN THOMAS: If it's about the noise – that's not me.

MAN FROM UPSTAIRS: It's about clothes lines.

JOHN THOMAS: Oh.

MAN FROM UPSTAIRS: Yes.

JOHN THOMAS: I lost three shirts from a clothes line in Colwyn Bay once – my own fault I gave them to someone else to be responsible for – if you want a job doing ... a circus got them. Vagabonds are wearing them.

MAN FROM UPSTAIRS: You use them then?

JOHN THOMAS: No.

MAN FROM UPSTAIRS: But you'd know where to find a clothes line.

JOHN THOMAS: Of course.

There's one down the bottom of the garden ... that dandelion jungle full of red hatted pixies looking ...

MAN FROM UPSTAIRS: One pair of panties blue – one pair of panties yellow – two pair of drawers Aertex.

JOHN THOMAS: ... looking at me.

MAN FROM UPSTAIRS: All missing overnight.

JOHN THOMAS: Don't look at me mate.

MAN FROM UPSTAIRS: You use them for dusters – that's it isn't it?

JOHN THOMAS: What are you asking me for? I've got nothing to hide ... have a search round and see. Not me officer. I'm a school teacher.

MAN FROM UPSTAIRS: I'm not going to look around.

JOHN THOMAS: Yes ... come on.

MAN FROM UPSTAIRS: I can't look around. I've got far too much on my plate.

JOHN THOMAS [*Licking his lips – nervously*]: Look in the wardrobe if you like – that's where I'd put them isn't it?

MAN FROM UPSTAIRS: You want to get me in that wardrobe.

JOHN THOMAS: Well – have a look ... satisfy yourself.

MAN FROM UPSTAIRS: You'll get me looking in that wardrobe for female raiment and slam the door – me inside. You'd like to get me shut up.

JOHN THOMAS: Not me mate.

I'm perfectly clear about you. You've got to ask questions and I've got to answer them – you've got to look and I've got to open the doors.

That's what we live in this country for. You'd better have a look.

MAN FROM UPSTAIRS: No – I'll take your word for it.

It's not sexual?

JOHN THOMAS: No. You must sublimate.

MAN FROM UPSTAIRS [*Triumphantly*]: I haven't got a warrant – you can't demand a search without a warrant. Ask me if I've got a warrant.

JOHN THOMAS: You haven't got one.

MAN FROM UPSTAIRS: Yes – but ask me.

JOHN THOMAS: This search of yours – through the house and my coat pockets. Have you got a warrant?

MAN FROM UPSTAIRS: Come now sir.

JOHN THOMAS: No – have you possession of a warrant?

MAN FROM UPSTAIRS: We can get a warrant.

JOHN THOMAS: You haven't got one though.

MAN FROM UPSTAIRS: Are you insisting? We'll kick your teeth in when we get you down to the station.

JOHN THOMAS: Veiled threats.

You can't force your way into a man's home and search through it without a warrant in this country ... all talk.

MAN FROM UPSTAIRS: That's right.

JOHN THOMAS: You'd do well to leave.

MAN FROM UPSTAIRS: No hard feelings ...?

JOHN THOMAS: You've got your job to do.

MAN FROM UPSTAIRS: That's mighty white of you Blackie.

JOHN THOMAS: That's all.

Don't come here doing it again – that's all.

MAN FROM UPSTAIRS: You asking sir?

JOHN THOMAS: No. I'm telling.

MAN FROM UPSTAIRS: You don't happen to be sexual then sir?

JOHN THOMAS: No more than anyone else.

MAN FROM UPSTAIRS: Don't give me that.

JOHN THOMAS: No.

MAN FROM UPSTAIRS: I've seen.

JOHN THOMAS: I don't know what you mean of course.

MAN FROM UPSTAIRS: I've seen you.

JOHN THOMAS: Unlikely.

MAN FROM UPSTAIRS: And I've seen you in the tube train.

JOHN THOMAS: What are you talking about?

MAN FROM UPSTAIRS: You.

JOHN THOMAS: Me?

MAN FROM UPSTAIRS: With the populace.

JOHN THOMAS: People?

MAN FROM UPSTAIRS: Don't echo.

JOHN THOMAS: No you haven't.

MAN FROM UPSTAIRS: Chin ...

JOHN THOMAS: No.

MAN FROM UPSTAIRS: ... on your shoulder.

JOHN THOMAS: Some other bloke.
   You've never stood ...

MAN FROM UPSTAIRS: I've stood ...

JOHN THOMAS: ... behind me?

MAN FROM UPSTAIRS: ... chin on your shoulder – that near.

JOHN THOMAS: Oh yes?
   I don't think so.

MAN FROM UPSTAIRS: Claw me – seen you purchasing.

JOHN THOMAS: I can hardly think so.

MAN FROM UPSTAIRS: Surely.

JOHN THOMAS: Can't help you out.

MAN FROM UPSTAIRS: Certainly.

JOHN THOMAS: For instance – what?

MAN FROM UPSTAIRS: For instance – various.

JOHN THOMAS: No – come on. You're so bright.

MAN FROM UPSTAIRS: And another thing.

JOHN THOMAS: That's another thing altogether.

MAN FROM UPSTAIRS: The match.

JOHN THOMAS: No – I will stay by my guns. No – I will not be
   sidetracked by red herrings.
   You say ... let's get it right because you are here at a disadvantage
   without your warrant to show.

MAN FROM UPSTAIRS: Don't rely on that.

JOHN THOMAS: I had got you on one leg there.

MAN FROM UPSTAIRS: Don't take advantage of my handicap.

JOHN THOMAS: No – be fair. You are in England.

MAN FROM UPSTAIRS: You can't deny I've come across you at the match.

JOHN THOMAS: White Hart Lane ... and another.

MAN FROM UPSTAIRS: And it's in.

JOHN THOMAS: And another.

MAN FROM UPSTAIRS: Give it to him.

JOHN THOMAS: Hock him.

MAN FROM UPSTAIRS: Dirty.

JOHN THOMAS: Decision.

MAN FROM UPSTAIRS: Centre.

JOHN THOMAS: Now.

MAN FROM UPSTAIRS: Now.

JOHN THOMAS: Whooooooooooraaaaaaaa.

MAN FROM UPSTAIRS: Whoooooooooraaaaa.

[*They laugh together excited.*]

JOHN THOMAS: Let off steam.

MAN FROM UPSTAIRS: Shake off.

JOHN THOMAS: Dirty water.

MAN FROM UPSTAIRS: A good shout.

JOHN THOMAS: Always good for a good night's sleep.

MAN FROM UPSTAIRS: A good rasping roar.

JOHN THOMAS: They're a study.

MAN FROM UPSTAIRS: When I roar – you roar.

JOHN THOMAS: I like studying them.

MAN FROM UPSTAIRS: I like a good game.

JOHN THOMAS: An education.

MAN FROM UPSTAIRS: Very real to some.

JOHN THOMAS: In their eyes. Very real to some. A good swing along pat on the back did you see that throat to tab roar.

MAN FROM UPSTAIRS: They get carried away.

JOHN THOMAS: I like a good game.

MAN FROM UPSTAIRS: Keeps you off the streets.

JOHN THOMAS: Through the streets.

Letting off steam.

A good swing along belt along shuffle fast along through the streets shoulder to wall roar ...

MAN FROM UPSTAIRS: When I stamp.

JOHN THOMAS: Run up.

MAN FROM UPSTAIRS: When I roar ...

JOHN THOMAS: Cower in the brick.

MAN FROM UPSTAIRS: Hands flat.

JOHN THOMAS: Shudder.

MAN FROM UPSTAIRS: Flutter on the grey brick.

JOHN THOMAS: Toe and clip.

MAN FROM UPSTAIRS: Boots you see – we all wear boots.

JOHN THOMAS: Glass.

MAN FROM UPSTAIRS: Crack it.

JOHN THOMAS: Black night.

MAN FROM UPSTAIRS: Flash it.

JOHN THOMAS: Red.

MAN FROM UPSTAIRS: Blue tinkle of cold broken glass.

JOHN THOMAS: Hand on mouth.

MAN FROM UPSTAIRS: Hand on snatch.

JOHN THOMAS: Hand on furry jewel.

MAN FROM UPSTAIRS: And you say it's not sexual?

[Long pause.]

JOHN THOMAS: Yes – I say that.

MAN FROM UPSTAIRS: Do you want to talk to me about it son?

JOHN THOMAS: You'd be the last.

MAN FROM UPSTAIRS: That's been said before.

JOHN THOMAS: I'd have to be very hard up.

MAN FROM UPSTAIRS: If I had five bob ...

JOHN THOMAS: I suppose it was those early films. I saw a lot of early films with my old man – he gave me a taste for it – before he died ... which he did ... in very tragic circumstances after *Birth of a Nation* ... for the umpteenth time.

MAN FROM UPSTAIRS: Bury me with a clean white spade.

JOHN THOMAS: The thing was – the thing that I'm trying to say was that we had to queue a lot for everything ... I suppose it was that early queueing gave me a taste for the common people thick on the ground. In those queues my old man used to come up like a sunflower – use them boy, when they're dead, they rich the ground and trees spring up, use them living like so much hot compost – so much sweet fertilizer ... to grow up out of ... spring up spring up with the trees. Up up for the strength to tolerate ... tower as a giant.

He was never coarse – fertilizer, he meant dung ... he was a very powerful mind ...

MAN FROM UPSTAIRS: I hope you're not going to go into a long and involved story without a word of truth in it to explain your lapse. Note that I say lapse.

JOHN THOMAS: Yes.

MAN FROM UPSTAIRS: There's no explanation.

JOHN THOMAS: No.

MAN FROM UPSTAIRS: And if there was – it's not evidence.

JOHN THOMAS: You'll have to take it into account.

MAN FROM UPSTAIRS: Why?

JOHN THOMAS: Because they do.

MAN FROM UPSTAIRS: You've been seeing too many early films with your old man before he died – as you laughingly put it – in tragic circumstances.

JOHN THOMAS: Just because you didn't.

MAN FROM UPSTAIRS: Not yet.

JOHN THOMAS: If I say I'm sorry. If I express my regret.

MAN FROM UPSTAIRS: Yes. Try that.

JOHN THOMAS: I've never yet been out ... while I don't go out ...

MAN FROM UPSTAIRS: Ah, but down there? You see you might. When I roar – you roar?

JOHN THOMAS: Ah now – that was just party games – make them feel involved ... Wasn't it?

MAN FROM UPSTAIRS: So you say – sir.

JOHN THOMAS: You'll stop and say sir again?

MAN FROM UPSTAIRS: You asking?

JOHN THOMAS: Yes.

MAN FROM UPSTAIRS: Or telling?

JOHN THOMAS: I'm going out.

MAN FROM UPSTAIRS: That's as well.

I'm having some people round.

JOHN THOMAS: Oh yes?

MAN FROM UPSTAIRS: Nobody you know.

JOHN THOMAS: I'd like to meet them.

MAN FROM UPSTAIRS: Really.

JOHN THOMAS: Yes – they sound very interesting – might take me out of myself.

MAN FROM UPSTAIRS: I'd say – bear in mind sir it's only a friendly warning such as I'd give to anyone in similar circumstances to yourself ...

JOHN THOMAS: Most grateful.

MAN FROM UPSTAIRS: Steer clear of the crowds.

JOHN THOMAS: It's not sexual officer.

MAN FROM UPSTAIRS: So you say sir.

JOHN THOMAS: No – honest.

MAN FROM UPSTAIRS: And another word of advice – when you're on the roads late at night – stick to sports coat and flannels.

JOHN THOMAS: You asking?

MAN FROM UPSTAIRS: I'm telling.

JOHN THOMAS: Out

Get out.

MAN FROM UPSTAIRS: See my meaning sir?

JOHN THOMAS: I have my rights. Leave.

MAN FROM UPSTAIRS: Are you sure?

JOHN THOMAS: Get out.

MAN FROM UPSTAIRS: Remember your old man died in very tragic and very untidy circumstances.

JOHN THOMAS: I think you ought to leave now. I've got to get dressed.

MAN FROM UPSTAIRS: Oh yes – in that case I'll have those boots you're so proud of.

JOHN THOMAS: They're my own.

MAN FROM UPSTAIRS: Let's have them.

JOHN THOMAS: My dad gave them to me.

MAN FROM UPSTAIRS: I've no doubt sir – let's be having them.

JOHN THOMAS: What will I do without the boots?

MAN FROM UPSTAIRS: I can't help that sir.

JOHN THOMAS: It's not worth bothering without boots.

MAN FROM UPSTAIRS: Look son. I've had a lot of experience of this kind of thing ...

JOHN THOMAS: No.

MAN FROM UPSTAIRS: I shall have to have them sir.

JOHN THOMAS: It's all silly without boots.

MAN FROM UPSTAIRS: You'll see son – you'll get used to it – like you got used to not going to those early films – you'll see it's for the best.

JOHN THOMAS: Can I have them back?

MAN FROM UPSTAIRS: I can't promise anything sir – the climate may change and we might all find ourselves in need of a change ...

JOHN THOMAS: I haven't even had a go with them. Not even once – inside.

MAN FROM UPSTAIRS: Just as well son. You won't miss 'em. Who ever saw a camel in boots. In all the literature of the ages for kiddies who ever depicted a camel booted? The scabby oont in size eight boots – on his back is where they'd be. That's what I say to that kind of woolly thought. Or placed smartly up his dirt box – for the twice as quick to Damascus.

Could you do that?

JOHN THOMAS: The camel has a swaying nobility – the ship of the desert.

MAN FROM UPSTAIRS: No. He's base ... on his knees to be lumbered.

JOHN THOMAS: I can have them back though?

MAN FROM UPSTAIRS: You want to take me on?

JOHN THOMAS: I have a horror of hitting.

MAN FROM UPSTAIRS: Very noble of you Jack – and bring your children up the same.

JOHN THOMAS: Here.

[*Gives the Man from upstairs the boots from the table.*]

MAN FROM UPSTAIRS: Thank you – and size?

JOHN THOMAS: Eight large.

MAN FROM UPSTAIRS: That's it. Only don't go blethering it around with letters to all and sundry and the local rag ... or I shall have something to say – yes? [*He takes the boots and slams the door shut.*

JOHN THOMAS *kicks the bottom of the door once and not very hard.*]

JOHN THOMAS: When I first started teaching I had the usual twitcher, the usual winker and the usual hard case head scratcher ... and Rombard.

As I grew more experienced I added a couple of weak bladders, a back row sexual demon, a foul farter ... two more twitchers and another Rombard. I said to Rombard the other day I said Rombard you're very impure and you've got a hare lip, not like King Arthur, Clive of India or Prince Philip. A couple of months ago I counted fourteen twitchers, twelve winkers some ambidextrous, a four-some of back row sexual demons, a quartet of foul farters and to my astonishment, a loud compulsive breather; I want to kick Rombard on his big head simply because he has got a big head ... and two more Rombards.

All four of them locked me in the cupboard.

You've got the boots – have the shirt to go with it.

[*Throws shirt upstairs.*]

At the beginning of this week when I was limp with baiting, my head was ringing with winks, twitches, farts and my eyes were swivelled so they cut the cord-roots watching for stinging on-coming chalk missiles ... I counted ten members of the class who were not Rombards and they were the back row sexual demons. Thirty Rombards locked me in the toilet and showered me with water from the faulty tank, they knew about ... Tomorrow they'll all be Rombards – even the now exhausted sexual demons who reached the front today and before my very swivelling eyes jigged and jogged in ecstasy.

You're very impure Rombard all you Rombards.

It's not that they're impure though – which they are ... it's that they will not listen.

You've got the boots ... you might as well have the breeches to go with it.

[*Throws breeches.*]

It's that they will not learn.

I said to Rombard – now he is a case in point always bringing in some article to taunt and turn in ... you've got a fat face Ayres, and it's greasy Ayres, Rombard. I don't wonder that you haven't got a gland condition from the size of your gross white body ...

you're impure and turn that syncopation off – I will not have the wireless during my lessons ... show me your leg Hamblin, Ayres, Rombard. Not getting any better is it? For all your sucking a vacuum with your hare lip round the edge of that milk bottle ... free milk for which I pay for will not make up for faulty breeding and twisted watery spermatique flow – drag your limb over here Rombard ... I'm entering you for the school sports. [*A knock on the door.*] Go away.

VOICE: The belt. I might as well have the belt.

JOHN THOMAS: You've got the belt.

VOICE: Would I ask for it?

Let's have the belt.

JOHN THOMAS: Hold on. [*He opens the door to the Man from upstairs. The Man comes in holding up his breeches. He is dressed in the shirt and breeches and boots. The shirt has devices on it.*] Must have got mislaid.

MAN FROM UPSTAIRS: You'd best unmislay it hadn't you? They come to me ... in my capacity as a civic dignitary – houses – they're not fit for houses ... I say wait. All in good time – wait.

I can't afford houses.

JOHN THOMAS: The belt.

MAN FROM UPSTAIRS: Thank you.

How do I look ...?

JOHN THOMAS: Quick – who's that?

[*The mirror gag.*]

MAN FROM UPSTAIRS: Oh yes.

JOHN THOMAS: Quick who's that?

MAN FROM UPSTAIRS: Me.

JOHN THOMAS: Thank goodness – I thought it was me.

THE MAN FROM UPSTAIRS [*bursts out laughing; thumps* JOHN THOMAS *hard on the back*]: Oh stone me – oh that's a good one ... stone me that's rich.

JOHN THOMAS: Yes. [*He manages a weak grin under the chummy belting.*] I thought it was me.

MAN FROM UPSTAIRS: John Thomas ... oh no – you haven't got the boots for it have you?

CURTAIN

SCENE ONE

Hanging in tatters, fluttering, looking most old-time, historical - Grey standards, guidons and Regimental colours. They dress front to rear in order of fade; this being indicative of seniority or no time under the sun at all which counts the same. At the back are the last to join still sexy round the pole from the touch of a Royal tart's hand. They swing as battens do when dropped in quick.

> [*Dust floats down.*
> *Somebody might be walking across the grid.*
> *Making* DICKIE BIRD *sneeze.*
> *Ranked in file facing, half a dozen long paces between to make a path for encouraging heroes (born) who before it got dangerous used to pass up and down with the warlike chat meaning to encourage the heroes (pressed) to go on to join heroes (copped it) ... like for a quick game of shinty or old time arme blanche chopping ... stand dressed up tailors' dummies.*
> *Dressed in Red, Blue, Black, Green, all the spiv martial colours plus brass and Khaki. Sodden and pinked neutral from sweat fear of heroes (born, pressed, copped it) weak, lost gushing bladder fears ... But that's long ago and they do go to the cleaners regular now.*
> *The smell makes* HARRY *sniff.*
> *They both sneeze.*
> *The movement of them sneezing separates the living from the old time/long time dead in two ranks facing*]

DICKIE BIRD: Up your throat.

HARRY: Camouflage nets.

DICKIE BIRD: Smell worse when they're wet then.

HARRY: They get wet?

DICKIE BIRD: They been wet – he for instance wet hisself grotesque at Waterloo. [*At dummy.*]

HARRY: Smells all like camouflage nets or webbing.

77

DICKIE BIRD: Riddled with dust.

HARRY: I joined for the lust not the dust.

DICKIE BIRD: It's a full time job keeping it something like.

HARRY: Bound to be – Lili Marlene.

DICKIE BIRD: Let's not beat about the bush ...

HARRY: No I won't what I'll do is out with it ... underneath the lamplight.

DICKIE BIRD: Don't tell your hard luck story by devious all round the houses my son ... we'll be here all night.

HARRY: I aren't devious ... Old Riley's Daughter.

DICKIE BIRD: Now then – stop kicking it down.

HARRY: Far from it ... Rose, Rose, I love you.

DICKIE BIRD: Do you hear?

HARRY: He can't hear you ... Nurse Cavell?

DICKIE BIRD: 'kin 'ell.

HARRY: Think he can?

DICKIE BIRD: I hopes not for his sake – things I've called him. . .

[*A nervous giggle and an upward glance by* BIRD. *Another fall of dust makes him attack the nearest dummy in a frenzy of dusting zeal.*]

HARRY: Windy?

DICKIE BIRD: Now then, now then. [*Aggrieved at another fall of dust.*]

GARIBALDI [*from among the dummies*]: Sweating.

DICKIE BIRD: Oh my God – sneaking about again – oh my dear good God ... What's mean sweating?

GARIBALDI: Never you mind.

HARRY: He sneaks about don't he – you sneak about.

GARIBALDI: That's why I have my boots soled soft – rubber.

DICKIE BIRD: Everybody sneaks – not a straight answer from any-one ... I keeps asking – no secrets with me – why en it universal?

HARRY: I lets you in.

GARIBALDI: Two's up.

HARRY: Don't I?

DICKIE BIRD: Thee dost. Got no choice.

HARRY: Anything I hears.

DICKIE BIRD: Got no choice – nig's got to talk to someone.

HARRY: That's it.

DICKIE BIRD: Only one thing I'm sweating on ...

HARRY: That's it.

GARIBALDI: I know what you're sweating on ...

HARRY: Do not come to me Jack.

DICKIE BIRD: I was going to say – only one ...

GARIBALDI: ... sweating on promotion.

DICKIE BIRD: ... hardly sweating on promotion.

GARIBALDI: ... on the dog's hind leg – broken lance Bird ... one who acts as corporal.

DICKIE BIRD: And I could. No – to be strictly factual there's only one thing I'm sweating on ...

HARRY: You're sweating on him stopping ...

GARIBALDI: Get some in.

DICKIE BIRD: And that for a game of soldiers – I'd be back in that box with the instructions 'fore you can say F.F.I.

GARIBALDI: That's your sweat.

DICKIE BIRD: Don't come to me Jack. I'll be too busy sorting out rations.

[*They are both suddenly angry at Harry putting their fear into words.*]

HARRY: One thing ... I aren't devious. I'll tell my story to any bloke – straight out.

GARIBALDI: Stop kicking it down.

DICKIE BIRD: I'll belt his arse one day ...

GARIBALDI: I'll catch the bleeder ...

DICKIE BIRD: He won't take any notice ... bend him back and let him go he won't notice he's been there.

HARRY: I'm just hot that's all. Comes of being young.

GARIBALDI: Know what today is?

DICKIE BIRD: Certainly.

GARIBALDI: What's today then?

DICKIE BIRD: There's no change. They're all the same to me Jack.

GARIBALDI: What's today.

HARRY: Do you think of it all the time?

DICKIE BIRD: What's this Harry?

HARRY: Do you think of them all the time, walking clip, clop in bright high heels? No, I see them very lively in slinky kit, by the barrack square. Marlene Dietrich.

DICKIE BIRD: There's all sorts.

HARRY: I think of them all the time, when I left home it wasn't for not having a job, it was … I thought broaden your outlook my son … Mademoiselle from Armentieres … all over the world you'll go, Tokyo Rose. Only one thing, take care no harm comes to you in a certain way – you see my meaning? So long as you keep it wrapped, keep it under self-control … not tonight, Josephine, there's no reason why you shouldn't enjoy yourself, mind you watch cups and towels. Because you are going to have to watch it … Mata Hari.

DICKIE BIRD: That's it. Casn't go far wrong there.

GARIBALDI: They say you're not a soldier till you've caught a cold.

HARRY: Singapore Sal.

DICKIE BIRD: Or done a twist in the kotwalee.

HARRY: Gibraltar Nell. It's all that penicillin now in it?

GARIBALDI: Get fell in.

DICKIE BIRD: Stop kicking it down.

HARRY: I didn't fancy the old umbrella treatment not one jot.

[DICKIE BIRD *and* HARRY *fall in side by side still talking and not in any way disturbed by being told to fall in. They stand at ease or rather easy and carry on the chat.*]

DICKIE BIRD: They got rid of that. That's out.

HARRY: I know that.

DICKIE BIRD: No it's just like a cough now.

GARIBALDI: Squad … shun.

DICKIE BIRD: No trouble at all.

[*They come to attention without any effort.* SPRATT *talks out of the ranks facing when* CORPORAL GARIBALDI *slides up to him and at attention reports.*

When he moves out SPRATT *is a very commanding person. He might be General one day – at the moment he is Squadron Sergeant Major.*

He is dressed in Cavalry Number Ones and very splendid at first glance … just scruffy when you scratch him waiting for a bus.]

GARIBALDI: One on leave …

HARRY: Who's on leave?

DICKIE BIRD: Him up there's on leaf.

GARIBALDI: One absent.

HARRY: Oh – who's absent?

GARIBALDI: One on duty ...

HARRY: Duty?

DICKIE BIRD: Your mate up there's on duty ...

GARIBALDI: One regimentally employed ... otherwise present and correct SIR.

HARRY: I was going to cover up for him.

DICKIE BIRD: Don't try covering up for him.

SPRATT: That's four.

GARIBALDI: Well – what else can you say sir?

SPRATT: Ignore it.

DICKIE BIRD: He won't cover up for you.

GARIBALDI: I would – only it gets up your throat though – you can't ignore it.

DICKIE BIRD: I said that.

HARRY: You said it first.

GARIBALDI: How else would you describe it?

SPRATT: It's your choice of phrase I quarrel with corporal – if he's on leaf he's not absent and if he's R.E. he's maybe on leaf all well and good but hardly likewise absent.

He's sick ... on duty – medicine and duty.

DICKIE BIRD: He's not sick.

HARRY: I wouldn't have thought it.

DICKIE BIRD: No – he's fly.

SPRATT: Now I'll go back and you try it again.

GARIBALDI: Sir.

DICKIE BIRD: He's making him do it again.

HARRY: I'm sick if he's sick.

DICKIE BIRD: You're not sick.

GARIBALDI: One sick ...

HARRY: I am ...

GARIBALDI: Otherwise present ...

DICKIE BIRD: And me ...

GARIBALDI: ... correct ...

HARRY: ... if he is.

GARIBALDI: ... ready for your inspection sir.

DICKIE BIRD: ... if you are.

SPRATT: Thank you corporal ... fall in on the right. Three ranks ... N.C.O.s on the right ...

[GARIBALDI *with the maximum fuss falls in on the right of Harry and Dickie Bird.*]

DICKIE BIRD: Made you do it again then ...

HARRY: He's far from being sick, up your throat.

GARIBALDI: I'm sick.

SPRATT: By the right ... NUMBER ...

GARIBALDI: One ... sick and tired.

DICKIE BIRD: Two – try again corporal.

HARRY: Three – tired of covering up – four.

GARIBALDI: Chocker with that rubbish coming down.

SPRATT: On the command march even numbers will take one place to the rear odd numbers will take one pace to the front ...

DICKIE BIRD: Stop covering up for him.

HARRY: He's my mate.

GARIBALDI: He's sick.

SPRATT: Trooooop MARCH.

[*They do that.*]

DICKIE BIRD: He's sick, I'm snuffed it.

HARRY: Made you look silly corporal.

GARIBALDI: How would you describe him then ...?

SPRATT: On the command march.

DICKIE BIRD: Puggled.

SPRATT: ... right marker will not march.

HARRY: Cushy.

SPRATT: Troop – right and left – left and right TURN.

[*This they do.*]

SPRATT: ... he will merely mark time.

HARRY: I'd describe him as very fly.

SPRATT: Rear file will wheel into position behind the last man of the forward file who will mark time on the command march.

DICKIE BIRD: And he's sick – I've got the eye of a needle ...

SPRATT: Trooooop ...

DICKIE BIRD: ... squitters.

SPRATT: ... MARCH.

 [*They do and end up just as they were before except that* HARRY *is now second man – all marking time in time.*]

GARIBALDI: I've had that – if you'd had that you wouldn't piss take about it.

DICKIE BIRD: I've had it.

HARRY: Well I aren't had it.

DICKIE BIRD: Because you ain't been in long enough.

GARIBALDI: You ain't bin in long enough for the Catterick cough.

SPRATT: Troop HALT.

 [*BANG.*]

HARRY: Too long. I've been in too long.

SPRATT: Troop will advance – left TURN.

GARIBALDI: Actually – it's a lovely drill movement done properly ...

DICKIE BIRD: Sizing.

GARIBALDI: Need the numbers though see.

DICKIE BIRD: I've seen it done by the Brigade of Guards.

HARRY: All of them? Mandy.

SPRATT: Dressing – right DRESS.

 [GARIBALDI *turns to the right – marches out three paces and about turns.*]

DICKIE BIRD: Can't you get your mind off kyfer?

HARRY: Sorry. No I can't.

DICKIE BIRD: No – don't think I don't like em. I likes em well enough ... all the time ...

GARIBALDI: Bird stick your gut in – Harry gut out – arse in ... front rank stand still.

HARRY: It's because I'm young.

SPRATT: I've had more rabbit than you've had in your dixie.

DICKIE BIRD: He's never had it yet

GARIBALDI: Centre rank stand still.

SPRATT: I've had more Chinese labour reaming than you've had spit in your porridge.

DICKIE BIRD: He's cocky sir.

GARIBALDI: Rear rank stand still.

 [GARIBALDI *marches back to his position.*]

SPRATT: Trooooop – eyes FRONT.

[*They do that. And bang their arms down. Or rather* DICKIE BIRD *does it because he's the only one with his arm up. Due to the fact that* HARRY *is right marker ... for this occasion.*]

GARIBALDI: He's going to tell us about what today is.

DICKIE BIRD: I don't want to know what today is.

HARRY: You been trying to tell us what today is ...
  I know what today is.

SPRATT: Stand at EASE. Stand EASY.

GARIBALDI: He looks at you and says you don't know what today is corporal?

DICKIE BIRD: All the same to me.

SPRATT: Now then ... anybody know what today is? Corporal Garibaldi?

GARIBALDI: Sir.

SPRATT: You don't know what today is corp. ...

HARRY: Balaclava Day Sir.

DICKIE BIRD: How do you know?

GARIBALDI: Stand to attention when ...

HARRY: He told me.

DICKIE BIRD: You been chatting him?

HARRY: He's my mate.

DICKIE BIRD: Hadn't noticed.

SPRATT: That's right ... Balaclava Day.

GARIBALDI: In it marvellous how it can go by without you blokes noticing.

DICKIE BIRD: Oh that's it then – it's lovely Balaclava Day – all gets pissed Balaclava Day. You'll lap up Balaclava Day – has a bramah time back in the regiment on such a day.

SPRATT: How did you know Trooper? Thought you'd be the last to know – last to join last to know not to your detriment ... how did you know?

HARRY: My mate.

SPRATT: Him upstairs?

HARRY: Him sick. He was there with Florence Nightingale.

SPRATT: Oh yes. [*Disbelieving.*] Right then, next time you see him ... tell him to stop kicking that rammel down will you?
  [*Long pause.*]

DICKIE BIRD: Go on – talk to him.

HARRY: I can't talk to him.

GARIBALDI: Go on – he's waiting.

HARRY: How can I talk to him?

DICKIE BIRD: You could tell them then sir.

GARIBALDI: That's it ... you could tell us some stories sir.
[*Another pause.*]

HARRY: Yes – I bet you could yes – an old chubby duster.

DICKIE BIRD: Don't take the piss.
[*Pause.*]

GARIBALDI: Try not to keep the Sergeant Major waiting.

HARRY: I've got nothing to say to him – I've said some words to
him ... you heard what I said.
[*Another pause.*]

SPRATT: Don't believe all the stories you hear about me Harry.
[*Pause.*]

HARRY: No sir – I haven't heard any stories about you sir.

DICKIE BIRD: I could tell you some stories about him.

GARIBALDI: You're trying to corrupt something that is fine, good
and noble, Bird.

DICKIE BIRD: I'm not trying to corrupt anything fine, good and
noble. I'm trying to prevent him getting his fine good and
noble snatched.

SPRATT: You seen me in ceremonial dress Harry?

GARIBALDI: I have sir. Very fine.

HARRY: No sir – only denims and blues and number twos.

SPRATT: Combat dress. You've no doubt seen me in combat
dress.

HARRY: Of course. Pity you're in blues now sir.

SPRATT: Why's that Harry?

HARRY: With all that coming down.

SPRATT: Stop knocking all that ...

DICKIE BIRD: He won't hear you.

GARIBALDI: He'll hear my boot when I catch him sir.

DICKIE BIRD: Have to catch him first.

SPRATT: I could tell you some stories. Gather round. In a half circle
round me ... MOVE.

GARIBALDI: Spread yourselves out ...

[*They do move round Spratt. And sit and wait.*]

GARIBALDI: You could tell us some stories. Sir.

DICKIE BIRD: Remind me to tell you some stories Harry.

GARIBALDI: Balaclava Day.

DICKIE BIRD: Holiday – Balaclava Day. Everybody gets tanked Balaclava Day Harry. Gets dressed up see – young lad like you would dress up as a tart most like because of your pink face and a tantalising little bitch.

SPRATT: I've seen some stories.

GARIBALDI: It's a day off in it? Everybody goes hatchah and slippery pole and shinty match officers and sergeants ...

DICKIE BIRD: Everybody gets cut ...

GARIBALDI: What happens is they wrap a turban round their heads and paint their eyes ...

DICKIE BIRD: Dresses up and has sing songs in the canteen.

SPRATT: Sing sing – or show your ring.

GARIBALDI: ... up to them whether they bothers about a suggestion of form.

SPRATT: Sing sing – or show your ring.

GARIBALDI: That it sir?

HARRY: If it's a day off ...

DICKIE BIRD: First off.

HARRY: ... should sod off.

DICKIE BIRD: Taters up for first off.

HARRY: In bed or out of barracks. I aren't in.

GARIBALDI: Bound to be.

SPRATT: No no – sing sing.

DICKIE BIRD: Right then taters up for first off.

GARIBALDI: Dress up though.

DICKIE BIRD: All that dust.

SPRATT: Young Harry. He's a good lad.

GARIBALDI: Tank up though.

DICKIE BIRD: Taters up.

SPRATT: What's his story?

DICKIE BIRD: Are we going to have this sing song? Pass the time away won't it?

SPRATT: Ought to dress up have a good time Balaclava Day ... make a good tart young Harry here.

GARIBALDI: Paint his face a bit.

HARRY: Not me.

SPRATT: Only a laugh.

DICKIE BIRD: I know some bramah ones.

SPRATT: Show the small of his back.

GARIBALDI: That's it – war games.

SPRATT: That's it – stone me ... only a laugh and it's Balaclava Day. Nobody gets charged on Balaclava Day see ... you can go through the camp like the titter and no slapping on the hooks. I promise you. Kotwalee is closed for the duration.

DICKIE BIRD: And it's Balaclava Day – where was my rum and coffee this morning? In the regiment you do get rum and coffee brought round by the orderly wank and you do get it in bed ... that's it – where was it then?

GARIBALDI: Sippers sir.

SPRATT: Don't touch the stuff.

DICKIE BIRD: Where is it Harry?

HARRY: Be all right if we had some bint – now I'd join you with some walking talking live – I'd be pleased to join you ...

GARIBALDI: You know Harry.

SPRATT: War games we ought to have.

GARIBALDI: You a general sir.

SPRATT: Plenty of time.

DICKIE BIRD: Your mate should know – he creeps around ...

GARIBALDI: Think we ought to have war games sir?

SPRATT: Try you out – see how your map reading and similar is going. There's this scientist to be smuggled through at dead of night. Escape and evasion.

DICKIE BIRD: And a free beer per man at dinner.

HARRY: Not all that again. I've captured, sacked, looted, and dug bog pits on Silk Hill so many times I know the local fairies for tantalising little flutter by nights. I call the left flank of Dumbell Wood my home – and it would sadden me to battle for Imber Crossing yet again. Up and down the plain from Blue to Red and back again to Blue I've chased Northlanders with atom secrets

– scientists in the hands of a foreign power, terrorists from the territorial army ... and once at dark I saw a bush become a Naafi bint waving leafy promise. I've stood all night and watched the stones start crawling ... four hills where one was tumuli starred on the map ... dew pearls on the tip of my cap motto ... I aren't getting involved in all that again without it's real – unless it's action action action and then I hope to be on leave and satisfied. Hamburg Hannah. All right if I falls out.

SPRATT: No.

[*They are astonished at the outburst.*]

GARIBALDI: It's not all right if you falls out.

DICKIE BIRD: Balaclava Day you spends with your muckers.

SPRATT: Getting up to jollity. We'll have a gay old time I can tell you.

DICKIE BIRD: He feels the same as I do no doubt sir – it's hardly the same without the wallop.

SPRATT: Don't touch the stuff.

DICKIE BIRD: Lying bastard.

SPRATT: Now then – esprit de corps.

DICKIE BIRD: Well – that's what you are. We know you keeps slightly oiled ... we know you drives off the scorpions – where's it to?

HARRY: There's a bottle in that bloody gun.

DICKIE BIRD: That's it.

HARRY: Why do I always have to say – dropped in it now aren't I? I don't touch the stuff ...

DICKIE BIRD: Which gun is that? All right if we gets it sir.

SPRATT: I don't touch the stuff.

HARRY: Now he's mad at me again – last time I got all the fires for a week ... he won't say anything now ... why is it always I? You knows where he keeps it as well as I.

DICKIE BIRD: It's that mate of yours – he lets you in on it see ... we only know where he had it last – you know where he has it now – take my meaning?

GARIBALDI: All right if we get it sir – they won't rest happy till they do sir. You don't need it I know sir ... but dutch courage.

SPRATT: Fall out then. But I despise you.

DICKIE BIRD: I despise myself.

[*They do – and go through the dummies and the trophies finding bottles under hats, in packs. Up sleeves and trouser legs. Until* DICKIE *has an arm load.* HARRY *sits where he is.*]

SPRATT: Don't have the chance to be alone with the young soldiers very much …

HARRY: Look sir – I don't enjoy these games …

SPRATT: Why is that?

HARRY: Well – they're a bit silly aren't they?

SPRATT: You want to fall out do you?

HARRY: It's not that …

SPRATT: This is the day you see Harry … you know the story? The Russians had the guns – right?

HARRY: What's it like sir? No – can we talk while we're talking like this … these blokes here just laugh when I ask … what's it like to have intercourse?

SPRATT: You taking the piss? Just watch points lad. These Russkies had the guns … right? The regiments rose early that day and it was remarked that they seemed in the most extraordinary spirits …

GARIBALDI: I remarked to Dickie Bird here sir – it would be good if the Sergeant Major told THE STORY.

DICKIE BIRD: When we getting round to the sing song …?

SPRATT: … whistling and joking amongst themselves as soldiers do – even complaining in that fine old way that British soldiers have …

DICKIE BIRD: … we got the wallop – how about the sing song or show your ring?

GARIBALDI: Wrap up Bird … always ticking.

SPRATT: … at the last moment the regiment was joined by the regimental butcher with poleaxe and apron fresh from the shambles … hearing his regiment was about to engage … he had asked to take his place with a troop …

GARIBALDI: Would not be left out.

DICKIE BIRD: Puggled.

HARRY: Here Dickie – all this talk … you've experienced it … is it all they say it is …?

SPRATT: … at the last moment Captain Nolan of the regiment dashed across the front … he seemed about to utter … clapping.

DICKIE BIRD: This is the bit I like ...

SPRATT: What he was saying ...

DICKIE BIRD: ... was never known.

SPRATT: ... was never known.

GARIBALDI: Macabre.

SPRATT: ...At the last moment a cannon shot decapitated the gallant Nolan ... or was it that other?

DICKIE BIRD: ... whipped his bleeding head off. Officers – there's one then.

SPRATT: ... The gallant Mason?

DICKIE BIRD: Two – twice as lovely.

GARIBALDI: ... I think it's macabre sir.

SPRATT: ... after the engagement ... we'd do it again sir!

GARIBALDI: Just say the word, sir.

HARRY: ... what do you do in the between bit? I mean you can't just ... you'd look so daft undoing your braces – don't they think you look daft?

DICKIE BIRD: He's stopped kicking that ...

SPRATT: There. [*He points off –* GARIBALDI *leaps to his feet ...* DICKIE BIRD *and* HARRY *turn over on their bellies and put their hands on the back of their necks.*]

GARIBALDI: On your feet. Where is he sir ...?

SPRATT: Eleven o'clock. Base of tall coniferous tree.

GARIBALDI: Get him.

DICKIE BIRD: Where?

GARIBALDI: Eleven o'clock. Base of tall coniferous tree. Now I want you to come with me Bird. Harry we're going to winkle him out – stay here until we're in position and then a frontal attack as soon as you hear three bursts.

SPRATT: Frontal?

GARIBALDI: That's it sir.

SPRATT: I'm not going to say you're right. I'm not going to say you're wrong. We've all got to learn the hard way. Right ... at the double.

[DICKIE BIRD *and* GARIBALDI *shoot out into the right hand file ... of Dummies and freeze.*]

SPRATT [*bends down over Harry and waits*]: All right son?

HARRY: Bloody no.

SPRATT: What's up son?

HARRY: I'm not sure.

SPRATT: Bit windy son?

HARRY: I've never had it see sir ... I might get my head decapitated before I have it ...

SPRATT: You'll be all right son. Now remember – three bursts and up you go like the clappers ... they'll put down smoke most like – stand up and walk for a bit ... till the last hundred yards when the smoke should still be covering you. You'll be all right – try not to bend double – you make a bigger target that way.

HARRY: I don't want to do that sir – I want to make a small target sir ...

SPRATT: They can't see you when the smoke's down son.

HARRY: Will it be thick smoke sir?

SPRATT: Very thick son ... I doubt if they'll get through with armour piercing son it's so thick.

HARRY: I'll get through it though sir?

SPRATT: And through the other side with cold steel. [*A shot whips out of the darkness. SPRATT ducks lower almost on a level with Harry.*] Armour piercing they're using son ... don't worry ... that's only for tanks.

HARRY: Sir. Were you frightened – your first time?

SPRATT: We're all frightened first time son. I don't think much of a man who is not frightened son. It's lovely to be frightened and conquer it son.

[*All sorts of smoke, dust, bangs and old rope are flying about. Lights among the dummies. Then it stops and nothing. This is more frightening than the noise.*]

HARRY: What's that?

SPRATT: What's what?

HARRY: Three bursts?

SPRATT: No. [*A scream ... and some sobbing.*] Your first thought there should be happy days son ... happy days that it's not you.

HARRY: That is my first thought sir.

SPRATT: There. What did I tell you. Glimpse of home and honey.

HARRY: I'll be all right sir.

[*A pause. No sound.*]

SPRATT: You'll be all right son.

HARRY: I'll be racing sir.

[*Three short bursts.*]

SPRATT: Three short bursts ... away you go. Now don't forget to shout.

HARRY: Right.

SPRATT: Three short bursts.

HARRY: Right. What we fighting for?

SPRATT: – what we fighting for?

HARRY: Yes – what we fighting for?

SPRATT: What we fighting for? To ... What?

HARRY: Yes – what we fighting for what we fighting for what we fighting for ...

SPRATT: Yours is not to reason why ... To stop that bloke kicking it down. Yes?

HARRY: But he's stopped.

SPRATT: That's right. That's what we're fighting for.

[*Three more short bursts.*]

HARRY: He's my mate.

SPRATT: Three more short bursts.

HARRY: Yes – only he's my mate.

SPRATT: Not any more he's not. He's foul.

[*Three more.*]

SPRATT: Come on – come on – or he'll come at us. At me ...

HARRY: Right. Does it hurt?

SPRATT: Don't feel it.

[HARRY *stands up gingerly and stands like he's messed his trousers which he has.* SPRATT *stays low.*]

SPRATT: Go on go on ...

HARRY: Yes ... right then. I should have gone mad headed shouldn't I? Right then. And the bastards ... [*With a weak little cry and holding an imaginary rifle and bayonet* ... HARRY *hops skips and jumps into the smoke.*]

Hurrah. Vera Lynn.

[*When the smoke clears and the drums stop beating and the old rope stops flying and the guidons, standards and colours stop fluttering,* DICKIE BIRD *sneezes.* HARRY *does too – only he's not* HARRY *now he's* FREDDIE.]

DICKIE BIRD: Gets up your nostrils.

FREDDIE: Gets up your throat.

DICKIE BIRD: That's right Freddie – that's what I mean. This place is crawling with dust ...

FREDDIE: Stop kicking it down.

DICKIE BIRD: Who dost thee think thee bist?

FREDDIE: I'm telling him – makes our job twice as hard.

DICKIE BIRD: He don't take notice of nigs. He casn't hear I – leave alone take notice of sheer youth.

FREDDIE: That's as well then en it George? Things I've called him it's as well he don't read me.

DICKIE BIRD: Jack to Spratt next won't un?

FREDDIE: And he's a skiver. Take a turn at duty make a change all round.

DICKIE BIRD: Thy first duty'll be the first.

FREDDIE: And you get a trade.

DICKIE BIRD: And me? And me! I was topping up my mussybot when you was pulling at your tittybot – I was jungli when you was hardly ...

FREDDIE: Still are very scruffy. Get stabilized.

DICKIE BIRD: I've seen some my son.

FREDDIE: I done more shiv and lacing down the King's Head than you done for the Queen. Get scientific.

DICKIE BIRD: I lost more time in the kotwalee than you got entered up ...

FREDDIE: Why don't you stop kicking it down?

DICKIE BIRD: I wish he would – change your tune ... soon change his tune wouldn't it?

FREDDIE: Sort out the men from the old men won't it?

DICKIE BIRD: I do suppose I shall feel sorry for thee. I always do feel heartbroke for thee ... at least I always have done up to now.

FREDDIE: Sort out the windy from the randy won't it?

GARIBALDI: Who's windy?

FREDDIE: You always sneak about like that? Like that?

DICKIE BIRD: I'm windy. Windy about swords – out here – more talk than walk when it comes to it.

FREDDIE: You're windy about him. Get mechanized.

GARIBALDI: Get fell in.

[*They fall in.*]

FREDDIE: You always sneak about like that Corporal?

GARIBALDI: I try to.

DICKIE BIRD: Thee's sticking thy neck out then.

FREDDIE: Secrets, radar ...

DICKIE BIRD: I got no secrets ... I'll tell my story to any bloke straight out.

GARIBALDI: Stand properly at ease.

[*They do.*]

FREDDIE: Garibaldi – that's a biscuit in it?

DICKIE BIRD: That's right.

GARIBALDI: Squad – shun!

[*They do.*]

GARIBALDI: Troop present and ready for your inspection sir ... apart from the usual.

SPRATT: What sort of report is that?

GARIBALDI: Incomplete sir.

SPRATT: Is he absent?

GARIBALDI: No he's here.

SPRATT: Where?

FREDDIE: Kicking it down, heavy interference.

SPRATT: Right then ... go back and try again. I'd class him as very sick in body and intention.

GARIBALDI: Sir. [*He goes back – turns round and starts again.*]

FREDDIE: I don't believe he is sick. I regard him as a bleeding nuisance. One sick, one on leave and one a bleeding nuisance. Jamming up the scanners.

GARIBALDI: And me – sooner he stops ... one sick otherwise present and ready for your inspection sir.

SPRATT: Thank you Corporal Garibaldi. Fall in on the right.

[GARIBALDI *does so and* FREDDIE *nudges him quickly* ...]

FREDDIE: Garibaldi – that's a biscuit in it?

GARIBALDI: That's right – with currants in it.

DICKIE BIRD: Made you do it again didn't un?

GARIBALDI: Belt up in the ranks.

DICKIE BIRD: And you.

SPRATT: Stand at ease.

[*They do.*]

SPRATT: Drummer take post.

[THE DRUMMER – *a splendid figure in Blues, but a boy, marches across the stage in front of the Squad. He halts near Spratt.*]

GARIBALDI: Who's that?

FREDDIE: I didn't know we had that. Prototype?

DICKIE BIRD: This'll sort out the soldiers from the sailors.

SPRATT: How's your taradiddle?

DRUMMER: Very fair – how's yours?

FREDDIE: With music – no less. Is it on issue?

GARIBALDI: He's a rose cheeked asset then sir.

SPRATT: I'm sorry about the mess to your uniform.

DRUMMER: That's all right, sir – when's he going to stop kicking it down?

SPRATT: When you going to reach man service …?

DRUMMER: I hopes he doesn't stop before I reach man service sir …

SPRATT: Plenty more lad – plenty more.

FREDDIE: When's he going to stop?

SPRATT: Now.

[THE DRUMMER *rolls on his drum and taps once. They brace up.*]

SPRATT: As on sentry – to the front salute.

[*To taps on the drum the* THREE SOLDIERS *come to attention – slope arms – take a pace forward and give a double butt salute – then they take a pace to the rear – order arms and stand at ease again.*]

DRUMMER: It's a lovely movement done properly sir.

FREDDIE: Up two three – across two three – down two three …

DICKIE BIRD: Who you telling?

FREDDIE: Thought you might have forgot. Where's your horse?

SPRATT: You like it do you son …?

DRUMMER: That old one's not very good.

SPRATT: Bird – you're holding that rifle like a princess.

DRUMMER: A princess?

SPRATT: A princess holding a navvy's prick. [*The* TROOP *has stopped.* DICKIE BIRD *looks suitably unabashed. But he's rattled.*] Do it again.

DICKIE BIRD: Again?

SPRATT: As on sentry – to the front salute. Again Bird and try to put some spunk into it.

DICKIE BIRD: Just I?

SPRATT: Just. Now.

[THE DRUMMER *rolls. And taps out the drill movement as before.*]

FREDDIE: Hey bandboy – tight it up. Full revs.

DRUMMER: Faster?

FREDDIE: He made you do it again then ... up two three – you do look baggy from the rear. Is it your aerial?

DICKIE BIRD: Why don't you ...?

GARIBALDI: Why don't you get it right?

FREDDIE: Get technical – bandboy.

SPRATT: You'll get your chance son, there's a place for specialists.

[BIRD *is back. But he drops his feather duster rifle. Just before* SPRATT *says ... 'There'. And they drop ...* FREDDIE *and* DICKIE BIRD.]

DICKIE BIRD: Now then – now then.

GARIBALDI: On your feet.

FREDDIE: Come back when you got spit in your tail. And your O Level.

SPRATT: There – one o'clock base of small bush. Drummer – FALL OUT.

[THE DRUMMER *marches off and stands in the dummies, still.*]

GARIBALDI: Right – one o'clock ... base of small bush.

DICKIE BIRD: Right. Soon as we're in position – three bursts. Frontal?

GARIBALDI: Frontal.

SPRATT: You'll never learn will you?

GARIBALDI: Right – skates on Freddie.

SPRATT: Up and at him Dickie.

DICKIE BIRD: Me?

SPRATT: You.

FREDDIE: Get trade tested it's all mechanical.

[GARIBALDI *goes with a grinning* FREDDIE.]

SPRATT: That bloke will never learn – corporals I've shit 'em ... Never make an N.C.O. as long as he's got a hole in his arse. There's no place for the dim in the streamlined army.

DICKIE BIRD: Me? I've never seen my chicko sir.

SPRATT: You're not married son.

DICKIE BIRD: But I might have a chicko – I aren't never seen him.

SPRATT: Smoke down ... touch of L.M.G. keep their heads down – won't know what's come amongst them ... chubby duster like you. Know what today is?

DICKIE BIRD: How thick's the cock sucking smoke?

SPRATT: Twice as thick as hot burgoo – and what day is today?

DICKIE BIRD: My day – my day. How far's the first bleeding bound?

SPRATT: Start Line – Jellalabad Day.

DICKIE BIRD: Jellybob? All gets pissed Jellybob day.

SPRATT: First Bound – Ghanzee. At which we remember the storming of the Citadel ... with special reference to ...

DICKIE BIRD: Sonner Roger's arm?

SPRATT: Major General Sale's contusions. Second Bound – Hill of Trukee ... with special reference to ...

DICKIE BIRD: Acker Lovelace – reached the top and was killed, no medals.

SPRATT: Private Anthony Burke – reached to top, killed three of the enemy, shot one, did bayonet the other, broke his musket on the head of a third ... two medals.

[*Three bursts.*]

SPRATT: Go.

DICKIE BIRD: Private Rogers lost his arm.

SPRATT: At Ghanzee – first bound ... GO.

[*Three bursts.*]

DICKIE BIRD: I know better than stand and stare. [*He stands up – wide eyed.*]

SPRATT: That's it – you know better.

DICKIE BIRD: Acker Lovelace cashed his pieces ...

SPRATT: Trukee – second bound ... had his name laid before the Duke of Wellington.

[*Three more bursts.*]

DICKIE BIRD: Keep upright see – pumping, pumping ...

SPRATT: That's it – you've done it.

DICKIE BIRD: I've done it. Right, right then ... here thee bist then.

[DICKIE BIRD *stands up and stands and stands and then with a throat grabbed cry he hops skips and jumps into the smoke and the hot yelling and flying old rope.*

Silence.]

SPRATT: Ghanzee, Jellalabad, Trukee.

One general, one garrison, thirty regimental Courts Martial ... lashes awarded, two thousand five hundred. Lashes inflicted, one thousand eight hundred and seventy-seven.

Strip sir. When the offender was tied or rather hung up by his hands; his back ... from intense cold and the effects of previous floggings did present a blue black appearance ... On the first lash – the blood spurted out some yards ... After fifty ... his back from neck to waist was one continued stream of blood. The sufferer, who was Irish and foul mouthed, on this occasion uttered not a single murmur ... but bore the whole of his punishment ... chewing on a lead teeth-marked lead, dead, bullet. He was obliged to be carried to the hospital in a dooly ... they couldn't bend his arms back they were stuck out like Jesus ... Crooked them later though and shot his teeth marked ... dig deep ... while the lash sticks the blood glue on your back ... bullet into his head and out the other side.

After Ghaznee, the Brigadier was graciously pleased to recommend restoration of service forfeited by desertion, to Private Rogers who lost an arm at the storm of Ghaznee and performed good and gallant service.

After Jellalabad, the Queen was graciously pleased to appoint Colonel, Sir Robert Henry Sale (performing good and gallant service in the rank of Major General in Afghanistan) to be a Knight Grand Cross of the Most Honourable Military Order of the Bath. Why can't you stop kicking the shit down?

CURTAIN

JAMES BROOM LYNNE

The Trigon

First presented in London at the British Drama
League Theatre on Sunday, 28 April 1963 by In-
Stage with the following cast:

ARTHUR	Timothy West
BASIL	Anthony Hall
MABEL	Prunella Scales
CHARLES	Simon Oates

Directed by Charles Marowitz
Designed by Frank Phelan
Lighting by Gerald Bedrich

First presented at the Arts Theatre, London, on
Wednesday, 27 May 1964 with the following cast:

ARTHUR	Timothy West
BASIL	Anthony Hall
MABEL	Prunella Scales
CHARLES	Keith Baxter

Directed by Charles Marowitz
Lighting by Joe Davis

CHARACTERS

ARTHUR: A stoutish, short nanny-man of thirty-five. House-proud. Sense of martyrdom. Keeps idle hands busy. Secretly greedy. Cherishes memory of Scout days.

BASIL: Thin, dark and neurotic. Same age as Arthur. Waspish. Dresses to concept of last-ditch hero/duellist. Consciously irascible. An anxious, taut man.

MABEL: A puzzled girl-woman of twenty-seven. Has waited for things to happen to her – is bewildered because they haven't. Strong sense of family and duty. Sentimental. Practical.

CHARLES: Tallish. Forty. A dissipated intellect. Holes in socks. An elongated Rumpelstiltskin with sad memories. Seeks environments in which he will shine as lover and sage.

ACT ONE

SCENE ONE

The set is the living-room of a flat on the top floor of a tall Victorian house somewhere in London. The backstage wall has two doors, side by side, which lead to the bedroom and landing respectively. Between the doors hangs a large, old barometer. Various pictures hang on the walls; a hunting scene in bright colours and, at various points round the walls, pictures of the painting-by-numbers type. A sideboard stands against the wall, on its top a radio and a portable, hand-wound gramophone. In the centre of the stage, a solid Victorian dining-table round which stand four dining-room chairs of the same vintage as the table. To the right, a solid, old-fashioned sofa; to the left, a deep, modernish arm-chair and a wooden kitchen arm-chair. The left-hand wall of the set contains a window with heavy, nondescript curtains hanging from ceiling to floor, and a door leading to the kitchen. Near the window is a small table on which rest a number of model aeroplanes made up from plastic kits. Somewhere on the stage, an old rocking-horse and a dressmaker's dummy on which is draped an Army officer's uniform with well polished buttons and glistening Sam Browne harness. Table lamps, a shaded top-light and a varied clutter of bits and pieces give the room a not uncomfortable feeling – a little drab, perhaps, but it is a room in which people live.

[*As the curtain rises,* ARTHUR *and* BASIL *are at breakfast. At least,* ARTHUR *is, for* BASIL *sits slouched in his chair moodily tapping the table with a thick slice of bread, in a beat deliberately at variance with the music scratchily issuing from the gramophone. It is the 'Dance of the Sugar-Plum Fairy'.*

BASIL *wears a white open-necked shirt, slim-cut black trousers and highly polished brown leather chukka boots.*

ARTHUR *is dressed in a maroon, short-sleeved sports shirt, over-long khaki shorts, thick fawn socks with green Scout tabs and heavy brogue shoes. As* ARTHUR *busily gets on with his breakfast,* BASIL *grows more and more bad-tempered. 'The Sugar-Plum Fairy' comes to an end and* ARTHUR *speaks between chewings and swallowings.*]

ARTHUR: Well – the sun's shining.

BASIL: So the sun's shining. It's about time ... but what's the glass doing?

ARTHUR: I haven't tapped it.

BASIL: Tap it then!

ARTHUR: After breakfast ... I will after breakfast.

BASIL: I want to know now!

ARTHUR: Then tap it yourself!

[BASIL *increases the pace of his bread-slice tapping, then, in a sudden paroxysm of bad temper, hurls the slice at the barometer. It hits it squarely in the face.* ARTHUR *squints at it.*]

It still says 'Change' ... Well – that's all right then, isn't it?

BASIL: 'Change'! ... Which way? Up or down? Change to what?

ARTHUR: I don't know. Neither up nor down. 'Fine', probably.

BASIL: 'Fine', you think? Why not 'Wet'? Answer me that! Why not 'Wet'?

ARTHUR: I don't mind what it does. I look on the bright side, that's all. I've come to terms. I've got an umbrella, I've got sun-glasses ... I've come to terms.

BASIL: You take everything lying down. Flat on your back – that's how you take it!

ARTHUR: I've seen people knocked down. They've had their noses in the air and didn't see what hit them.

BASIL: You mean me?

ARTHUR: I mean nobody in particular.

BASIL: That means you – a nobody in particular. [*A silence as* ARTHUR *gets on with his breakfast.* BASIL *scowls.* ARTHUR *pours a cup of tea.*] Give me a cup!

[ARTHUR *ignores him and sips his tea noisily.* BASIL *suddenly thumps his fists on the table.*]

ARTHUR: Oh, I know you when your temper's up! Don't I know it! Temper. That's all it is. Look at the last few days – the two of us, on holiday and all cooped up. All right – that's all right ... But because you can't stop the weather changing when it feels like it, you nearly kill me. Twice you nearly kill me. Once with your hands and once with the hammer. That's twice in three days! If I hadn't begged for my life ...

BASIL: Crawling hysteria!

ARTHUR: Like all cross people, you're sentimental.

BASIL: One day I'll finish you!

ARTHUR: When?

BASIL: When I feel like it.

ARTHUR: That's not answering my question – when?

BASIL: When your stupid tears roll off my back and I can't hear your sobs.

ARTHUR: I'll scream the next time. I'll try screaming.

BASIL: Crawling little bastard!

ARTHUR: That's abusive! That's very abusive! [*Pause.*] What I've got is a high fear-and-pain threshold. Did you know that? A high fear-and-pain threshold. And that's a difficult thing to have. You wouldn't like to have it. Oh, no! you'd hate it. You couldn't bear it the way I do.

BASIL: You've got hobbies. And that's all you've got ... Hobbies. Little aeroplanes made of plastic – high-impact plastic. And painting by numbers. My hackles rise when I see you at it!

ARTHUR: You and your hackles! You haven't enough to occupy your mind. I've nearly got it worked out!

BASIL: Got what worked out?

ARTHUR: What it's all about. I know how to cope with adversity. When it strikes I ask myself all the right sort of questions. It rains, so I ask myself 'What good is rain?' And back comes the answer – quick as a flash: 'It helps lay the dust.'

BASIL: Christ!

ARTHUR: So I welcome the rain as much as the sun ... as long as there's not too much of either.

BASIL: Can't you think of me? You know how I hate the rain! How it affects me ...

ARTHUR: I know all right. You rant and bellow, swear up and down the room, and do violence to my person when things don't fit into the pattern of your liking.

BASIL: I'll take nothing lying down!

ARTHUR: You'll see. Wait till the end comes. You'll lie down.

BASIL: The end isn't yet.

[ARTHUR *cuts a slice of bread and butters it.* BASIL *stares moodily into nothing.*]

ARTHUR [*chewing*]: Anyway ... you're feeling better? You're feeling all right?

BASIL: I can feel the energy building up in me. There's a dynamo going it somewhere inside me. Building up an energy – [*He looks fiercely at Arthur.*] – that could serve a hundred women, then stretch-gallop the bloodiest-minded horse until it dropped dead. In a little while, there'll be nothing I can't do ... [*Pause.*] I've pity for you. A big, foxy pity.

ARTHUR: Why?

BASIL: You'll find out.

ARTHUR: I know what you mean. I can guess all right.

BASIL: I wouldn't be too sure.

ARTHUR: Mabel?

BASIL: Mabel. [*Count of five.*] She wants a man, not a castration complex.

ARTHUR [*winces*]: What Mabel wants is an understanding man. Kindness, that's what she's looking for. Kindness. Understanding. I can give her that.

BASIL: She wants someone to bash the sexual daylights out of her. A black eye and kept awake all night, that's what Mabel wants. And she'll get it! ... From me. I'll give it to her all right!

ARTHUR: If you ever got as far as that with Mabel, who d'you think she'd turn to for loving-kindness?

BASIL: She wouldn't know which way to turn.

ARTHUR: She'd turn to me! What a chance you'd stand then! I know you! If it came to the point, you'd fall off your stretch-galloping horse flat on to your face.

BASIL: What the hell do you know about it? The nearest you've got to knowing a woman is the Boy Scout's Manual on How to Live a Clean Life.

ARTHUR: That was a good book!

BASIL: Written by a man married to a Scout.

ARTHUR: You say every abusive thing that enters your head!

[*They brood in silence.* BASIL *lights a cigarette and throws the match on the floor.*]

Do you have to throw dead matches all over the floor? After all, I'm the one who has to do all the cleaning.

BASIL: Leave it where it is! Ask yourself one of your questions.

[ARTHUR *picks up the match and places it in the ash tray.*]

ARTHUR: I do. Oh, yes, I ask a question ... Whenever you leave rubbish lying around I ask myself, 'Is it good to leave rubbish lying around?' And I can never find a single point in its favour. Untidiness irritates me.

BASIL: I like it.

ARTHUR: But it's not good for you! It's undisciplined action ... You're undisciplined!

BASIL: If you'd seen me in the war, you wouldn't have said that. I disciplined those men. Oh, yes – they knew it when I was around. And nothing was too dangerous. Discipline and danger. I lived with them for five years ... and never faltered! Never lost my nerve ...

[ARTHUR *looks at him with admiration.*]

ARTHUR: I wish I'd known you then! You must have been magnificent.

[BASIL *looks more cheerful.*]

BASIL: Some of us lived in that war.

ARTHUR: I can just see you.

BASIL: I enjoyed those five years.

ARTHUR: I didn't enjoy *my* war.

BASIL: You're made differently. You're good for peace. I'm bad for it.

ARTHUR: Oh, no, you mustn't think that. You keep people like me on our toes.

[BASIL *rises and goes to the window.*]

BASIL: Well, you kept out of the war all right.

ARTHUR: What do you mean? I didn't keep out of the war! I may have been a civilian, but I was in the middle of it!

BASIL: Worked it then.

ARTHUR [*very indignant*]: I didn't work anything! What I did took conscience – real conscience! If you think that didn't take courage – !

BASIL: There's nothing wrong in being afraid.

ARTHUR: I wasn't afraid!

BASIL: Then you ought to have been!

ARTHUR: I was – apprehensive. Of certain things … You could say I was afraid of doing the wrong thing. If that's fear, then I admit it – I was afraid.

BASIL: Moral cowardice!

ARTHUR: It wasn't!

BASIL: Diarrhoea of the conscience.

ARTHUR: It was never that. [*Cradles his head in his hands.*] There was no enjoyment in it for me. It hurt too much – in a way you'd never understand. Oh, I've got over it. Like the phoenix, I rose out of the ashes … I had to do what I did. There was no other way … At least, I couldn't see any other way.

[*During* ARTHUR'S *soliloquy* BASIL *has moved to the gramophone. He selects a record, puts it on the turntable and sets it going. The music starts at the end of* ARTHUR'S *speech. It is 'The British Grenadiers' played by a brass band.*]

BASIL: That's the stuff!

[ARTHUR *taps his foot in rhythm with the march, though he still looks miserable. After a few bars, the needle sticks on 'Though all the world's great heroes' and the phrase is repeated until* BASIL, *with anger, crosses to the gramophone and stops it. He looks at Arthur with venom.*]

Well?

ARTHUR: It seemed all right so I didn't get it seen to. My records are all right on it. Not a single scratch. So don't blame the machine, even though I didn't get someone to look at it. It seemed all right, Basil – so I didn't bother.

BASIL: You didn't bother. Christ! He didn't bother. [*Moves to the window and, after a silence, begins to whistle tuneless Morse.*] – ··· ––– ··· ––– ··· ––– ··· ––– ··· ––– ··· –––

ARTHUR: That's SOS, isn't it? Do you know what SOS means?

BASIL: Silly old sod.

ARTHUR: It means Save Our Souls.

BASIL: Amen.

[ARTHUR *picks up a fork and taps out Morse against the side of his cup. He stops.*]

ARTHUR: No – that's not right … [*Taps again, listening intently.*]

BASIL: Shut up.

ARTHUR: I was only trying to remember the alphabet ...

BASIL: Then forget it! [*Goes to the radio. Turns it on and twiddles with the knob. No sound. He stares long at Arthur.*] – It seemed all right, I suppose?

ARTHUR: I forgot.

BASIL: Nothing works. Nothing. All that seems to work is the conversion of food into energy and waste matter.

ARTHUR: I'm surprised you call it waste matter.

BASIL: And what do we use the energy for? Nothing. We don't even manure the land. When I was a child, we had an earth closet in the garden. Grew nasturtiums round it. You should have seen the size of those leaves! Big as plates. Wonderful! ... What happens now? We join the great sewer and reach our destination to be rendered harmless and inorganic and made into – Christ knows what – Plastics, I suppose. [*Is suddenly amused by this thought.*] I'd like that. If I could be sure that's what happens. [*Suddenly cheerful, he walks over to Arthur and stands before him, hands on hips.*] When's Mabel coming?

ARTHUR: Some time this morning. Any time – I don't know.

BASIL: I'm taking her to the park this afternoon. Alone. Do you understand?

ARTHUR: Can't I come?

BASIL: No.

ARTHUR: Doesn't she want me to come?

BASIL: You're not coming.

ARTHUR: Doesn't she want me to come? Don't be afraid you'll hurt me. I only want to know. So you'd better tell me. Doesn't she want me to come?

BASIL: I didn't ask her.

ARTHUR: Does she know you're taking her to the park without me?

BASIL: No.

ARTHUR: I thought we'd take a trip down the river to Greenwich. On a boat. With sandwiches and a thermos.

BASIL: No.

ARTHUR: I'll ask her which she'd rather do.

BASIL: Why do we always have to ask Mabel? Everything that comes up – we have to ask Mabel!

ARTHUR: We always do.

BASIL: What have I done that I should know only you? Other men have an ageing mother – fat sisters with fat husbands – men to drink with. What have I got? A wet nurse. A short-arsed Crawfie!

ARTHUR: Goodness knows what you'd do if you didn't have me to fuss you around. You'd go hungry – shirts dirty – holes in your socks. What would you do without me? What would you do without Mabel?

BASIL: Oh, shut up!

ARTHUR: I know we haven't many friends ...

BASIL: We haven't *any* friends.

ARTHUR: And why haven't we? Because you put people off. I'd like to have a few friends. We could ask them round for coffee or something. Just for an evening's talk now and again. Just one or two friends. That'd be nice. I'd like that. It's rather sad, isn't it? – when you come to think about it.

BASIL: Let's cry our eyes out and sing the 'Organ Grinder's Monkey'! ... The other day, I asked a breath-whistling, smegmatic old car-park attendant to have a drink with me. The old bastard refused ... Refused! 'Jest orf ter meet the boys,' he said. He gave me a dirty look. He gave me the 'I know your sort, mate' look. A car-park attendant! ... We're cut off from people. Isolated.

ARTHUR: We're not cut off – we're just insular. Mark you, insularity can be carried too far. We don't want to be lost in a crowd, do we? No, we don't want that. But we've seen the warning light and we've made a move in the right direction.

BASIL: We won't see *him* again. You and your cards in shop windows!

ARTHUR: He liked the flat.

BASIL: He won't come back.

ARTHUR: He'll come back. He'll be here on the dot. [*Consults his watch.*] He said he'd be here by ten.

BASIL: Put something decent on. Take those bloody shorts off and put on something decent. Look at yourself – just look at yourself.

ARTHUR: I'm on holiday. I always wear shorts on holiday. Every year for fourteen days, I wear shorts.

BASIL: Like an obscene fat schoolboy.

ARTHUR: I'll wear what I like!

BASIL: If I were you, do you know what I'd do?

[ARTHUR *is silent.* BASIL *draws a finger across his throat.*]

That's why he's not coming. The queer sight of you put him off.
Our bit of company! He reflected ... He sat down and reflected.
So he's not coming ... And I don't blame him.

[BASIL *suddenly raises his head and listens.* ARTHUR *looks at him
questioningly.*]

Well – answer it.

ARTHUR: Answer what?

BASIL: The door. I heard a ring.

ARTHUR: There wasn't a ring.

BASIL: I tell you, I heard a ring!

ARTHUR: Noises in your head.

[*Both listen intently for a count of five.*]

Anyway, Mrs Bamber would let him in.

BASIL: Shut up!

[*They listen again.* ARTHUR *sneaks an amused glance at Basil.*]

What are you smirking about?

ARTHUR: I think you want him to come, don't you?

[BASIL *looks at Arthur with distaste.*]

Do you want him to come, Basil? I mean, is it important to you
that he lives with us? You said you didn't mind, but that's not the
same as wanting it, is it? You've got to be sure. You mustn't make
a mistake. Do you want him to come?

BASIL: If he keeps you out of my way, he's welcome. Oh, he'll be
welcome all right if he can do that.

ARTHUR: He seemed a kind person. He liked the pictures and he was
– interested. Yes, he was interested. I thought that was important.
Very important.

[*A knock on the door, which* ARTHUR *answers. There is no one there,
just a large brown-paper parcel lying on the floor.* ARTHUR *carries
it in, leaving the door open.*]

It's the laundry. Only the laundry. [*Opens the parcel on the table
and begins to check the contents.*] Two shirts. [*Finds two shirts.*] Two
pants. [*Finds two pairs of pants, then pauses and looks up.*] I wonder
if I'd have time to make up his bed before he arrives.

BASIL: Let him make his own bed.

ARTHUR: I don't mind doing it. Must make him welcome.

[*Over the last two lines of dialogue,* CHARLES *appears in the doorway.*]

CHARLES: You've done that already. Very welcoming you were. [*Enters the room, carrying a suitcase.*] What a sunny morning! How are you both?

[*A count of five.*]

ARTHUR: I was going through the laundry. Sometimes they send the wrong things.

CHARLES: Better than the stuff you sent?

ARTHUR: Basil had a beautiful check shirt once. Beautiful. He kept it. Very dishonest of course, but it suited him so well. He wore it for weeks ... then we had to send it back.

CHARLES: Of course.

ARTHUR: Basil thought you weren't coming.

CHARLES: On the stairs, I met a shrouded woman, all grey skin and black.

ARTHUR: That's Mrs Bamber. The housekeeper. She's a bit strange, you see – a bit strange ...

BASIL: We're all bloody strange.

[CHARLES *sits down in the arm-chair.*]

CHARLES: It *is* a sunny morning. Are you enjoying your holiday? You did say you were on holiday, didn't you?

BASIL: He said we're on holiday – if you can call fourteen days C.B. a holiday. Listen, when we fix our holiday for the year, the same thing happens. A Plan comes up. It was Spain last year ... We'd go together, live simply, see the country ... We never got to Spain. It was Germany's turn this year. But are we going to Germany?

ARTHUR: We couldn't afford it.

BASIL: So here we stay. Next spring, the Plan will hit us again and if all goes well, we'll have another fourteen days at home.

ARTHUR: It's not so bad.

BASIL: Each fortnight is worse than the last and it takes a whole year to prove it. Fourteen days of uncertain weather sandwiched between three hundred and fifty-one glorious-by-comparison days.

CHARLES: Well – the sun's shining now.

BASIL: It won't for long.

ARTHUR: We might be in for a sunny spell. You never know.

BASIL: Whenever you say that, it rains. The clouds start building up. The rain is sweeping into the suburbs just because you think we're in for a sunny spell.

ARTHUR: I look on the bright side. That's all. We might have a vulture perched on the door to hear you talk.

BASIL: You'd call it a canary.

[*A short silence.* CHARLES *looks at the hunting picture.*]

CHARLES: What an attractive picture.

ARTHUR: It was here when we came.

CHARLES: And you've kept it because you are both sportsmen?

ARTHUR: Basil doesn't like it.

BASIL: You hold your tongue!

ARTHUR: Well – I don't like it, either.

CHARLES: A bright splash of colour ... don't you think?

ARTHUR: I'd take it down to the basement if I had my way.

CHARLES: Why don't you?

ARTHUR: It's part of the room.

CHARLES: The Berkshire Hunt?

ARTHUR: It's left a mark on the wall.

CHARLES: And on many a case-hardened sportsman.

ARTHUR: All those red coats ... Where's the fun in killing for sport?

BASIL: I shot a hare once ... We were out on reconnaissance and there he was, leaping and running, first this way, then that. I gave him a quick burst of fire ... You never saw anything stop existing so quickly. Then all the other men had a go at anything in sight.

ARTHUR: How could you? I couldn't ... I couldn't do that.

BASIL: And they didn't hit a thing – not a thing.

CHARLES: Sport, eh?

ARTHUR: I couldn't do it!

BASIL: Only a hare. A leaping, comic hare.

ARTHUR: So alive!

BASIL: So dead! It didn't know it had stopped living. A good shot, that was. A damned good shot.

ARTHUR: Were you hungry?

BASIL: No.

ARTHUR: In a temper?

113

BASIL: No.

ARTHUR: Were the others hungry?

BASIL: No.

ARTHUR: Did the hare frighten you or something?

BASIL: Hah!

ARTHUR: Then what gave you the right to take its life?

BASIL: I didn't take it. I ended it. Just left it where it was. Boomp! I ended it – like that. You've got to show your hand sometimes – exercise your rights – or you forget you ever had them.

CHARLES: Well, anyway, it's a good picture of a hunt. A fine, bold display of the courage of old England – the white, scarlet-gashed pantaloon faces of the women; the wine-dark gentlemen with finely veined noses, riding the mounts of faded privilege. Tally Ho! – and off they go to run the proletarian fox to his hole. And it doesn't matter if Maud, the General's daughter, comes off at the jump, breaks her neck and expires on the field – she gave her life to a noble cause and what dashed bad luck – what dashed bad luck!

[BASIL *and* ARTHUR *stare at him. An uneasy pause.*]

ARTHUR: Will you like it here, do you think?

CHARLES: I feel quite at home. You make it feel like home.

ARTHUR: It's very quiet. There's no one above us, you see. No feet stomping around.

CHARLES: I like quiet.

BASIL: Sometimes it's too bloody quiet.

CHARLES: Then make your own noise.

ARTHUR: We've got a wireless, but it's broken.

CHARLES: We'll have it mended.

ARTHUR: It's not worth it.

CHARLES: Not worth it? Not worth it? The whole world beating its electronic wings on your window, clamouring to be admitted, waiting to delight you and you don't think it's worth it? Does Hilversum mean nothing to you? Doesn't the magic of a wavelength awe you? How long is a wavelength? Well?... You see, you don't know. Why deny yourselves the pleasures of this world? When did you last hear Ludwig Koch? Uncle Mac? Music while you work? Perhaps you don't like music while you work. Or the musical whisper of W. R. Rodgers giving you the latest memory of the Irish bog as you iron the smalls. Or being posed the problem, 'Is there an honest God?' as you clear away the supper things. Why, you'd be with it all the time if you opened the window and let the waves in.

ARTHUR: We would?

CHARLES: I would like to suggest that you allow me to furnish you with a really magnificent multiple-purpose machine. A television set with automatic contrast control, with new stereo sound realism in which, with the new high-sensitivity valves and circuit design, there will be no disparity due to weakness of signal. And, if we have V.H.F. radio built in – my word! What I have in mind are such riches, plus – a stereogram! Four speeds, for all types of records – or do you prefer to say discs? Twin amplifiers – ah, yes! twin eight-by-six speakers which will, can you believe it, bring the Philharmonic into your room! Amazing! Fantastic! Doesn't it seem odd to you both that so few people really want such wonders?

[ARTHUR *and* BASIL *are lost in wonder at Charles's speech. There is silence.*]

ARTHUR: I think, if it's all the same to you, we'll keep the radio.

BASIL [*turning on* ARTHUR]: Why shouldn't we have something that really works? Are you serious about this machine?

CHARLES: So serious that, I promise you, it will be installed before the week is out.

BASIL: That's settled then. I'd like it very much.

CHARLES: Arthur?

ARTHUR: I didn't want to impose on you.

CHARLES: There is no imposition.

ARTHUR: I'd like to think about it.

BASIL: For God's sake let's not think about it! Or nothing will happen.

[*There is a silence.* BASIL *is fierce,* ARTHUR *worried,* CHARLES *quizzically interested.*]

CHARLES: I'll get it then. What marvellous evenings we'll have. We'll watch a play. Have a snack, and then settle down to a concert. A symphony, perhaps – or some chamber music. A round of Guinnesses and then, if we have any time left, we'll round the evening off with one or two of our favourite records. The Laughing Policeman. A Charlie Kunz selection. And to finish, what could be nicer than a few ear-splitting *Lieder* from Madame Schumann-Heink?

ARTHUR: We must tell Mabel. We haven't told him about Mabel yet.

BASIL: Well, tell him.

ARTHUR: Mabel. Well – Mabel is a friend ... Of ours. A mutual friend, you might say ... She comes round to see us. Hardly a day passes without a visit from Mabel. Well ... most days she comes round. We're very fond of her. She's a very nice girl. And always the same.

BASIL: Do you know what he thinks? He thinks he's going to lay her one day. All nice and legal, of course. What a dream of glory!

ARTHUR: And what do you want to do, eh? Brutalize her. That's what you want to do – brutalize her. Turn her into a broken slut! ... I won't let you do it! I'll put a stop to it.

BASIL: Can you hear the Boy Scout bugles blowing? Try to make fire with a damp stick – that's the weight of his chance of making it with Mabel.

ARTHUR [*very deliberately*]: If I thought Basil could give to Mabel all that she needs – security, understanding – I'd stand aside. I would! I'd stand aside. For her good, I'd waive my claim ... And I have a claim ... If I'm lucky enough ... Basil will never want for a home. I can promise him that. I won't let my friends down. She'll have to choose ... One day ... But Basil will never want for a home. Never.

CHARLES: Perhaps she needs you both.

BASIL: That's what I tell the Patrol Leader here. When I fix things with Mabel, I tell him, he can have a room with us. Then, when she's feeling brutalized, she can have a nice, cosy chat with Baden-Powell and be made sweet again for me.

ARTHUR: Whatever happens, I'll make the best of it. I'll stand by. I can wait. Oh, never fear – I can wait ... and stand by.

BASIL: Stand by. Action. Like the war ... Something happening all the time. Explosive! Contrasts! Christ, it was terrific! Have you ever seen a man with all the muscles of his body corded and strong, his eyes shining and feeling such brute life in him that he has to

sing all the obscenities he ever learned and then – suddenly – crack!
He's dead ... And so still, you have to whisper when you talk over
his body. Have you seen that, either of you? That's something
worth seeing. I could see it again and again.

[CHARLES *and* ARTHUR *have given him their full attention during
Basil's speech. He finishes in fine, cheerful, cocky violence and then, as
his audience remain silent, he goes broody. He thrusts his hands in his
pockets, turns his back and looks through the window.*]

There'll be changes when I fix things with Mabel. Excitement! A
great whacking excitement, that's what it's going to be. I'll be
brutal ... And won't she love it!

CHARLES: Have you ever thought of owning a dog?

BASIL: What would I do with a dog?

ARTHUR: The poor thing would be dead in a week.

BASIL: I asked him the question.

CHARLES: You'd be such a good master. You'd lavish violence and
love on it. You'd beat it and pat it and you'd only have a pair of
liquid eyes to tell you how much it feared and loved you. Better
than a woman.

ARTHUR: I'm not having a dog in the flat.

BASIL: If I want a dog. I'll have one.

ARTHUR: It would have to be a small one.

BASIL: A big one. The biggest bloody dog I can find. A Great Dane –
a walloping smelly St Bernard.

CHARLES: But you'd rather have Mabel?

BASIL: She'll do.

CHARLES: When am I going to meet her?

ARTHUR: Any moment now. She comes every day.

BASIL: I've suddenly thought of Mabel as a bitch.

CHARLES: Association of ideas.

ARTHUR: We used to play a game at Jamboree rather like that.
We'd sit round in a circle and someone would start the ball rolling
by saying, well – 'Oxo', or something, and then the next person
would say the first thing that came into his head ... Like 'Beef' ...
Then someone would say 'Bulls' ... 'Cows' ... 'Meadows' ...
'Buttercups '... 'Daisies' ... Um ...

BASIL: Udders.

ARTHUR: Why?

BASIL: Cows are called Daisy. Cows have udders.

ARTHUR: We'd play the game for hours ... I did enjoy it ... very much.

BASIL: Then they'd all have a jolly sing-song and the King would come round as they crouched over the cooking-fires and say, 'Ah – bangers'.

ARTHUR: I was never there when the King came round.

BASIL: Neither was I, thank God! Look at me – I've never been near a Boy Scout Rouser, yet I can see the whole scene ... It hits me right where it makes me vomit. Like your hobbies. As soon as you set them out each evening I feel the nausea rise.

ARTHUR: You'd be happier if you had a hobby. Anything. Stamps, car numbers, match-box labels. Anything.

BASIL [directly to Charles]: First it was painting by numbers. Then it was model planes. Then it was both. Painting by numbers ... When he comes to a bit marked 9, he looks it up. Burnt Sienna, it says. So he whips up a bit of burnt sienna and carefully, with his lips pursed in concentration, carefully fills in the outlined piece on the outlined picture entitled, for those who want to know, 'Cloistered Calm'. Christ!

ARTHUR: What can you do? Answer me that. What can you do? How do you keep your mind occupied?

BASIL: I think. I plan. It's all in my mind ... Take high speeds. To travel at high speed and if you don't get there, you're dead ... And revolution. I think revolution when all the people are screaming for action. And I lead them ... You should hear the volcanic rumble and crump as they trample over the bodies of dowager Boy Scouts. You should hear the old trouts scream. Whooooops! [In falsetto]: You – you poor booby with your painting by numbers ... By numbers! You bring me back to reality with stupid questions ... 'Isn't this shaping nicely?' you ask – Why do you hold me back?

ARTHUR: I don't. That's unjust, Basil, that's very unjust. I admire you. Honestly. I like your strength. But your violence! It makes me choke. When you talk of smashing this and smashing that, I feel you're smashing me!

BASIL: You! [*Grips hold of chair and kicks it over.*] Have I kicked a chair? Oh, no – I've just kicked Arthur up the arse! [*Picks up the chair and lays it across his knee. Spanks the seat.*] Now I'm giving the naughty boy a good spanking for misunderstanding his beloved playmate. [*Appeals to Charles.*]

– Why? Can you tell me why?

CHARLES: It's all a matter of perspective. If you could both see yourselves in perspective – and I'm sure you will – everything will be pleasant. Oh, very pleasant. There are many ways of putting it. We can use a simile. We can use metaphor ... Not seeing the wood for the trees ... The trees for the wood ... And a chair has arms, legs, back, feet ... And a bottom – or seat. It is also a poetic reality to identify oneself with certain objects ... I am a Tower of strength ... A dynamo ... A shy, shrinking violet ... My heart has turned to stone ... My heart has wings ...

[BASIL *and* ARTHUR *listen with peculiar concentration during this speech, mystified, but interested.*]

Lion-hearted ... The milk of human kindness! Let us drink at the mother fountain and remember the land of our birth.

[BASIL *and* ARTHUR *suddenly look towards the door as a key grates in the lock. The door opens and* MABEL *enters.*]

MABEL: Here we are then! [*Sees Charles and goes quiet.*]

BASIL: Any clouds coming up, Mabel?

MABEL: I didn't notice any.

ARTHUR: Mabel – this is Charles.

CHARLES: I'm very glad to see you – I've heard so little about you.

MABEL: Oh? [*A slight pause.*] – Well – it's a lovely day.

CHARLES: The sun's shining.

MABEL: You need it on holiday.

CHARLES: How right you are.

MABEL: I'm having my fortnight now. The same as Basil and Arthur.

CHARLES: That makes four of us.

MABEL: You too?

[CHARLES *nods.*]

Are you staying? I mean, right away?

CHARLES: Right away.

MABEL: Well – that's nice. I expect you'll keep Basil and Arthur in good temper.

CHARLES: I have dedicated myself to that task.

MABEL [*a little surprised by the manner of his answer*]: Pardon?

CHARLES: Sharing can be very pleasant.

MABEL: Oh, you'll have to share me, too ... I suppose. I'm always coming round. Quite the bad penny, I am ... Well – I'll have to treat you like one of the family, won't I? [*Her embarrassment grows as she flounders on.*] Well – that'll be four of us ... We can play whist. Or rummy. I mean, it's better than being three – being four ... One and two makes three and it's odd man out. We're an even number ... Well – it'll be nice, won't it? ... The four of us.

CURTAIN

SCENE TWO

The next day. Late afternoon. The sun is shining. CHARLES *sits in the arm-chair pouring out a Guinness. Three empty bottles lie at his feet. On the bedroom door is pinned a crude drawing, some six feet in height, of a figure just recognizable as St Sebastian if only for the red arrow pinned to the chest of the figure. The figure is drawn on a length of ceiling paper.*

> [CHARLES *finishes pouring, holds the glass up to eye-level and looks at its colour. The door opens and* MABEL *quietly enters. She hesitates as she sees that Charles is alone, then closes the door and comes forward to the table. Without turning his head,* CHARLES *speaks to her.*]

CHARLES: They've gone out.

MABEL: I thought they had. Together?

CHARLES: How else?

MABEL: They never know when I'm coming.

CHARLES: They expect you all the time.

MABEL: I suppose they do ... Have you had all those bottles?

CHARLES: I'm drinking the fourth now.

MABEL: Is that a lot?

CHARLES: No. Would you like some?

120

MABEL: Oh, no – thanks. [*There is a silence and* MABEL *looks idly round the room. She sees the St Sebastian drawing and, puzzled, walks over to inspect it.*] What's this?

CHARLES: It's a game Basil invented. A variation of putting the tail on the donkey. Only this game is called, Putting the arrow in St Sebastian. Basil at his most sadistic. A blasphemous little game, but most successful for its effect on Arthur. He was most hurt – but for the sake of peace, Arthur tried his luck and scored a bull's eye every time which, oddly enough, pleased him ... But Basil – he couldn't get anywhere near it. Arthur became quite cheerful, and Basil very bad-tempered.

MABEL: Did you play as well?

CHARLES: No. I encouraged them and drank Guinness while they played. It was funny while it lasted.

MABEL: I don't think you ought to encourage Basil.

CHARLES: The score was equalized when Arthur played one of his records and the needle stuck. The room was filled with dozens of identical Sugar-Plum Fairies.

MABEL: Poor Arthur.

CHARLES: Poor Basil. But don't let us wear our widow's weeds – the coffin may be empty.

MABEL: Are you really going to stay on? With Basil and Arthur?

CHARLES: I think so. We get on well, it seems, and it's a relief to put one's feet up ... It gave me a faint feeling of pleasure to see their cheerfulness when their morning's tiff was forgotten. Basil seemed quite sunny and Arthur was chattering with happiness. They both gave the glass a good tap before they went out. So I think I shall stay on ... Do *you* think it's a good idea?

MABEL: Well – I don't know. I mean, I don't know you very well, do I? You see, I'm not very good at summing up people. But – do you like them?

CHARLES: They like me and that puts me well on the way to liking them. You can watch their trust growing. I had no idea my father-image was so bright. They made me a proposition.

MABEL: What?

CHARLES: They asked me to take over the responsibility of paying the rent. Basil's idea. He even went down into the crypt to tell Mrs Bamber.

MABEL: Whatever made Basil do that?

CHARLES: The rent seemed to be bothering them so I offered to pay the whole of the quarter. I suggested that they pay me weekly. They were very touched. Thought it very kind of me. Thank you very much! Then Basil said he thought it would be only fair if I became the official tenant ... So I'm the landlord.

MABEL: Then, they're staying with you, really?

CHARLES: Technically speaking, I suppose they are.

MABEL: Funny, isn't it?

CHARLES: I suppose it is.

MABEL: It doesn't take much to change a situation, does it?

CHARLES: Nothing at all.

MABEL: It's like Basil and Arthur and me. If I fell – you know – if I fell in love with one of them, that would change things very much.

CHARLES: It would shatter them both!

MABEL: I don't think I'll ever like them in that way.

CHARLES: Don't you feel anything for them?

MABEL: I like them better than anyone else. That's something, isn't it?

CHARLES: That's certainly something. It's useful to like people.

MABEL: I get impatient. If I could feel something more, like being sure of something so that I don't feel any doubt ... It's very worrying ... It makes me impatient.

CHARLES: I'd wait if I were you.

MABEL: Wait?

CHARLES: Until it happens. Just wait patiently.

MABEL: Oh, I've done that for years. For years and years. A bit like Basil and Arthur, I suppose.

CHARLES: Basil says he's going to do something soon. I'd watch out if I were you. He means business. He's going to swoop down on Arthur's rocking-horse and carry you off.

MABEL: Oh, that's just talk. Basil won't do anything ... I don't want him to ... It wouldn't work. I know it wouldn't work ... [A silence.] But I'd like to feel that way about someone.

CHARLES: You will.

MABEL: I never have, you see. I know girls who were married at seventeen ... What they must have felt! I think about it – quite a lot ... About what they feel. And then I think about what I don't feel. Then I know I'm missing something ... Like having lots of money ... I don't really know what I should think. When I read a book I find out what other people think. But it's not the way I think.

CHARLES: Well, I shouldn't worry. Just lie in bed and gorge yourself on the sort of dreams books get banned for.

MABEL: I wouldn't know how to start. It's like knowing which knife and fork to use, or the correct way of addressing an archbishop. You've got to know whether you're on the right lines ... Like knowing right from wrong. I mean you might dream the wrong thing and then where would you be? I wish I knew.

CHARLES: I can't tell you, of course.

MABEL: Oh, no, I know that. I'd get all the wrong ideas, I expect. Charles? How do you tell if they're the right ideas?

CHARLES: Try 'em out.

MABEL: In real life?

CHARLES: Yes. You'll be surprised how skilled you'll become.

MABEL: Supposing I was wrong?

CHARLES: Some surprised man would go screaming up the wall ... Or call the police.

[*Count of five.*]

MABEL: You don't fit in with Arthur and Basil, somehow. I don't know what it is, but you don't – quite fit in.

CHARLES: Must I fit in?

MABEL: Do you like steak and kidney pudding?

CHARLES: No.

MABEL: They do. I do, too.

CHARLES: Well?

MABEL: If we're having it one day, what will you have?

CHARLES: If there's nothing else, I'll have steak and kidney pudding.

MABEL: But you wouldn't like it.

CHARLES: That wouldn't be important.

MABEL: Well ... I always thought it was. It's important to know what people like and don't like ... If they're going to fit in, that is.

CHARLES: We'll have to give and take, won't we?

MABEL: That's what we'll have to do. Then we'll all fit in – Arthur and Basil. You and me.

[CHARLES *flashes her an amused glance.*]

– Were you ever married? If you don't mind my asking. I do go on a bit, I know, but it's nice to know about people ... So it just came into my head to ask you ... Because I don't know.

CHARLES: I was married.

MABEL: I suppose she died.

CHARLES: She was like an old soldier ... She served her country faithfully and well ... then faded away ... A fine woman. With luck, she is being enjoyed somewhere. With luck, and – we must hope – with love. A fine soldier.

[*Puzzled,* MABEL *considers him for a space.*]

MABEL: Don't you ever see her?

CHARLES: No.

MABEL: Don't you want to?

CHARLES: No.

MABEL: Do you know where she is?

CHARLES: No.

MABEL: She might be dead. You might go on thinking she's alive somewhere when all the time she's dead. Funny to think that ... I suppose people do all the time ...

CHARLES: A bit of immortality never did anyone harm ... Gone to Jesus but still in our hearts ... Is there anyone there? Knock once for yes, twice for no. Is there anyone there? [*Bends down and knocks the floor once.*] Is there a message for us? [*One knock.*] Well, keep it! ... And some poor chap knocks on the ectoplasmic gates, begging for a bit of immortality ... Hello, Mum ... Hello, Dad ... You'd love it here, Mum – flowers all the way. And, Dad – you remember old Rover? Run over when I was a kid? He's here too. He still runs after the old stick. Quite like old times, it is. Saw Gran the other day. Still a bit deaf. Sends her love. Well, see you soon, Mum and Dad. You don't know it, Dad, but it's sooner than you think, ha-ha! Sorry to dash away but I've just seen Uncle Ted in the distance ... Whereupon Dad says "Ere, Ted's still alive. Why I only spoke to 'im last week.' ''E must 'ave passed on,' says Mum.

'I'll pop round and ask Tilly.' So she pops round and finds that Uncle Ted is well and truly – guess.

MABEL: Dead?

CHARLES: Alive and kicking.

MABEL: Do you like me? Or shouldn't I ask that? It's easy to ask you questions. I don't always understand your answers, but ... do you like me?

CHARLES: I'm aware of you.

MABEL: What does that mean?

CHARLES [goes to her]: It means that I know exactly how your face is shaped. [Holds her chin.] – That you have lips that show much more than you imagine ... [Places both hands on her shoulders. At this point, the lights dim and a spotlight isolates their heads and shoulders on the darkened stage.] Your neck and shoulders ... [Goes down on one knee and his hands slide down her arms and cover her hands where they rest in her lap.] And how provocative your body is ... [Raises a hand as if to touch her breast, but halts and looks up at her.] And from this moment I shall think of you in a very organic way.

MABEL: Organic?

CHARLES: In bed.

[Lighting floods back to normal and CHARLES climbs to his feet. MABEL blinks, as if dazzled by the return of normal lighting. She rubs one of her eyes with her fingertips.]

MABEL: You mustn't let Basil hear you say things like that.

CHARLES: Would he lose his temper and break up the place? And wouldn't he enjoy it. Or he'd take it out of Arthur. Arthur would then begin to enjoy it more than Basil.

MABEL: You should see Arthur when there's been a row. He cries like a baby. And that makes Basil angry. So Arthur gets worse and so it goes on until something breaks. I don't know what it is that breaks ... but it breaks ... And they go quiet ... until the next time. Just like a baby, he cries ... So you mustn't say things like that when he's here.

CHARLES: And when he isn't here?

[She looks at him for a count of five, then lowers her eyes.]

MABEL: When will they be back?

CHARLES: I don't know. Any time.

MABEL: It's a pity they can't afford a proper holiday. They nearly had a nice holiday last year. Leigh-on-Sea, I think it was ... Well, it could have been nice ... They could go out for days. Coach trips or something ... Sevenoaks ... Or Whipsnade, to look at the animals ... By Green Line ... What fruit do you like?

CHARLES: Guavas, litchi, pomegranates, and passion fruit.

MABEL: I've had pomegranates, I don't know the others. Have you been round the world?

CHARLES: Not all of it.

MABEL: It must be nice to travel.

CHARLES: It's all right.

MABEL: I had an aunt ... she's dead, now. When I was fifteen – or was it fourteen? – well, I was fairly young. She told me about a holiday she'd had in Skegness. It didn't rain once, she said. The sky was blue all the time. The best holiday she'd ever had. I've often thought of going there. I'd like to go ...

CHARLES: Don't.

MABEL: I want to go there. Blue sky and hot sun ... My aunt dozing in a deckchair and the sea all glittering and all those people on holiday too so you wouldn't feel lonely. And the beach ... warm golden sand ... it's all so clear ... I'll have to go there.

CHARLES: I'll take you there.

MABEL: We could all go. We're all on holiday.

CHARLES: I don't think this is the best time.

MABEL: Why isn't it?

CHARLES: Listen ...

[*A rumble of distant thunder.*]

A storm coming up ... I like a good storm.

[*They listen intently as the thunder increases in volume. The light slowly changes; becomes dark and ochre in colour and their faces are picked out in the light from outside. There is a bright flicker of lightning.*]
Listen!

[*A drumming rain begins and a loud roll of thunder.* MABEL *draws nearer to Charles. He puts an arm round her.*]
Frightened?

[*The rain increases and the theatre is filled with the sound. They stand watching the lightning flicker outside the window.*

With a loud crash, the door bursts open and ARTHUR *lurches in. In a terrible panic he makes for the window and madly pulls the curtains across. With panic-stricken face, he looks towards the door, where* BASIL *appears livid and menacing. He makes for Arthur who ducks behind the curtains, gathering them to his face. As* BASIL *passes the table, he picks up the knife used to cut the bread. He reaches the curtains and draws back his arm to strike. In his progress from door to curtain he shouts at the concealed Arthur.*]

BASIL: You liar! You creepy, little, bastard liar. Liar! Liar! I'll cut your bloody little heart out! ...

[He is about to strike, when CHARLES, *in two swift movements, picks up an empty Guinness bottle and strikes Basil precisely on the head. Simultaneously, there is a great crash of thunder.*

BASIL *very slowly sinks to the floor and lies huddled, head cradled in his arms.*

To the sound of drumming rain, the curtain slowly descends.]

ACT TWO

SCENE ONE

The living room, 11.45 a.m. the following day. The sun is shining in full strength. BASIL *lies on the sofa, cold compress on head.* CHARLES *sits in the armchair, very cheerful and bright.* ARTHUR *arranges a bunch of yellow flowers at the table.* MABEL *sits at the table watching* ARTHUR *do the flowers.*

[BASIL *groans.*]

BASIL: What happened after you hit me?

MABEL: We put you to bed.

BASIL: No – before that?

CHARLES: You fell like a soldier with the life draining out of him and seemed to die in grief.

BASIL: Did I cry out?

CHARLES: Not a sound.

BASIL: I'm glad of that.

ARTHUR: I felt the blow right through my head!

BASIL: Bugger your head!

CHARLES: Does it ache?

BASIL: I'm fighting it.

CHARLES: It will pass soon.

BASIL: It hurts like hell!

CHARLES: That's the spirit ... I'm sorry, of course. I thought you really were going to use that knife.

BASIL: So I was.

ARTHUR: When I think of it! I couldn't cry out! My voice was strangled. Petrified!

MABEL: I was going to scream for you, Arthur, when Charles stepped in.

BASIL: Didn't anyone scream?

CHARLES: No one. The storm thundered and rolled and shook the house and we stood silently watching your huddled body. Inert, quiet. It was a pregnant moment ...

[*A silence.*]

ARTHUR [*fusses with the flowers*]: If only I had a bit of fern.

MABEL: Get a bit in the Park.

BASIL: That'll be the day.

ARTHUR: Just a couple of pieces here and there. Make all the difference.

CHARLES: Do you always do the flowers, Arthur?

MABEL: They don't often have flowers.

ARTHUR: We had a cactus, once. *Opontia Microdasys* it was called. I've never forgotten its name. It was on a little wooden tab stuck in the pot.

CHARLES: Rabbit Ears.

ARTHUR: Eh?

CHARLES: That's its other name.

ARTHUR: It was a big one. [*Looks towards Basil.*] Wasn't it, Basil? ... We put it out one night on the window-sill. Thought the rain might do it good. It was a bit dusty ... but it fell off in the night, and killed Mrs Bamber's cat in the basement.

BASIL: I pushed it.

ARTHUR: It hit the cat right on the head ... Death was instantaneous, I should think ... Poor cat ... It haunted me for weeks. It was my fault. I shouldn't have put it on the window-sill.

BASIL: I pushed it!

ARTHUR: I buried it in the Park next morning ... Poor cat. And I never liked it.

CHARLES: Did the cactus pull through?

ARTHUR: I repotted it, what was left, but it was never the same. It didn't live. A double tragedy, really. I wish it had lived. I wonder what it died of?

BASIL: Myxomatosis.

MABEL: Arthur used to wash it with a sable brush and warm water.

ARTHUR: I liked that cactus.

[BASIL *suddenly groans.*]

MABEL: Head hurt, Basil?

BASIL: This compress is warm. What good is it, warm?

MABEL: I'll get you another.

BASIL: Don't bother.

ARTHUR: I'll get it.

BASIL: I don't want one!

[CHARLES *goes to the sideboard and takes out two bottles of Guinness and a glass. He returns to his chair.*]

CHARLES: Well – who'd like some?

MABEL: I would. Can I, Charles?

[CHARLES *gives her a searching look. Then he clips the cap off.*]

ARTHUR: Mabel!

CHARLES: Who drinks of my blood shall live for evermore! [*Pours the Guinness into a glass and hands it to Mabel.*] Is this the first time, my child?

[*Puzzled, she takes it and has a sip. She grimaces and lowers the glass.*] Abandon yourself to it. Take a deep draught. It will prepare you for the life to come.

[*She takes a deep draught.*]

MABEL: I like it better now.

CHARLES: You'll come to like it as much as I do.

[*She beams at Basil and Arthur.*]

MABEL: Well – we're all good friends again, aren't we? We'll have no more trouble ... So let's all have a drink together –

CHARLES: The four of us. Basil? [*Starts for the sideboard to get more bottles and glasses.*]

BASIL: My head aches too much. It'll make it worse. I can just fight it as it is.

ARTHUR: I don't like beer.

[CHARLES *waits, head cocked on one side.* BASIL *shakes his head.*]

BASIL: No, I'm hungry – not thirsty. Send Arthur out for some food.

ARTHUR: All right – I'm going. [*Rises a little crossly.*]

MABEL: I'll come with you, Arthur. [*Picks up her handbag.*] We'll have fish and chips. I know you like that. What sort do you want? Skate, haddock, rock salmon, cod? You have just what you want – if they've got it, of course. So you'd better choose two, just in case. Would you like rock salmon? And if they haven't got it – what? Skate?

BASIL: I want a gun. A ·45. A loaded gun smelling of gun-oil.

MABEL: Don't be silly, Basil. What sort of fish do you want?

BASIL: I don't give a damn! Anything!

[MABEL *shrugs and moves to the door with Arthur.*]

I want plenty of chips!

[*The door closes on Mabel and Arthur.* CHARLES *cocks an eye at Basil.*]

CHARLES: Sure you won't have one?

BASIL: No.

CHARLES: It'll cheer you up. [*No answer.*] What a woman is Mabel. Her buttocks revolve round their centre like moons round the sun. It's good to watch them. Do you think Arthur notices them?

BASIL: He's a bloody eunuch.

CHARLES: Come, now. He's modestly sexed. Mm? It's an absorbing study how men variously deal with the never-ending itch ... Does Arthur scratch himself very much? I haven't noticed it. Thinks of higher things, no doubt. The Greeks ... Why have you stayed together so long?

BASIL: He gets the food – cleans the flat – does the laundry – all the things I can't be bothered to do myself. I can put up with him when things are all right ... He's bearable some of the time, but not all of the time ... You've seen how it is.

CHARLES: One thing surprises me. His little models all lying quite undamaged on the table there. [*Crosses to the table, picks one up and returns to Basil.*] They're so fragile – easily broken. Why don't you smash them, Basil? In one of your spasms, why haven't you smashed them?

BASIL: Too easy. Oh, I could smash them all right, but he'd forgive me and enjoy putting them together again. Constructive. I can smash them any time I like. Don't think I'm afraid ... Besides, there's no blood in them ... And there has to be blood ...

CHARLES: But if you imagine – this – [*He is a few paces from Basil; he points the model like a dart.*] Give yourself to this idea. Concentrate fiercely.

[BASIL *obeys.*]

You are Wing-Commander Basil, Hawk of the Upper Air, Killer, Ace – fierce, angry, excellent –

[*The lighting dims and a spotlight picks out the two figures.*]

On patrol, at eighteen thousand feet, you seek vengeance. Your iron-gloved hand grips the control column –

[BASIL *grasps an imaginary joy-stick. He looks in deadly earnest.*]

– thumb ready on the trigger button of your synchronized guns ...
Suddenly – the enemy bears down on you – [*Walks slowly up to
Basil who is focusing all his attention on the model.*] – Icy cool, you
wait for the crucial moment when you know you cannot miss ...
The enemy's bullets are flittering past your thundering angry
machine ... Screaming ... Thundering ... But you wait – wait ...
Until ...

[*The model is only a foot away from Basil's eyes.*]

the moment comes ... Now!

[BASIL *raises his fist, his face vicious ... He hesitates – and lets his
hand drop. Normal stage lighting slowly returns.*]

Well?

BASIL: I can't do it.

CHARLES: Why?

[BASIL *turns his head away and into the cushion.*]

BASIL: It's not raining.

CHARLES: Shall we go through it again and pretend that it's raining?

BASIL: I'm fighting the pain in my head. [*Clasps his head with both
hands.*] What does the glass say?

CHARLES [*walks to barometer and taps it*]: The needle didn't budge a
fraction.

BASIL: Still on 'Change', is it?

CHARLES: Still on 'Change'.

BASIL: I've watched that bloody machine for three years and I've
never caught it on 'Fine'. Two points this way – two points that ...
But always on 'Change'.

CHARLES: I always rely on a fir-cone.

BASIL: It must point to 'Stormy' sometimes ... Or 'Very Dry' ... I
can never catch it at the right time ... I bet you, if I went out in
a storm – God forbid – then rushed back here in the middle of it –
like yesterday – the glass wouldn't say 'Stormy', because the storm
will have stopped by the time I enter this room ... and the glass
will say 'Change'. It's odd, that. Very odd.

CHARLES: I wonder what would happen if I poured my Guinness
into the works.

BASIL [*much agitated*]: No! Don't do that! It's got to be accurate. It's
no good if it isn't accurate.

CHARLES [*very deliberately*]: What would Mabel do if you parted from Arthur?

BASIL: I don't know. Never thought about it. Probably see me one day and him the next ... Or me in the morning and him in the afternoon ... Or vice versa ...

CHARLES: She'd find it hard to keep it up – being kind to you both and not telling you what she did with Arthur and not telling him what she did with you.

BASIL: I wouldn't want to know.

CHARLES: Oh, yes you would. You'd pump her. Mental hydraulics put to practical use ... Little acorns into big trees ... Nothing innocent ... Suspicions dominated by the Master Bed ... The greatest drama of all ... In bed, afterwards, the soft, languid, fleshy afterwards ... Talking about you, pitying you – 'poor old Basil, look what he's missed ... We must be nice to him, dear ... Therefore, let us have a quiet time in honour of poor Basil who cannot be with us tonight ... Just five minutes, dear – for we have things to do.' ... It is not bearable ... at any time!

BASIL: I'd fight it. It wouldn't be like that. I'd fight it – tooth and claw.

CHARLES: Did you notice what Mabel didn't say when she left with Arthur?

BASIL: No, what?

CHARLES: She didn't ask me what fish I would like.

BASIL: Nothing in that. She only asked me because she was sorry for my head. She guesses what you like. She's treating you like one of the family. You'll like what she gets for you.

CHARLES: When I struck you, her face registered nothing but interest. Interest in the bottle held in my hand.

BASIL: She felt it all right ... Not the way Arthur said he did, but she felt it.

CHARLES: Women have an affinity with violence.

BASIL: That's what I tell Arthur – Mabel likes her bit of blood.

CHARLES: I've seen them at bull-fights. When the crisis comes, they bate their breath and lean forward with tight breasts as the phallic sword hovers ... points ... steadies ... then enters the bull up to its hilt. And as the bull crumples its forelegs and dies, they let out a great sigh ... of satisfaction ...

BASIL: I've watched them at wrestling matches. They howl for blood at the wrestling. Two great ugly bastards face each other and grapple with clawed hands under a white sizzling light. When they draw blood, the women love it! They egg the uglies on ... tell them what to twist – what to kill ...

CHARLES: In hospital, it was the same. Sights that made men sick that the blood and mess emanated from themselves, were mopped up by the women, dealt with, and removed with such equanimity that you began to doubt your own vision.

BASIL: I'll never go to hospital. I'll die before that happens ... Can you imagine what it would be like surrounded by bloody Arthurs all day and all night? He'd have the upper hand in hospital ... All those types fussing around ... Enemas ... temperatures ... scab-washing. And the do-gooders with Joy Hours every Sunday morning ... Are you with Christ, my son?

CHARLES: Are you in a State of Grace, my child?

BASIL: When did you last see your Father?

CHARLES: All together now –

Rock of Ages, cleft for me –

[*They sing together.*]

Let me hide myself in Thee:
Let the water and the blood
From Thy riven side which flowed,
Be of sin the double cure,

[CHARLES *stops singing.* BASIL *carries on.*]

Cleanse me from its guilt and power! ...

CHARLES: We have been blasphemous.

BASIL [*uncomfortable*]: You started it!

CHARLES: You're right to fear blasphemy.

BASIL: D'you think I'm afraid of the consequences?

CHARLES: Well, aren't you?

BASIL: No.

CHARLES: It's a zealous God that strikes the blasphemer.

BASIL: I don't care.

CHARLES: You're the man for Mabel – no doubt about that.

BASIL: It's obvious, isn't it?

CHARLES: Then what are you waiting for?

BASIL: A sign. I'm waiting for a sign.

CHARLES: You'll know it when it comes, of course?

BASIL: I'll know it.

CHARLES: You're sure the sign didn't creep into your mental crypt some time ago and, unrecognized, creep out again?

BASIL: No. I'd have known ... It's not far off ... because I keep feeling danger. I can smell it. Not far off ... It's been coming for days ... I shall make the decision ... A big decision ...

CHARLES: I've felt that about you. Your instincts poised and alert ... Feeling proximities with your sensitive, delicate and terrible mechanism of nerves ... Choosing methods ... Gauging distance ... Counting down to that orgasm of action which means life or death ... It's terrible ...

BASIL: You see that in *me*?

CHARLES: Yes – and it's magnificent.

BASIL [*puts out a hand which* CHARLES *shakes very gravely*]: I should like to thank you.

CHARLES: Contrariwise, I should thank you. It's not often one has the chance of studying a man of action. Especially in action.

BASIL: When the time comes, I will not be watched.

CHARLES: Wouldn't it help to have someone around as an insurance policy? ...

BASIL: You can stuff your bloody insurance.

CHARLES: How about God? He might intervene.

BASIL: Chief Scout!

CHARLES: No God?

BASIL: You ought to meet Arthur's God. Straight out of *Reader's Digest* ... 'The Greatest Magician I Ever Knew ...' 'It Pays To Be with God ...'

CHARLES: All the same, you never know when God's going to pounce. Some memory jogs at the very moment you're about to commit the best of the all star seven, and before you can say 'Amen' you're on your knees.

BASIL: Has that happened to you?

CHARLES: I don't engage the way you and Arthur do.

BASIL: There's no God in my childhood. No God at all.

CHARLES: How about Mother?

BASIL: Dead.

CHARLES: Father?

BASIL: No!

CHARLES: Brothers – sisters?

BASIL: There was an aunt ... Aunt Jessie ... she's dead now. You wouldn't mistake her for the voice of God. Every Saturday, when I was a boy, she'd take me shopping. Baked beans on toast in a Lyons tea-shop, then round Woolworths ... And she'd help herself – you know, small things. A packet of hairpins, jar of face cream, a pencil or two. She never got caught. Those were good times. I looked forward to those trips. But she wouldn't let me try my hand. A very moral woman. I think of her quite a lot ... now, she eggs me on. Go it, boy, she says – go it. Chance your luck. Last night, when I went after Arthur, she came into my head ...

CHARLES: If I'd known your Aunt Jessie was in attendance, I wouldn't have interfered.

BASIL: It wasn't the right time – I can see that.

CHARLES: When you part company, Arthur will miss you.

BASIL: Let him! Let him miss me as much as I'd like to miss him ... Sometimes he's not so bad ... Only you've got to be very fit. Or something. Because if you're not, he's unbearable ... He's too good a target. Always asking for it. He reminds me of the things I've missed. Not people, but objects. Objects acquired and lost, stolen, or strayed ... As if he were responsible, like a bloody magpie. After the war, I had a Luger, a ·38 Smith & Wesson, a Colt I lifted from a gin-soaked Snowdrop and a beautiful, shining lady's pistol I found on a manicured Nazi. They were beautiful weapons ... My landlady got scared and asked the police was it all right for me to keep them in my room, cleaning and handling them ... They gave me a receipt. It's in the pocket of my uniform over there ... I often think of those pistols. Arthur makes me think of them. I don't know why. It's as if ... if you cut off the top of his head, there they'd all be. All the things I've had taken from me, or mislaid. One Luger. One ·38 Smith & Wesson. One Colt ·45. One lady's pistol. One filigree gold watch given me by my mother. A toy train, OO gauge. One father. Sisters, never born. Assorted medals,

including the V.C. and M.C. A legacy worth ten thousand pounds. One Samurai sword with ivory-and-gold hilt. One commission – Brigade of Guards. And ... the Freedom of the City of Bristol.

[CHARLES *moves to the window during Basil's speech. He has listened intently.*]

Are they coming back?

CHARLES [*looking through window*]: They've just turned the corner. Arthur is trotting on the inside like the gentleman he is, carrying the fish-and-chip bundle.

BASIL: I'm getting up. [*Rises from the sofa and makes for the bedroom door.*]

CHARLES: In your sleep last night, you were singing 'Mac the Knife' ...

[BASIL *halts by the bedroom door. He turns to Charles.*] Do you remember?

BASIL: I never remember dreams.

CHARLES: And then you started crying because you said you were a Mac without a knife.

BASIL: I don't remember.

CHARLES: Arthur giggled when he heard you.

[BASIL *scowls, opens the bedroom door and slams it shut behind him. Hands in pockets,* CHARLES *waits the return of Arthur and Mabel. He whistles 'Mac the Knife' monotonously.* MABEL *enters, followed by* ARTHUR. *She takes the bundle from him.* ARTHUR *catches the tune* CHARLES *is whistling. He giggles.*]

MABEL: I'll just put the fish in the oven to keep warm.

ARTHUR: Keep the newspaper round them.

[MABEL *exits to kitchen.* ARTHUR *sits down at table.* CHARLES *stands, rocking on his heels, lightly amused.*]

CHARLES: I had a cosy talk with Basil while you were out.

ARTHUR: I thought you would. I said to Mabel, I bet Basil's telling Charles all his troubles ... it'll help get things off his chest, I said ... What did he talk about? I'm sure you did him a lot of good.

CHARLES: He talked about his childhood.

ARTHUR: Anything else?

CHARLES: Nothing else.

ARTHUR: Didn't he go on about me?

CHARLES: You're part of his childhood.

ARTHUR: I didn't know him then.

CHARLES: You misunderstand me.

[ARTHUR *lapses into puzzled silence.*]

What a deprived fellow he is.

ARTHUR: I try to make things easier for him. Always thinking of him ... I'd never let him down. You can get very fond of a person, you know. I mean, in the fish shop just now, Mabel ordered only one and sixpenceworth of chips and I remembered that Basil wanted lots of chips. I told her to buy *two* and sixpenceworth.

CHARLES: That's really thinking of the other man.

ARTHUR: Well, it's a little thing, but it does indicate a state of mind.

CHARLES: How you have the patience to keep it up!

ARTHUR: I've always been the same.

CHARLES: Do you know what I think? I think you've endured some pretty harsh experiences.

ARTHUR: You've noticed that, have you?

CHARLES: Yes.

ARTHUR: Bitter expériences, some of them. It helps to know that you see in me some of the scars. I've no visible war-wounds. No medals. But during the war, I came into a complete set of Thomas Hardy's works and a book called *Martyrs*. Hardy bored me – but the *Martyrs!* I read it *seven* times! Hardly a day passed when I wasn't humiliated. Such humiliation ... More than I deserved ... But those Martyrs! How *they* suffered! My humiliation was nothing by comparison. Their agonies! Stretched on the wheel, burned alive, torn with hooks, disembowelled, hung by the neck, shot slowly to death with arrows ...

CHARLES: St Sebastian!

ARTHUR: I loved that saint! ... I began to bear with humiliation. I got through ... but only by the skin of my teeth.

CHARLES: You take a lot from Basil, don't you?

ARTHUR: It's the price of friendship.

CHARLES: Is it worth paying?

ARTHUR: There's no other way. I don't have to put up with it. But what else is there? Before you came we hadn't even a friend ... No one to talk to but each other ...

CHARLES: He hates the Scout Movement.

ARTHUR: I enjoyed the Scouts ... You didn't have to prove your manhood by the number of women you'd mucked about with. Just your capacity for service and your ability to get on with the other chap. It was healthy, too ... And safe. I've never known such safety.

CHARLES: Why did you leave?

ARTHUR: The war came and I had to break my Scout oath. You know, King and Country.

CHARLES: How you must miss the Troop.

ARTHUR: I did. Until Basil and I started to share ... Oh, I still miss the innocence of the good old times ... St George's Day, camp, Church Parade ... Do you know, I really enjoyed Church Parade?

CHARLES: You felt like a soldier of Christ.

ARTHUR [after a pause]: I suppose I did. [Is suddenly desolate. Memory has flooded back in him and he is invaded by the terror of the war years.] After the war, everything seemed taken away from me ... There was nothing I could talk about. All my war memories were the wrong memories ... If I'd gone into the Army I might have enjoyed it ... But the idea of their brutality horrified me ... I wasn't afraid of being kicked, or bashed about ... but they'd have demanded that I did the same things ... Whoring, blaspheming, defecating all over the place ... Once I went to a public convenience during an air raid. I caught a North Country private in the act of writing on the wall 'Brigadier Pepper pissed here' ... Why did he have to do that? They'd have wanted me to do the same. And I couldn't – not in a month of Sundays.

CHARLES: I think you had guts.

ARTHUR: It wasn't fair! [Wanders over to the rocking-horse.] It wasn't fair! [Climbs and sits astride the rocking-horse.] All the others who stayed out because they had weak hearts or missing limbs, or were too old, too deaf, too stupid, or too blind – they were encouraged to think of themselves as the gallant Home Defenders ... Crusaders, fighting a Holy War. Didn't I do the same jobs? I comforted the dying ... cleared up the dead ... helped people to safety ... I was a pariah dog ... [Climbs off the rocking-horse and sits down at table.] Anyway, it was grossly unfair.

CHARLES: How you've emerged. It's splendid, how you've emerged. All those years of misery ... and then you meet Basil ... and are kind to him ... A record to be proud of. How *did* you find Basil?

ARTHUR: I'd been working for the Company, not very long, when I noticed this chap brooding alone in the canteen. Never eating much and scowling if anyone sat down at his table. It worried me, seeing him day after day, sitting alone ... I wouldn't be put off – you can guess the sort of things he said to me. Then, he got talking ... Something started him off ... He'd really lived in the war – he's got quite a few medals, you know. He's lost them, but he had them. Quite a few ... What he'd lived through! A wonderful record. But what has he left?

CHARLES: His medals and an old war-wound?

ARTHUR: Nothing. For five years he gave of his best – doing all the glorious things my conscience wouldn't let me do. And the promise was broken. He became a soldier without an army. His blood had run cold ... [*Looks at his hands.*] It was different for me. I promised myself brickbats and degradation in exchange for a clear conscience ...

CHARLES: Did you get it?

ARTHUR: There was never a moment when I could rest and examine it. One thing led to another, you see. The day Peace broke out, I'd made up my mind to fight. And it was too late.

CHARLES: Last night – after the ball was over – what did you think?

ARTHUR: Oh, I thought a lot – a great deal. Last night, I really thought Basil was going to go too far. That he *was* going to do me. Thought so this morning, too. But now, after going out for the fish and chips, and the sun shining, I don't think he meant it ... I'm sure he didn't mean it. Did he?

[*MABEL enters from the kitchen.*]

MABEL: I can't find the bread knife. Have you seen it, Arthur?

[*ARTHUR, embarrassed, reaches inside his inside pocket and draws out the knife. Holding the point he hands it to Mabel.*]

That's a funny thing to do. [*Returns to the kitchen.*]

CHARLES: That wasn't a good idea.

ARTHUR: It was just an impulse. It was cowardly, I know, but I couldn't help it.

CHARLES: It wasn't cowardly, but you mustn't let him see you're frightened. Never show fear.

ARTHUR: I didn't want him to be tempted.

[MABEL *returns*.]

MABEL: What have you done to this knife? It's blunt.

[*She and* CHARLES *look at* ARTHUR, *who shifts uncomfortably*.]

ARTHUR: I came in this morning, early, and the knife seemed so sharp. The edge was razor-keen and it made my flesh creep. It seemed so sensible at the time to go downstairs and blunt it on the doorstep. It didn't take a minute, though I suppose the time it took doesn't matter ...

MABEL: It's all right, Arthur, I can manage. Don't you worry.

[*Over* MABEL's *words*, BASIL, *now fully dressed, appears through the bedroom door, where he has obviously listened to the last part of* ARTHUR's *conversation with Charles*.]

BASIL: Give it to me, Mabel, I'll sharpen it.

[*Surprised, they look towards Basil*.]

I'll make it sharper than it's ever been.

MABEL: I shouldn't worry about it, Basil – I can manage, honestly.

BASIL: Give it to me.

[*Silently, she hands over the knife to* BASIL *who runs his finger along the edge and tests its point. He looks at Arthur with contempt*.]

BASIL: Where's the sharpener, Arthur? Have you seen it, Arthur? Or have you hidden it – Arthur? Arthur? Where's the hone, Arthur? Arthur? Arthur? ...

ARTHUR: It's in the left-hand drawer.

[BASIL *moves towards the sideboard*.]

But I shouldn't bother about it now, Basil – Mabel can manage.

BASIL: Must you blunt *everything* I touch?

[*He hurls the knife at Arthur. It misses him and clatters on the floor. They all freeze. Then* MABEL *walks over to the knife and picks it up. Without a glance at the men, she walks to the kitchen, speaking over her shoulder*.]

MABEL: Basil, lay the table, will you?

[*Silently,* CHARLES *follows her into the kitchen*. BASIL *walks slowly to the sideboard, opens a drawer and takes out a tablecloth. He turns to the table and viciously spreads it*. ARTHUR *just manages to whip*

*away the vase of flowers before the cloth settles. He sits in silence,
vase on his lap.* BASIL *returns to the sideboard and gets knives, forks,
and salt-cellar, which he puts in his pocket, and bottle of sauce. He goes
to the table, throws the knives and forks down, bangs the sauce bottle
on the table and sorts out the cutlery into places. He pushes a knife and
fork towards Arthur.*]

BASIL: Lay your own bloody place!

ARTHUR [*sighs miserably and looks down into the flowers*]: I forgive you
for last night.

BASIL: You do, do you? Is *your* head aching? Do you have an abra-
sion with an attendant swelling that pulses like a heart?

ARTHUR: I'm ready to admit that it was my fault.

BASIL: You said it would be fine!

ARTHUR: I thought it would be. Honestly, Basil – I truly thought it
would be fine. I was quite sure ... I know I was wrong.

BASIL: Keep your mouth shut in future. [*Takes the salt-cellar from his
pocket and bangs it down on the table.*]

ARTHUR: Now your pocket's full of salt.

[BASIL *comes close to him.*]

BASIL: The knife means nothing! Nothing, do you hear? Nothing!
It could have been a sword ... Or an axe with two sharp edges ...
But, whatever it was, it was nothing ...

[ARTHUR *raises his head and looks sadly at him.*]

BASIL: And those flowers are the colour of pus.

ARTHUR: They're buttercup yellow.

BASIL: So's pus.

ARTHUR: That doesn't make these flowers pus.

[BASIL *sits in his place at the table.*]

I went out this morning and bought them to cheer you up.

BASIL: Bloody fool! ... What did you pay for them?

ARTHUR: You shouldn't ask.

BASIL: I hate yellow.

ARTHUR: I tried to get red. I tried two places, but they only had yellow.

BASIL: Couldn't you have got blue?

ARTHUR: Only yellow.

BASIL: They saw you coming ... 'Here comes a little yellow man,'
they said, 'to buy some yellow flowers.'

[ARTHUR *remains silently unhappy.* MABEL *and* CHARLES *enter.* CHARLES *carries a tray of loaded plates,* MABEL *a plate of bread and butter.* CHARLES *puts down the tray and hands out the plates.* ARTHUR *puts the vase on the table.* MABEL *sits down.*]

CHARLES: Shall I say grace?

ARTHUR: We always said grace in the old days.

MABEL: I've forgotten how.

CHARLES [*raising his hand in pontifical manner with two fingers pointed*]: In nomine Patris, et Filii, et Spiritus Sancti ...

MABEL: That's a funny grace.

CHARLES: One of the three.

BASIL: Faith, Hope, and Charity.

CHARLES: Or, to be accurate, all three.

BASIL: That was Latin, wasn't it?

MABEL: What does it mean?

BASIL: You wouldn't understand.

ARTHUR: The only one I ever knew was: 'For what we are about to receive, may the Lord make us truly thankful.'

    [*Count of five.*]

MABEL [*very seriously*]: Would you say that again, Arthur?

ARTHUR [*with feeling*]: For what we are about to receive, may the Lord make us truly thankful ...

    [CHARLES *knocks off one of Arthur's models, deliberately, from the sideboard, and treads on it.*]

CHARLES: Sorry, Arthur, I didn't see it.

CURTAIN

SCENE TWO

The same room. Afternoon. The curtains are partly drawn against the light. The room is shady, with sunlight entering the room in shafts.

    [MABEL *is lying on the sofa, hands behind head. She is humming 'Mac the Knife'. Suddenly she is alert and stops singing. She takes a quick glance towards the door. Her head is back in the original position as the door opens and* CHARLES *enters. He closes the door slowly behind him and stands with his back against it.*

After a pause, MABEL *speaks, without turning her head.*]

MABEL: Where did you leave them?

CHARLES: In the Park.

MABEL: Something told me you'd come back.

CHARLES: I told you.

MABEL: You said you'd be back, all of you, at six. It's only about four thirty.

CHARLES: My intentions reached you clearly enough.

MABEL: I thought you'd come back.

CHARLES: Intentions are odd ... Sometimes they coincide with a basic need. And the message goes singing out ... The fugue of a musical bedstead.

MABEL: Charles? Can a person be crude *and* intelligent?

CHARLES: Mm?

MABEL: Because when I think you've said something crude, you'd only have to tell me that it isn't crude for me to think that what you said was intelligent.

CHARLES: I am never crude.

MABEL: You make fun of me, I think ... I don't mind, because it's gentle.

CHARLES: It's a method of love-making ... [*Moves slowly to the centre of stage.*] The playful tap – the love tap ... The giggling romp ... A bit of prelude to the serious business ... And here we are talking, apparently with all the time in the world. So let's be quiet for thirty seconds and I'll ask you a question.

[*A silence. The lighting slowly grows dim over the next few lines of dialogue until the right moment of sexual tension is reached when both figures are spotlighted and there is concentration on their faces and hands.*]

What are you thinking about?

MABEL: Skegness.

CHARLES: That's a thought.

MABEL: I was thinking how I shall go there one day.

CHARLES: This is the day for Skegness.

MABEL: No, it's too late.

CHARLES: Say the word and we'll leave right away.

MABEL: Another day.

CHARLES: We'll rush to the station on the off-chance of there being a train, and if there isn't one, we'll wait until there is ... We can go this minute, if you say the word.

MABEL: You've no intention of taking me to Skegness today. You're saying one thing and meaning another. You've no intention of taking me ... to Skegness. I always know when you mean something different from what you are saying.

CHARLES: It's because you're a sensitive woman.

MABEL: I am sensitive, you know? I didn't think I was – until recently. I think it's dangerous, but I can't help it.

[CHARLES *crosses to the window and looks through the curtains to the street.*]

CHARLES: Why did you draw the curtains?

MABEL: The light was too strong.

CHARLES: Or did your thoughts make better shapes in the dark?

MABEL: I felt quiet – and pleased ... I felt I was all one piece and there was nothing wrong. Even the doubts I had were only there to think about. Not worry about ... just think about.

CHARLES: If I drew back the curtains and switched on all the lights, would it upset you? ...

MABEL: I don't know, but I don't want to risk it.

[CHARLES *crosses to the table near the sofa.*]

CHARLES: Are you thinking about Arthur and Basil?

MABEL: No ... not really.

CHARLES: Don't you think you should consider them?

MABEL: No ... Because I've considered them for so long ... that now I've got to stop for a while and consider myself ... There'll be a time later for Basil and Arthur. But not at this moment. All those years that have passed ... Tell me what I've been doing all those years.

CHARLES: Keeping strange company.

MABEL: Is that all?

CHARLES: Yes.

MABEL: All those years?

CHARLES: You did other unimportant things. What you thought was proper ... Following an undefined path. Getting older ... And hoping for the best without knowing what the best looked like.

MABEL: You can't help trusting to luck.

[*The stage is now in complete darkness, only the heads and hands of the two figures are spotlighted.* CHARLES *moves over to the couch and sits down on the edge. He reaches out a hand and touches her hair.*]

MABEL: Are you sorry for Arthur and Basil?

CHARLES: You've started thinking about them.

MABEL: Only because you made me consider the time I've spent with them and how little it's really meant. But, are you sorry for them?

CHARLES: No. I am no more sorry for them than I am for myself. It would be a stupid sorrow ... Like Arthur and Mrs Bamber's cat.

[*Count of five.*]

MABEL: What time is it?

CHARLES: Not yet.

MABEL: Oh!

[*He strokes her hair.*]

You think I'm inhibited, don't you?

CHARLES: A bit frightened.

MABEL: I'm not, you know – not really.

CHARLES: Perhaps not ... Don't you think this is the best part of love?

MABEL: It's nice, isn't it?

CHARLES: When you finally commit yourself to love there is an incredible descent into sensation ... The slow climb to a peak of wonderful ferocity. Then – suddenly – the spiralling, spinning down into a desireless pit ... like suicide.

MABEL: I don't understand that. I mean, with suicide, you don't come back.

CHARLES: After love, you wonder why you came back.

MABEL: That's silly – it isn't sad.

CHARLES: Up and down like a monkey on a stick – love. Until it wears out. And then –

MABEL: What?

CHARLES: You buy a new monkey on a stick.

MABEL: That doesn't sound like love. Not my sort of love ... You see ... I thought you waited and waited and then – it happened ... There it was ... You acted the way love told you and, no matter what you did, it was right because you acted out of love ... It's not that I think it's roses all the way. There's anger and worry ... And disappointment. That must be hard to bear – disappointment ... But to come so far and be afraid – well – that would be disappointing. So the thing is, not to be afraid. Even though I know it's not roses all the way, though I'm not saying it wouldn't be nice. But I know there's nothing I can do about it, except take a chance ... Not with you – but with love.

[*She places her hands on his shoulders.* CHARLES *leans over and kisses her. Gently at first and then with intensity as her hands come up to the back of his head and hold it to hers. Their kiss ends and she pushes him away with slow, deliberate force. She rises from the sofa and, as if in a trance, walks to the bedroom door. She opens it and goes through to the room. A moment's pause, then* CHARLES *follows, closing the door quietly behind him. There is absolute silence. Perhaps a few street noises penetrate, but an odd silence persists. There is a click as the front door opens.* BASIL *enters followed by* ARTHUR. *They look at the darkened room, their faces lit by an amber spotlight. There is something a little frightened in their manner.*]

ARTHUR: Charles? Are you in, Charles? [*They wait in bewildered silence.*]

[*Loudly*] Charles! We're back! [*Goes to the bedroom door, opens it and peers in.*] Charles? [*Takes one step forward, then retreats in horror as* MABEL's *voice screams out at him from the concealment of the bedroom.*]

MABEL: *Get out!* Damn you! Damn you! Get out! *Get out!*

[BASIL's *face drains of colour as* ARTHUR *continues to back away from the bedroom door and the curtain slowly falls.*]

ACT THREE

The next morning. CHARLES *is sitting at the table pouring out a cup of tea. It is breakfast time, but* CHARLES *is the only one taking food, which he is doing with great calm and enjoyment.* BASIL *sits at the window, head in hands. The room has been stripped of most of its contents; the pictures have gone with the exception of the hunting scene. The rocking-horse has gone – so have the radio and gramophone; the room has a part-furnished, uncomfortable look.*

> [ARTHUR *enters from the bedroom with a strapped suitcase, dumps it down and crosses stage to the kitchen. He returns with a small collection of bundles and carrier bags, and shoots Charles a dirty look.* CHARLES *watches his activity with amusement. After several journeys in outraged silence,* ARTHUR *addresses Charles as if in reply to a question.*]

ARTHUR: Would you stay? Would you demean yourself in our position? [*Snorts and stomps out of the room and returns immediately with a brown-paper bundle which he adds to the pile.*] You *would* stay, wouldn't you? That's how much pride you've got! I'm not thinking of myself, you know ... it's Basil I'm worried about. Look at him. Look what you've done to him. And don't think you can apologize – it's too late for that ... Where's your respect, that's what I'd like to know? Where's the common decencies? [*Pause.*] We've got some integrity, you know. *And* spirit. Basil had spirit – lots of it; now it's gone – gone! Because you didn't respect his spirit, it's gone. [*Packs papers into carrier bag.*] You'd call it a lot of wind, wouldn't you? It would be just like you to call it wind. And what about his pride? ... It's a fine thing – a very fine thing for a man to lose his pride. [*Looks at Basil tenderly.*] What's going on in his poor head now that you've robbed him of his pride? Can you tell me that? [*Pause. After waiting in vain for Charles to reply,* ARTHUR *looks back at Basil.*] All night long, he was awake on that settee. Not one word did he speak. Not one word all night long. Every time I woke up – [*guiltily*] when I dropped off, that is, and it wasn't very often – I went over to him ... Not one word all night. I got him some hot milk, but he

148

wouldn't drink it ... And all you can say is: 'His wind has gone!'
[*Takes chair, undoes ceiling light. Muttering*]: His wind has gone ...
[*Suddenly turning on Charles from above*]: You're the most callous
man I've ever known. [*Nearly falls off chair. Recovers his balance, then
climbs down, lamp-shade in hand, catches* CHARLES *smiling.*] I suppose
you think it's funny. A lot of nonsense. You think it's all nonsense,
don't you?

[*Pause.* CHARLES *stirs his tea.*]

You've taken Mabel away and left us nothing. It's outside for
Basil and me, and you call it nonsense ... [*Looks at Basil with pain.*]
I could be as quiet as Basil – but somebody's got to speak up for
our rights.

[CHARLES *butters a piece of toast.*]

[*Suddenly*] What are you and Mabel going to do?

[CHARLES *crunches toast in his mouth.*]

I suppose we have no rights? None of our business? What she said
to Basil and me last night! It was disgusting! Beastly! Grotesque.
Obscene! Like a beast of prey. But you're not put out at all, are
you? Not one little bit. Well, let me tell you: if we all behaved the
way you and Mabel did the world would be a jungle. [*Pause:
waits for a reply.*]

[CHARLES *sips his tea.*]

It's all right ... all right. I know marching orders when I see them
– but I won't be ordered out by you! I can take the initiative. You
didn't know that, did you? Oh, we could stay here living under
your heel and you'd like it. I know you – you'd like that. Well,
I'm not lying down for you to trample on. Oh no! I'm going to
make the best of it. Basil *and* me. We know how to make the best
of things.

[BASIL *bangs a fist down hard on the table.* ARTHUR *fusses to his side
and lays a hand on his shoulder.* BASIL *tightens inwardly.*]

Don't listen to him, Basil. He's just trying to goad you!

[BASIL *again bangs his fist down on the table.*]

I know what you're going through, Basil. Truly I do. [*Turns
fiercely on Charles.*] See what you've done? Have you seen grief
like this before? Well? Take a good look – you'll never see grief
like this again!

[CHARLES, *amused, sips tea.*]

I don't expect you to worry about us. That's the last thing I expect. Our qualities will pull us through, never fear. And Basil has qualities you'll never possess – not in a thousand years ... As for me – ha! ha! – I've lived through hard times. We're old friends, hard times and me. So don't worry about us. [*His fine indignation slowly leaves him. He saddens.*] She loathes us ... detests the sight of us. And it's all your doing ... And I thought you'd be good for Basil. I really thought you'd be good for him. I didn't care for myself; it was for him. He doesn't make friends very easily and when you came, all friendly and smiling and interested – drawing him out – it was a wonder to see, and I thought what a good idea ... When we were in the park yesterday, Basil went to sleep. Do you know what that meant? A restless man like Basil falling asleep in a deckchair?

It meant he was quiet. Inside. Quiet enough to sit with me, his old irritating sparring partner, and go to sleep ... I could feel the peace in him. And when he woke up, I thought of you with gratitude. I said to him 'What shall we do now?' and he said, 'Let's go back and have tea with Charles.' [*Looks bitterly at Basil. Then at Charles.*] How could you destroy him? You knew what Mabel meant to him – to me. What's left for us? Why ask even? You don't care about us. We're nothing. Just dirt to be swept out. Good riddance. Out you go – and don't come back. No further use for us.

CHARLES [*suddenly*]: What do you want me to say? Must I list the actions we can commit together? Card games? Bezique, rummy, poker, strip and stud, Old Maid, bridge, canasta, Beggar-my-Neighbour, knock-out whist, Happy Families, Snap, Pontoon, Brag ... Eating together? Baked beans on toast for three. Chips for three – and one extra portion for the scowling gentleman. One pot of tea for three ... And entertainments. Three two and ninepennys. We all like watching Alec Guinness. Three seats in a row. Seasonal get-togethers. Let us not forget the spirit of Christmas. Happy Christmas from Basil to Arthur. From Arthur to Basil and Charles to Arthur. And Basil to Charles and Charles to Basil. And Arthur to Charles ... Who's got the wishbone? Lucky fellow! May I really break it with you? Oh, how nice, I've got the biggest piece – I get

my wish. And co-operation … Do you mind if I use the lavatory
before you, old chap? No, not a bit – go ahead. Oh, thank you,
I'll do the same for you one day. Whose turn to get breakfast?
Supper? My turn to do the washing up? No, no, no – I insist …
Man, the list is endless … But for Christ's sake, don't ask me to
share your stupidity!

ARTHUR [*after a pause*]: How we've changed – now we're stupid! We
were stupid all right, not to see through you.

CHARLES: Then it's agreed; you are stupid. All you have to do now
is make up your mind and we can all have peace and quiet.

ARTHUR [*firmly*]: My mind is made up, don't worry.

CHARLES: And Basil? Has he made up his mind? Look at him, poised
on the edge, but holding back, I wonder why? Shall I tell you
things that will settle you both for good? That will knock the
stupidity out of you and leave you gasping? Because I can do that
with such ease. Well? Shall I? – [*Disgusted*] I can't put up with you
much longer.

[BASIL *rises slowly. There is something of his old truculence in his
manner, but he has become slower, deeper. Menacingly, he approaches
Charles.*]

Ah – the gallant Captain has come out of his stupor. Welcome
back to the Regiment!

BASIL [*quietly*]: I'll kill you. If you don't shut your mouth, I'll kill
you.

ARTHUR: Basil!

CHARLES: Now don't spoil Basil's big moment, Arthur.

BASIL: I tell you – shut up!

CHARLES: Better listen to your little friend, Basil. He knows you're
going to make a fool of yourself.

[ARTHUR *lays a restraining hand on* BASIL's *arm,* BASIL *violently
shakes it off, picks up an empty Guinness bottle, raises it like a club.*]
So there's nothing for it.

[BASIL *comes closer to* CHARLES *with bottle poised.*]
Come on then, Captain – into the valley of death!

[BASIL *lurches at* CHARLES, *who steps swiftly aside, grasps* BASIL
*in a simple but painful arm-lock and bends his arm until the bottle
falls out of his grip.*]

You see, Basil, it's no use. You're no good at the old violence lark. [*Contemptuously pushes* BASIL *aside.*] You've been out of character all your life.

[BASIL *sits down wearily.* CHARLES *picks up the bottle and suddenly lobs it over to Basil.*]

Catch, boy!

[*Instinctively,* BASIL *catches the bottle. Dumbly he stares at it, then, as he realizes that he has been tricked into a co-operative action, slowly places the bottle back on to the table.*]

You see, we can still do things together.

BASIL [*slowly raises his eyes and looks at Charles. Regards him in silence for a space, then speaks slowly, deliberately*]: How you win! Jesus, how you win! Always on the mark. Every time a bull. A bull's eye. I see what it all comes down to – the place in the middle for you. Always the place in the middle, and push every one else outside. You've rigged us, haven't you? – rigged us right up to the crow's nest ... And you can't be touched. Not by me. Not by Arthur. I don't know who could touch you. You're untouchable. I – know – what – you've been getting at. But Arthur doesn't. I could tell him but that would embarrass me. Very much. But does he have to know? Did I have to know? You asked me why didn't I smash his little aeroplanes. You said, if I hated his hobbies why didn't I smash them. You wanted me to smash them, didn't you? For the kicks. You wanted me to put the heel in, didn't you? I know how your message goes: 'Knock the little fat bastard over; knock him for six and if there's any left, feed it to the dogs.'

ARTHUR [*quizzically*]: Basil?

BASIL: Arthur, listen to me. Don't try to understand more than you want to understand. It's no good either of us thinking of Mabel. Or any other woman for that matter. We'll make plans for each other. No third party – it's too great a risk. [*Turns to Charles.*] I'd give anything to take the sting out of you. But you've spent too much time on yourself. You've devoted your life to it. Christ! What an ocean of time that must be! I can't match your muscle. I haven't had your training ... I'm not strong enough – or rich enough or whatever it takes to be a big man like you. But the waste! The bloody waste of time! Haven't you got your money's worth? Is there anything you've not yet done? Before we get out and exist without you? Because whatever we've got to look forward to is a bloody sight better than what you're left with. You can take the piss out of yourself in future. Or haven't you finished with us?

CHARLES [*for the first time, peeved*]: Not quite. I've yet to rub your noses in the mess.

BASIL: I don't deny you could do it. You could do anything and that's why you're untouchable. [*Turns sharply on Arthur.*] Come on, Arthur, pick up the stuff. There's not much time left. [*He lifts the suitcases.*]

ARTHUR [*puzzled*]: Basil?

BASIL: Stop asking questions and get on with it.

[ARTHUR *collects bundles and carrier bags.* BASIL *moves to the door, picking up an umbrella on his way.*]

CHARLES [*indicates the uniform on the dummy*]: Don't forget your ju-ju.

[BASIL *looks at the uniform, then at Charles.*]

BASIL: It's not mine.

[*Walks out carrying umbrella and suitcases.* ARTHUR *follows, pauses at door and looks at Charles.*]

ARTHUR: You can tell her she's a Jezebel.

[CHARLES *does not answer. With stony face he watches* ARTHUR *flounce out of the room and through the door.* CHARLES *sits in the chair, gazing at the open door. He looks round the room, taking in its stripped, de-humanized look. All amusement and mobility has left his face. It is now dead, impersonal – a diagram of a face. He rises and goes to the table, picks up the tea-pot and tries to pour a cup of tea, but the pot is empty and, after lifting the lid to look inside, he puts tea-pot down.*

Goes to arm-chair and sits heavily down and looks again at the open door.

MABEL *enters and looks round the room, slowly taking in the change with some bewilderment.*]

MABEL: Arthur? Basil?

CHARLES: They've gone.

MABEL: Gone where?

CHARLES: They packed their bags and left.

MABEL: But where did they go?

CHARLES: I don't know. The rain stopped and they went.

MABEL: Any messages?

CHARLES: No messages.

MABEL: Well ... I suppose it's for the best, really. I mean, we couldn't have gone on as if nothing had happened, could we?

CHARLES: Damn little did happen.

MABEL: I don't think that's right. Look at yesterday –

CHARLES: I wouldn't if I were you. Basil and Arthur looked at yesterday and didn't like it.

MABEL: Have they gone for good?

CHARLES: They packed their bags, Basil rummaged around, found an umbrella and off they went. Into the Unknown they went, imbued with new life ...

MABEL: As long as they're all right.

CHARLES: Forget about them.

MABEL: I could never do that.

CHARLES: Arthur called you a Jezebel.

MABEL: Me a Jezebel?

CHARLES: He accused you of breaking every law of decency. You really shouldn't have strung them along, you know.

MABEL: That's not fair! What have I done that's so wrong? I lost my temper with them, I know – and I shouldn't have spoken to them like that. But I'm sorry! I wanted to apologize, but they've gone off without giving me the chance ... And now, it's too late ... What have I done that's so wrong?

CHARLES: You were too realistic ... They couldn't bear the real thing because it was not for them. But I give Basil his due ... In the heroism of the moment he did a Nurse Cavell that surprised me. But no due to Arthur, except the thanks due to a pound of cooking fat ... You were too realistic and they couldn't bear it.

[*A count of five as* MABEL's *mind leaps back into yesterday.*]

MABEL: I was tremendously happy yesterday. It was all so right. Complete. And the waiting was good. You liked the waiting part, too, didn't you, Charles?

When do you think I'll get over them? I feel guilty, you see. I don't think I've done wrong, but I feel wrong. Inside ... Last night, when I was trying to sleep, I started thinking the way you said I would. About us, you know. And Basil and Arthur kept intruding ... I think that's how it was ... Kept coming in ...

I expect I'll get over it soon and I won't be silly ... I won't feel this guilt any more ... What I feel I ought to say is, can you do something to help me over this guilt? Or we could both do something, like – perhaps – well – just being friends for a few days ... I know it will be difficult, but we've got all the time in the world, haven't we?

CHARLES [*sharply*]: No!

MABEL: Oh, but we have! A few days won't make any difference ... I want to be excited about us again, you see. But there's this guilt feeling ... I don't think it will last long, so I'll be patient. A few days won't make any difference when we've so much time.

CHARLES [*with greater sharpness*]: I said No!

MABEL: You mean we haven't much time?

CHARLES: We have no time at all.

MABEL [*gets up from the table and goes to Charles. Lays a hand on his shoulder*]: I thought we had. I thought we had years and years ... Would you be nice to me, Charles? I don't know where I am ...
[CHARLES *rises from his chair, pushes past her and goes to the sideboard.* MABEL *watches him.*]

CHARLES: You have so many failings. So vulnerable – so lightly balanced with your touchwood and consecrated ground, that you fall flat on your fannies at the slightest push ... [*Takes a bottle of Guinness from the sideboard, and a glass. Holds up the bottle for Mabel to see.*] It's as if you maintain that this bottle, despite its label designed with the express purpose of telling you precisely what is inside the bottle, actually contains white wine! Not black stout, but crystal-clear wine! When you open it and the truth comes out, you're surprised. Offended. And down you go!

MABEL: I know I'm not very bright.

CHARLES [*with exasperation*]: I don't mean that! [*Returns to his chair and sits down.*] Your notions of love! ... One love – kept at white-hot pitch – you hope! And conquering all ... Love in one tatty basket ... For you alone and don't you dare love anyone else or I'll do you ... Why? Why are you all so stupid?

MABEL: I don't know.

CHARLES: Is there some virtue in it, this love? Some virtue I haven't seen? In keeping up a false virginity after the bird has flown? Go back to sleep, the whole damned lot of you!

MABEL: Why are you getting at me? This isn't like yesterday. I'm the same. I haven't changed.

CHARLES: Then change! This is another day! A new situation! Cope with it ...

MABEL: But, yesterday – in this room – it was different. I thought I felt different. I feel different now ... If I could see what was wrong, I could do the right thing, but I'm new to it. I'd go back if I could and start all over again but I don't know how to go back.

CHARLES: You don't have to go back.

MABEL: You mean I must wait?

CHARLES: If you like.

MABEL: A word from you will make it all right.

CHARLES: I can't give you the word.

MABEL: But why can't you?

[*There is a short silence, then* CHARLES *looks very calmly at her.*]

CHARLES: I don't feel like it.

MABEL: I see ...

CHARLES: If you do see, then you'll have an easy mind.

MABEL: I don't know what to say ... I don't know what to do ... I love you – that's certain. You haven't told me that yet, but it doesn't matter, although I depend on you to tell me. I've never really depended on anyone – not in the way I depend on you. Yesterday ... you made me feel I wasn't so stupid. That I might even be – well – attractive. I love you for making me feel that. And excitement. I liked that – I liked it very much. I'd give anything to go back to yesterday. [*Goes to the table and, with great stress, asks him*] Won't you tell me what to do? Please? I know you can tell me what to do. I'll do it! I won't question it! I'll just do it.

[*Insolently,* CHARLES *looks at her.*]

CHARLES: Give me the bottle-opener.

[*MABEL looks at the table, picks up the opener and, obviously hurt, looks at it; then, suddenly angry, throws it at his feet.*]

CHARLES [*picks it up and gives her an amused glance*]: If you had put that action into words, what would you have said? [*A silence to count five.*] It doesn't matter. I asked for the opener and you conveyed it to me. Desire fulfilled ... That's what it's all about. [*Proceeds to open the bottle.*]

MABEL: You wanted me yesterday, didn't you?

CHARLES: Yes.

MABEL: Do you want me now?

CHARLES: This is not the time.

MABEL: Do you want me now?

[*Count of three.*]

CHARLES [*takes swig from bottle*]: The savour has gone from it.

MABEL: Last night – thinking about you – what we would have done together – these thoughts ... Can I show you what I thought about?

CHARLES: No.

MABEL: You can tell me if they're the right ideas ... You said try them out.

CHARLES: This is not the time.

MABEL: It is for me ... Look! [*Goes to the windows, draws the curtains; the room darkens. Returns to Charles.*] Now it's like yesterday. You kissed me. Remember? Then I got up from the sofa –

[*She goes towards the bedroom door but* CHARLES *darts ahead of her, slams it shut and leans against it.* MABEL *stares at him – at the anger in his face.*]

Please Charles ... Please?

CHARLES: No!

[*She backs away from him.*]

MABEL: Isn't there anything I can do?

CHARLES: Just give up and leave me in peace.

MABEL: I know what it is – you're trying me out. I've got to act in a certain way and then you'll know I'm the sort of woman that – *I must try!* ... But it's so difficult – to know what to do ... You know what I have to do ... But you won't tell me. Please tell me what it is and I'll never forget ... So what is it?

CHARLES: Nothing!

[*There is such finality in his voice that* MABEL *turns from him and rests her hands on the table in an attitude of desolation. After a space, she reaches for her handbag where it lies on the table, picks it up and turns. As she does so, the clasp of the bag comes undone and some of the contents fall on to the floor. Slowly, dumbly, she bends down and scoops them back into the bag. She straightens her back and looks at Charles.*]

MABEL: Shall I come back?

[*He shakes his head.*]

I will if you want me to ... [*There is no answer and, very sadly, she makes for the door.*] Tomorrow – or next week, if you like ... I shan't be doing anything else ... [*Opens the door and stands for a moment looking back at the room and Charles.*] I'd like to come back ...
[CHARLES *does not answer. He takes a slow swig from the bottle.* MABEL *slowly turns and exits, closing the door softly behind her.* CHARLES *raises his head and takes in the emptiness of the room. A long look at the uniform, then he turns his head and looks at the audience with a long, hostile, accusative stare as the curtain descends.*]

JOE ORTON

Entertaining Mr. Sloane

First presented in London at the New Arts Theatre on 6 May 1964 by Michael Codron Ltd and at Wyndhams Theatre on 29 June 1964 by Michael Codron and Donald Albery, with the following cast:

KATH	Madge Ryan
SLOANE	Dudley Sutton
KEMP	Charles Lamb
ED	Peter Vaughan

Directed by Patrick Dromgoole
Designed by Timothy O'Brien
Costumes supervised by Tazeena Firth

CHARACTERS

KATH
SLOANE
KEMP
ED

A room. Evening.

> [KATH *enters followed by* SLOANE.]

KATH: This is my lounge.

SLOANE: Would I be able to use this room? Is it included?

KATH: Oh, yes. [*Pause.*] You mustn't imagine it's always like this. You ought to have rung up or something. And then I'd've been prepared.

SLOANE: The bedroom was perfect.

KATH: I never showed you the toilet.

SLOANE: I'm sure it will be satisfactory. [*Walks around the room examining the furniture. Stops by the window.*]

KATH: I should change them curtains. Those are our winter ones. The summer ones are more of a chintz. [*Laughs.*] The walls need re-doing. The Dadda has trouble with his eyes. I can't ask him to do any work involving ladders. It stands to reason.

> [*Pause.*]

SLOANE: I can't give you a decision right away.

KATH: I don't want to rush you. [*Pause.*] What do you think? I'd be happy to have you.

> [*Silence.*]

SLOANE: Are you married?

KATH [*Pause*]: I was. I had a boy ... killed in very sad circumstances. It broke my heart at the time. I got over it though. You do, don't you?

> [*Pause.*]

SLOANE: A son?

KATH: Yes.

SLOANE: You don't look old enough.

> [*Pause.*]

KATH: I don't let myself go like some of them you may have noticed. I'm just over ... As a matter of fact I'm forty-one.

> [*Pause.*]

SLOANE [*briskly*]: I'll take the room.

KATH: Will you?

SLOANE: I'll bring my things over tonight. It'll be a change from my previous.

KATH: Was it bad?

SLOANE: Bad?

KATH: As bad as that?

SLOANE: You've no idea.

KATH: I don't suppose I have. I've led a sheltered life.

SLOANE: Have you been a widow long?

KATH: Yes a long time. My husband was a mere boy. [*With a half-laugh*]: That sounds awful doesn't it?

SLOANE: Not at all.

KATH: I married out of school. I surprised everyone by the suddenness of it. [*Pause.*] Does that sound as if I had to get married?

SLOANE: I'm broadminded.

KATH: I should've known better. You won't breathe a word?

SLOANE: You can trust me.

KATH: My brother would be upset if he knew I told you. [*Pause.*] Nobody knows around here. The people in the nursing home imagined I *was* somebody. I didn't disillusion them.

SLOANE: You were never married then?

KATH: No.

SLOANE: What about – I hope you don't think I'm prying?

KATH: I wouldn't for a minute. What about – ?

SLOANE: ... the father?

KATH: [*Pause*]: We always planned to marry. But there were difficulties. I was very young and he was even younger. I don't believe we would have been allowed.

SLOANE: What happened to the baby?

KATH: Adopted.

SLOANE: By whom?

KATH: That I could not say. My brother arranged it.

SLOANE: What about the kid's father?

KATH: He couldn't do anything.

SLOANE: Why not?

KATH: His family objected. They were very nice but he had a duty you see. [*Pause.*] As I say, if it'd been left to him I'd be his widow today. [*Pause.*] I had a last letter. I'll show you some time. [*Silence.*] D'you like flock or foam rubber in your pillow?

SLOANE: Foam rubber.

KATH: You need a bit of luxury, don't you? I bought the Dadda one but he can't stand them.

SLOANE: I can.

KATH: You'll live with us then as one of the family?

SLOANE: I never had no family of my own.

KATH: Didn't you?

SLOANE: No. I was brought up in an orphanage.

KATH: You have the air of lost wealth.

SLOANE: That's remarkable. My parents, I believe, *were* extremely wealthy people.

KATH: Did Dr Barnardo give you a bad time?

SLOANE: No. It was the lack of privacy I found most trying. [*Pause.*]
And the lack of real love.

KATH: Did you never know your mamma?

SLOANE: Yes.

KATH: When did they die?

SLOANE: I was eight. [*Pause.*] They passed away together.

KATH: How shocking.

SLOANE: I've an idea that they had a suicide pact. Couldn't prove it of course.

KATH: Of course not. [*Pause.*] With a nice lad like you to take care of you'd think they'd've postponed it. [*Pause.*] Criminals, were they?

SLOANE: From what I remember they was respected. You know, H.P. debts. Bridge. A little light gardening. The usual activities of a cultured community. [*Silence.*] I respect their memory.

KATH: Do you? How nice.

SLOANE: Every year I pay a visit to their grave. I take sandwiches. Make a day of it. [*Pause.*] The graveyard is situated in pleasant surroundings so it's no hardship. [*Pause.*] Tomb an' all.

KATH: Marble? [*Pause.*] Is there an inscription?

SLOANE: Perhaps you'd come with me this trip?

KATH: We'll see.

SLOANE: I go in the autumn because I clean the leaves off the monument. As a tribute.

KATH: Yes.

SLOANE: That's the main task I set myself.

KATH: Any relations?

SLOANE: None.

KATH: Poor boy. Alone in the world. Like me.

SLOANE: You're not alone.

KATH: I am. [*Pause.*] Almost alone. [*Pause.*] If I'd been allowed to keep my boy I'd not be. [*Pause.*] You're almost the same age as he would be. You've got the same refinement.

SLOANE [*slowly*]: I need ... understanding.

KATH: You do don't you? Here let me take your coat. [*Helps him off with his coat.*] You've got a delicate skin. [*Touches his neck. His cheek.*]

[*He shudders a little. Pause.*]

KATH [*kisses his cheek*]: Just a motherly kiss. A real mother's kiss. [*Silence. Lifts his arms and folds them about her.*] You'll find me very sentimental. I upset easy. [*His arms are holding her.*] When I hear of ... tragedies happening to perfect strangers. There are so many ruined lives. [*Puts her head on his shoulder.*] You must treat me gently when I'm in one of my moods.

[*Silence.*]

SLOANE [*clearing his throat*]: How much are you charging? I mean – I've got to know.

[*He drops his arms. She moves away.*]

KATH: We'll come to some arrangement. A cup of tea?

SLOANE: Yes I don't mind.

KATH: I'll get you one.

SLOANE: Can I have a bath?

KATH: Now?

SLOANE: Later would do.

KATH: You must do as you think fit.

[*A door slams.* KEMP's *voice is heard off.*]

KEMP: You there?

KATH [*calls*]: I'm in here. Don't stand about. Sit down. Go on. We don't charge.

166

[SLOANE *sits on the settee.*]

That's a lovely shade of blue on your woolly. I'll fetch you one down later that I knitted for my brother.

[KEMP *enters.*]

[*loudly*]: We have a visitor, Dadda.

KEMP: Eh?

KATH: A visitor.

KEMP [*stares, lifts his glasses and stares again*]: Oh ... It's Eddie?

KATH: You are the limit. You show me up no end. It isn't Ed. [*Pause.*] You behave like a sick child. I'm just about tired of it. Afraid to have a guest or a friend in the house. You put them off, Dadda. Let him shake your hand. Go on.

[KEMP *shakes Sloane's hand.*]

KEMP: What's he want then?

KATH: Mr Sloane is going to stay with us.

KEMP: Stay with us?

KATH: That's what I said.

KEMP: He can't. We've no room.

KATH: Make an effort will you? What will the gentleman think? He'll think you're a rude old man. [*Exchanges looks with Sloane.*] I'm going to have to apologize for your boorish attitude. Do you feel embarrassed, Mr Sloane?

SLOANE: It's all right.

KATH: No, it isn't. [*To Kemp*] Pull yourself together! [*Silence.*] Can I trust you to behave yourself while I get something to eat?

[KEMP *does not answer.*]

Entertain Mr Sloane now. Give him the benefit of your experience. [*Pause.*] You want to learn manners. That's what you want. [*Picks up a basket of provisions from the floor.*] I'm a good mind to give you no tea. [*To* SLOANE] I'd not care to wonder what you must think of us. [*Takes a packet of crumpets from the basket. Hands it to Kemp.*] Here, toast these. Give yourself something to do. [*Exits.*]

[KEMP *goes to fire. Begins to toast crumpets.*]

SLOANE: Haven't we met before?

KEMP: Not to my knowledge.

SLOANE: Your face is familiar. Have I seen your photo in the paper? In connexion with some event?

167

KEMP: No.

SLOANE: Do you pop into the pub at the end of the road?

KEMP: I don't drink.

SLOANE: Are you a churchgoer?

KEMP: Not at the moment. I used to be. In the old days I'd knock up the Vicar at all hours. But then I lost touch.

SLOANE: I've seen you somewhere. I very rarely forget a face.

KEMP: Y've got me confused with another person.

SLOANE: Perhaps.

KEMP: Forget it, son. I'm not seen about much.

SLOANE [Pause]: You don't resent my being in the house, do you?

KEMP: Not at all.

SLOANE: I thought you did. Just now.

KEMP: No.

SLOANE: This seems a nice place. Friendly atmosphere. [Pause.] How many children have you?

KEMP: Two.

SLOANE: Is your daughter married?

KEMP: She was. Had a terrible time. Kiddy died.

SLOANE: You have a son, don't you?

KEMP: Yes, but we're not on speaking terms.

SLOANE: How long is it?

KEMP: Twenty years.

SLOANE: 'Strewth!

KEMP: You perhaps find that hard to believe?

SLOANE: I do actually. Not speaking for twenty years? That's coming it a bit strong.

KEMP: I may have exchanged a few words.

SLOANE: I can believe that.

KEMP: He was a good boy. Played some amazing games as a youth. Won every goal at football one season. Sport mad, he was. [Pause.] Then one day, shortly after his seventeenth birthday, I had cause to return home unexpected and found him committing some kind of felony in the bedroom.

SLOANE: Is that straight?

KEMP: I could never forgive him.

SLOANE: A puritan are you?

168

KEMP: Yes.

SLOANE: That kind of thing happens often, I believe. For myself, I usually lock the door.

KEMP: I'd removed the lock.

SLOANE: Anticipating some such tendencies on his part?

KEMP: I'd done it as a precautionary measure.

SLOANE: There are fascinating possibilities in this situation. I'd get it down on paper if I were you. [Goes to the window.]

KEMP: Admiring the view?

SLOANE: A perfect skyline you've got here. Lord Snowdon would give you something for a shot of that. Stunning it is. Stunning. Was this house a speculation?

KEMP: Not exactly.

SLOANE: Who built it then? Was he a mad financier? The bloke who conceived the idea of building a house in the midst of a rubbish dump?

KEMP: It was intended to be the first of a row.

SLOANE: Go on. What happened?

KEMP: They gave up.

SLOANE: Lost interest?

KEMP: There were financial restrictions.

SLOANE: What a way to carry on!

KEMP: We've tried putting in complaints, but it's no good. Look at it out there. An eyesore. You may admire it. I don't. A woman came all the way from Woolwich yesterday. A special trip she made in order to dump a bedstead. I told her, what do you want to saddle us with your filthy mess for? Came over in a shooting-brake. She was an old woman. Had her daughter with her. Fouling the countryside with their litter.

SLOANE: What you want is someone with pull on the council.

KEMP: If my boss were here I'd go to him.

SLOANE: Wealthy was he?

KEMP: He had holdings in some trust. He didn't go into details with me.

SLOANE: How old was he?

KEMP: Forty.

SLOANE: Early middle-age?

KEMP: Yes.

SLOANE: Dead is he?

KEMP: Yes.

SLOANE: Did he die for his country?

KEMP: No. He was murdered. On the unsolved crimes list, he is.

SLOANE: A murderer not brought to justice. That's a sobering thought. [*Pause.*] Why can't they find the murderer? Didn't they advertise?

KEMP: Yes. They took a piece in the local paper.

SLOANE: How long ago was all this?

KEMP: Two years.

SLOANE: Do they have any clue to the murderer's identity?

KEMP: He was a young man with very smooth skin.

SLOANE [*Pause*]: Was your boss a small man?

KEMP: Yes. Wavy hair. Wore a tweed tie.

SLOANE: What was his profession?

KEMP: He was a photographer. Specialized in views of the river.

SLOANE: You were employed in his service?

KEMP: Yes. As a general handyman. [*Pause.*] We gave the murderer a lift on the night of the crime.

SLOANE [*Pause*]: You saw him then?

KEMP: Yes.

SLOANE: Why didn't you go to the police?

KEMP: I can't get involved in that type of case. I might get my name in the papers.

SLOANE: I see your point of view. [*Pause.*] They won't find the killer now.

KEMP: I should very much doubt it.

SLOANE: No, the scent's gone cold.

[*He watches Kemp in silence.*]

Have you ever toasted a crumpet before?

KEMP: Yes.

SLOANE: I thought it was your first time from the way you're messing that about.

[KEMP *does not reply.*]

KEMP [*Pause*]: Come here.

SLOANE: Why?

170

KEMP: I want to look at you.

SLOANE: What for?

KEMP: I think we have met before.

SLOANE: No, Pop. I'm convinced we haven't. I must have been getting you mixed up with a man called Fergusson. He had the same kind of way with him. Trustworthy.

KEMP: You think that?

SLOANE: Yes. [*Laughs.*]

KEMP [*Pause*]: Fetch me a plate, will you?

SLOANE: Where from?

KEMP: The dresser. Back there.

[SLOANE *goes to the dresser. Fetches a plate. Comes to Kemp, bends down to give him the plate.* KEMP *seizes Sloane's arm, pulls him towards him.*]

SLOANE: What's this!

KEMP: We have met before! I knew we had.

SLOANE: I've never met you.

KEMP: On my life. I remember.

SLOANE: Your eyes aren't good.

KEMP: I could still identify you.

SLOANE [*Pause*]: Identify me?

KEMP: If it was necessary.

SLOANE: How could it be necessary?

KEMP: It might be.

SLOANE: Do lay off, Pop. You couldn't identify a herring on a plate!

KEMP: Don't speak to me like that, sonny. You'll find yourself in trouble.

SLOANE: Go on, you superannuated old prat!

KEMP: I'll have somebody to you. See if I don't.

[SLOANE *turns away.*]

SLOANE: Why don't you shut your mouth and give your arse a chance?

[KEMP *lunges at Sloane with the toasting fork.* SLOANE *gives a squeal of pain.*]

SLOANE: Oh, you bleeding maniac! My leg. My leg.

KEMP: You provoked me!

SLOANE [*sinks into an armchair*]: I'll be in a wheelchair for life. [*Examines his leg.*] Oh, you cow. I'm covered in blood! Call somebody!

KEMP [*goes to the door, shouting*]: Kathy! Kathy!

KATH [*runs on, drying her hands on her apron, sees Sloane, screams*]: What've you done?

KEMP: It wasn't intentional. [*Comes forward.*]

KATH [*shoos him away*]: Is there pain?

SLOANE: I can't move.

KATH: Are you hurt bad?

SLOANE: He's got an artery. I must be losing pints. Oh, Christ!

KATH: Come on. You'll be better on the settee. [*He allows her to guide him over. She settles him.*] What happened? Did he attack you? He's never shown signs before.

KEMP: I thought he was further off. I can't judge distances.

KATH: Let Mr Sloane speak for himself.

SLOANE: He ought to be in Colney Hatch. He's a slate off. Throwing things about.

KATH: Throw them did he?

SLOANE: I don't know what he did.

KATH: I'm ashamed of you, Dadda. Really ashamed. I think you behave very badly. Lie down, Mr Sloane. [*To Kemp.*] Go and get the Dettol and some water. Make yourself useful.

  [KEMP *shuffles off.*]

I never realized he was antagonistic to you, Mr Sloane. Perhaps he's jealous. We were getting on so well. [*Pause.*] Is it hurting you?

SLOANE: Can you get a bandage?

KATH: I will. [*Goes to the sideboard and rummages in a drawer. Rummages again. Repeat. Second drawer. Takes out and places on top of the sideboard a Boots folder containing snapshots and negatives, a reel of cotton, a piece of unfinished knitting, a tattered knitting pattern, a broken china figure, a magazine, a doorknob and several pieces of silk.*]

SLOANE [*calling impatiently*]: There's blood running on your settee. You'll have a stain, I can see it coming.

KATH [*runs back with a piece of silk. Lifts his leg. Spreads the silk under the bloody patch*]: This'll do. It's a piece of material my brother brought back. It's good stuff. I was intending to make a blouse but there's not enough.

SLOANE: What's he doing with that Dettol? Is he gone to Swansea for it?

KATH [*shouting*]: What are you doing Dadda? He gets that thick. [*Goes to sideboard.*]

[*KEMP enters with a bottle of Dettol.*]

KATH [*takes it from him*]: You done enough damage for one day. Make yourself scarce.

[*He shuffles off.*]

And don't be eating anything out there. [*Pushes past him. Returns with a saucepan full of water. After hunting in sideboard finds a torn towel. Comes to Sloane. Kneels.*] What a lovely pair of shoes you got. [*Unlacing his shoes she takes them off and places them under the settee.*]

SLOANE: I think I'm going to spew.

[*KATH hastily holds the saucepan under him.*]

No. I'll be all right.

KATH: I wonder, Mr Sloane, if you'd take your trousers off? I hope you don't think there's anything behind the request. [*Looks at him.*]

[*He unloosens his belt.*]

I expect you guessed as much before I asked. If you'll lift up I'll pull them off. [*Tugs the trousers free.*]

[*SLOANE tucks the tail of his shirt between his legs.*]

KATH: That's right. [*Pause.*] Where is it then?

SLOANE: Here. [*Pointing and lifting his leg.*]

KATH: He attacked you from behind? If you ask me it's only a deep scratch. [*Pause.*] I don't think we'll require outside assistance. [*Pause.*] Don't be embarrassed, Mr Sloane. I'd the upbringing a nun would envy and that's the truth. Until I was fifteen I was more familiar with Africa than my own body. That's why I'm so pliable. [*Applies Dettol.*]

SLOANE: Ouch!

KATH: Just the thing for the germs. [*Pause.*] You've a skin on you like a princess. Better than on those tarts you see dancing about on the telly. I like a lad with a smooth body. [*Stops dabbing his leg. Takes up the bandage. Rises. Fetches a pair of scissors. Cuts bandage. Ties it round Sloane's leg.*] Isn't it strange that the hairs on your legs should be dark?

SLOANE: Eh?

KATH: Attractive though.

SLOANE: Dark?

KATH: Yes. You being a blond.

SLOANE: Oh, yes.

KATH: Nature's a funny thing.

[*Ring on the doorbell.*]

SLOANE: Who's that?

KATH: Keep your voice down. [*Pause.*] It's probably her from the shops. I'll not answer it. She's only got one subject for talk.

SLOANE: She'll hear.

KATH: Not if you keep your voice down.

[*Prolonged ringing.*]

SLOANE: What about Pop?

KATH: He won't answer. I don't want her in here. She tells everybody her business. And if she found me in this predicament she'd think all kinds of things. [*Pause.*] Her daughter's involved in a court case at the moment. Tells every detail. The details are endless. I suffer as she recounts. Oh, Mr Sloane, if I'd only been born without ears. [*Silence. Finishes tying the bandage and squats on her haunches looking up at him. Pause.*] Is that bandage too tight?

SLOANE: No.

KATH: I wouldn't want to restrict your circulation.

SLOANE: It's O.K.

[*She picks up his trousers.*]

KATH: I'll sponge these, and there's a nick in the material. I'll fix it. [*Puts Dettol, bandage, etc, into the sideboard.*] This drawer is my medicine cabinet, dear. If you wants an occasional aspirin help yourself. [*She comes back.*]

[*He lies full length; she smiles. Silence.*]

KATH [*confidentially*]: I've been doing my washing today and I haven't a stitch on ... except my shoes ... I'm in the rude under this dress. I tell you because you're bound to have noticed ...

[*Silence.* SLOANE *attempts to reach his trouser pocket.*]

Don't move, dear. Not yet. Give the blood time to steady itself.

[SLOANE *takes the nylon stocking from between cushions of settee.*]

I wondered where I'd left it.

SLOANE: Is it yours?

KATH: Yes. You'll notice the length? I've got long legs. Long, elegant legs. [*Kicks out her leg.*] I could give one or two of them a surprise. [*Pause.*] My look is quite different when I'm in private. [*Leans over him.*] You can't see through this dress can you? I been worried for fear of embarrassing you.

    [SLOANE *lifts his hand and touches the point where he judges her nipple to be.*]

KATH [*leaps back*]: Mr Sloane – don't betray your trust.

SLOANE: I just thought –

KATH: I know what you thought. You wanted to see if my titties were all my own. You're all the same. [*Smirks.*] I must be careful of you. Have me naked on the floor if I give you a chance. If my brother was to know ... [*Pause.*] ... he's such a possessive man. [*Silence. Stands up.*] Would you like to go to bed?

SLOANE: It's early.

KATH: You need rest. You've had a shock. [*Pause.*] I'll bring your supper to your room.

SLOANE: What about my case?

KATH: The Dadda will fetch it. [*Pause.*] Can you get up the stairs on your own?

SLOANE: Mmmm.

KATH [*motions him back. Stands in front of him*]: Just a minute. [*Calls*]: Dadda! [*Pause.*] Dadda!

    [KEMP *appears in the doorway.*]

KEMP: What?

KATH: Turn your face away. Mr Sloane is passing. He has no trousers on. [*Quietly to Sloane.*] You know the room?

SLOANE: Yes.

    [*Silence.* SLOANE *exits.*]

KATH [*calling after him*]: Have a bath if you want to, dear. Treat the conveniences as if they were your own. [*Turns to Kemp.*] I want an explanation.

KEMP: Yes. Kathy ...

KATH: Don't Kathy me.

KEMP: But he upset me.

KATH: Upset you? A grown man?

175

Kath + Ed. →

KEMP: I've seen him before.

KATH: You've seen the milkman before. That's no cause to throw the shears at him.

KEMP: I didn't throw them.

KATH: Oh? I heard different. [*Picks up her handbag and takes out money.*] Go and fetch his case. It'll be about five pence on the bus.

[*Presses the money into his hand.*] The address is 39 St Hilary's Crescent.

KEMP: Where's that?

KATH [*losing her temper*]: By the Co-op! Behave yourself.

KEMP: A teetotal club on the corner is there?

KATH: That's the one. Only it is closed. [*Pause.*] Can you find it?

KEMP: I expect so.

[*There is a noise of tapping.*]

KATH [*goes to the window. Over her shoulder*]: It's Eddie.

KEMP: What's that?

KATH [*speaking to someone outside*]: Why don't you come round the right way?

ED [*outside the window*]: I rung the bell but you was out.

KATH: Are you coming in?

ED: I'll be round. [*Closes the window.*]

KATH: It's Eddie.

KEMP: I'm not going to talk to him!

KATH: I don't expect he wants you to.

KEMP: He knows I'm in always on Friday. [*Pause.*] I'm signing nothing you can tell him that.

KATH: Tell him what?

KEMP: That I'm not signing nothing.

ED [*entering*]: Is he still on? What's the matter with you?

[KEMP *does not reply.*]

Always on about something.

KEMP: I'm not speaking to him.

ED [*patiently*]: Go on, get out of it afore I kicks you out. Make me bad you do. With your silly, childish ways.

[KEMP *does not reply.*]

KATH: Do what I told you, Dadda. Try not to lose yourself. Follow the railings. Then ask somebody.

[KEMP exits.]

[KATH dips towel in saucepan, begins to sponge bloody patch on settee.]

ED [watches her. Takes a drag of his cigarette]: What's this I heard about you?

KATH: What?

ED: Listening are you?

KATH: Yes, Eddie, I'm listening.

ED: You've got a kid staying here.

KATH: No ...

ED: Don't lie to me.

KATH: He's a guest. He's not a lodger.

ED: Who told you to take in lodgers?

[Pause.]

KATH: I needed a bit extra.

ED: I'll give you the money.

KATH: I'm taking Dadda away next year.

[Pause.]

ED: I don't want men hanging around.

KATH: He's a nice young man.

ED: You know what these fellows are – young men with no fixed abode.

KATH: No.

ED: You know what they say about landladies?

KATH: No, Eddie.

ED: They say they'd sleep with a broom handle in trousers, that's what they say.

KATH [uneasy]: I'm not like that.

ED: You're good-natured though. They mistake it.

KATH: This young man is quite respectable.

ED: You've got to realize my position. I can't have my sister keeping a common kip. Some of my associates are men of distinction. They think nothing of tipping a fiver. That sort of person. If they realized how my family carry on I'd be banned from the best places. [Pause.] And another thing ... you don't want them talking about you. An' I can't guarantee my influence will keep them quiet. Nosy neighbours and scandal. Oh, my word, the looks you'll get. [*Pause.*] How old is he?

KATH: He's young.

ED: These fellows sleep with their landladies automatic. Has he made suggestions? Suggested you bring him supper in bed?

KATH: No.

ED: That's what they do. Then they take advantage.

KATH: Mr Sloane is superior to that.

ED: Where did you find him?

KATH: In the library.

ED: Picked him up, did you?

KATH: He was having trouble. With his rent. [*Pause.*] His landlady was unscrupulous.

ED: How long have you been going with him?

KATH: He's a good boy.

[ED *sees trousers, picks them up.*]

KATH: It was an accident.

ED: Had the trousers off him already I see. [*Balls his fist and punches her upper arm gently.*] Don't let me down, darlin'. [*Pause.*] Where is he?

KATH: Upstairs.

ED: You fetch him.

KATH: He hurt his leg.

ED: I want to see him.

KATH: He's resting. [*Pause.*] Ed, you won't tell him to go?

ED [*brushing her aside*]: Go and fetch him.

KATH: I'm not misbehaving. Ed, if you send him away I shall cry.

ED [*raising his voice*]: Let's have less of it. I'll decide.

[*She exits.*]

ED [*calls after her*]: Tell him to put his trousers on. [*Picks up the trousers and flings them after her.*] Cantering around the house with a bare bum. Good job I come when I did. [*Pause.*] Can't leave you alone for five minutes.

KATH [*off*]: Mr Sloane! Would you step down here for a minute? My brother would like to meet you. [*Re-enters.*] He's trustworthy. Visits his parents once a month. Asked me to go with him. You

178

couldn't object to a visit to a graveyard? The sight of the tombs would deter any looseness. [*Sniffs. Shrugs. Picks through the junk on the sideboard, finds a sweet and puts it in her mouth.*] He hasn't any mamma of his own. I'm to be his mamma. He's an orphan. Eddie, he wouldn't do wrong. Please don't send him away.

ED: It'd crease me if you misbehaved again. I got responsibilities.

KATH: Let him stay.

ED: Kid like that. Know what they'll say don't you?
[*Pause.*]

KATH: He's cultured, Ed. He's informed.
[ED *turns and lights another cigarette from the butt of the one he is smoking. Opens the window. Throws the butt out..*SLOANE *enters.*]

KATH: This is my brother, Mr Sloane. He expressed a desire to meet you.

ED [*turns, faces Sloane*]: I ... my sister was telling me about you.
[*Pause.*]
My sister was telling me about you being an orphan, Mr Sloane.

SLOANE [*smiling*]: Oh, yes?

ED: Must be a rotten life for a kid. You look well on it though.

SLOANE: Yes.

ED: I could never get used to sleeping in cubicles. Was it a mixed home?

SLOANE: Just boys.

ED: Ideal. How many to a room?

SLOANE: Eight.

ED: Really? Same age were they? Or older?

SLOANE: The ages varied by a year or two.

ED: Oh well, you had compensations then. Keep you out of mischief, eh? [*Laughs.*] Well your childhood wasn't unhappy?

SLOANE: No.

ED: Sounds as though it was a happy atmosphere. [*Pause.*] Got anything to do, Kath?

KATH: No.

ED: No beds to make?

KATH: I made them this morning.

ED: Maybe you forgot to change the pillowslips?

KATH [*going*]: Eddie don't let me be upset will you? [*Exits.*]

179

ED: I must apologize for her behaviour. She's not in the best of health.

SLOANE: She seems all right.

ED: You can't always go on appearances. She's ... well I wouldn't say unbalanced. No, that'd be going too far. She suffers from migraine. That's why it'd be best if you declined her offer of a room.

SLOANE: I see.

ED: When are you going?

SLOANE: But I like it here.

ED: I dare say you do. The fact is my sister's taking on too many responsibilities. She's a charming woman as a rule. Charming. I've no hesitation in saying that. Lost her husband. And her little kid. Tell you did she?

SLOANE: She mentioned it.

ED [wary]: What did she say?

SLOANE: Said she married young.

ED: She married a mate of mine – a valiant man – we were together in Africa.

SLOANE: In the army?

ED: You're interested in the army, eh? Soldiers, garrison towns, etc. Does that interest you?

SLOANE: Yes.

ED: Good, excellent. How old are you?

SLOANE: Twenty.

ED: Married?

SLOANE: No.

ED [laughs]: Wise man, eh? Wise man. [Pause.] Girl friends?

SLOANE: No.

ED: No. You're a librarian?

SLOANE: No.

ED: I thought she said –

SLOANE: I help out at Len's ... the tobacconist. Give him a hand. I'm not employed there.

ED: I was told you were.

SLOANE: I help out. On Saturdays.

ED: I see. I've been mistaken. [Silence.] Well, as I just said ... I don't think it'd suit you. What with one thing and another. [Pause.] To show there's no hard feelings I'll make it worth your while. Call it a gift.

SLOANE: That's decent of you.

ED: Not at all. [*Pause.*] I'd like to give you a little present. Anything you care to name. Within reason.

SLOANE: What's within reason?

ED [*laughs*]: Well ... no ... Jags. [*Laughs.*] ... no sports cars. I'm not going as far as that.

SLOANE [*relaxing*]: I was going to suggest an Aston Martin.

ED [*walks from the window looking for an ashtray. He does not find one*]: I wish I could give you one, boy. I wish I could. [*Stubs out his cigarette into a glass seashell on the sideboard.*] Are you a sports fan? Eh? Fond of sport? You look as though you might be. Look the ... outdoor type, I'd say.

SLOANE: I am.

ED: I'd say you were. That's what struck me when you walked in. That's what puzzled me. She gave me the impression you were ... well, don't be offended ... I had the notion you were a shop assistant.

SLOANE: Never worked in a shop in my life.

ED: No. [*Pause.*] I see you're not that type. You're more of a ... as you might say ... the fresh air type.

SLOANE: I help out on Saturdays for a mate of mine. Len. You might know him. Lifeguard at the baths one time. Nice chap.

ED: You're fond of swimming?

SLOANE: I like a plunge now and then.

ED: Bodybuilding?

SLOANE: We had a nice little gym at the orphanage. Put me in all the teams they did. Relays ...

   [ED *looks interested.*]

... soccer ...

   [ED *nods.*]

... pole vault, ... long distance ...

   [ED *opens his mouth.*]

... 100 yards, discus, putting the shot.

   [ED *rubs his hands together.*]

Yes, yes, I'm an all rounder. A great all rounder. In anything you care to mention. Even in life.

[ED *lifts up a warning finger.*]

... yes I like a good work out now and then.

ED: I used to do a lot of that at one time. With my mate ... we used to do all what you've just said. [*Pause.*] We were young. Innocent too. [*Shrugs. Pats his pocket. Takes out a packet of cigarettes. Smokes.*] All over now. [*Pause.*] Developing your muscles, eh? And character. [*Pause.*] ... Well, well, well. [*Breathless.*] A little bodybuilder are you? I bet you are ... [*Slowly.*] ... do you ... [*Shy.*] exercise regular?

SLOANE: As clockwork.

ED: Good, good. Stripped?

SLOANE: Fully.

ED: Complete. [*Striding to the window.*] How invigorating.

SLOANE: And I box. I'm a bit of a boxer.

ED: Ever done any wrestling?

SLOANE: On occasions.

ED: So, so.

SLOANE: I've got a full chest. Narrow hips. My biceps are –

ED: Do you wear leather ... next to the skin? Leather jeans, say? Without ... aah ...

SLOANE: Pants?

ED [*laughs*]: Get away! [*Pause.*] The question is are you clean living? You may as well know I set great store by morals. Too much of this casual bunking up nowadays. Too many lads being ruined by birds. I don't want you messing about with my sister.

SLOANE: I wouldn't.

ED: Have you made overtures to her?

SLOANE: No.

ED: Would you?

SLOANE: No.

ED: Not if circumstances were ripe?

SLOANE: Never.

ED: Does she disgust you?

SLOANE: Should she?

ED: It would be better if she did.

SLOANE: I've no interest in her.

[*Pause.*]

ED: I've a certain amount of influence. Friends with money. I've two cars. Judge for yourself. I generally spend my holidays in places where the bints have got rings through their noses. [*Pause.*] Women are like banks, boy, breaking and entering is a serious business. Give me your word you're not vaginalatrous?

SLOANE: I'm not.

ED [*Pause*]: I'll believe you. Can you drive?

SLOANE: Yes.

ED: I might let you be my chauffeur.

SLOANE: Would you?

ED [*laughs*]: We'll see ... I could get you a uniform. Boots, pants, a guaranteed 100 per cent no imitation jacket ... an ... er ... a white brushed nylon T-shirt ... with a little leather cap. [*Laughs.*] Like that?

    [SLOANE *nods. Silence.*]

Kip here a bit. Till we get settled. Come and see me. We'll discuss salary arrangements and any other business. Here's my card. [*Gives Sloane a card.*] Have you seen my old dad?

SLOANE: I spoke to him.

ED: Wonderful for his age. [*Pause.*] Call her in will you?

    [SLOANE *exits.*]

SLOANE [*off*]: I think you're wanted. [*Re-enters.*]

ED: You'll find me a nice employer. [*Pause.*] When you come to see me we must have a drink. A talk.

SLOANE: What about?

ED: Life. Sport. Love. Anything you care to name. Don't forget.

SLOANE: I'm looking forward to it.

ED: Do you drink?

SLOANE: When I'm not in training.

ED: You aren't in training at the moment, are you?

SLOANE: No.

ED: I wouldn't want you to break your training. Drinking I don't mind. Drugs I abhor. You'll get to know all my habits.

    [KATH *enters.*]

KATH: What you want?

ED: A word with you afore I go.

KATH: Are you staying, Mr Sloane?

ED: 'Course he's staying.

KATH: All right is it?

ED: He's going to work for me.

KATH [*Pause*]: He isn't going away is he?

ED: Offered him a job I have. I want a word with my sister, Sloane. Would you excuse us?

[SLOANE *nods, smiles, and turns to go.*]

KATH [*as he exits*]: Have a meal, Mr Sloane. You'll find a quarter of boiled ham. Help yourself. You better have what's left 'cause I see he's been wolfing it. An' you heard me ask him to wait di'n't you? I told him.

[*Exit* SLOANE. *Silence.*]

ED: You picked a nice lad there. Very nice. Clean. No doubt upright. A sports enthusiast. All the proper requisites. Don't take any money from him. I'll pay.

KATH: Can I buy him a shirt?

ED: What do you want to do that for?

KATH: His own mamma can't.

ED: He can buy his own clothes. Making yourself look ridiculous. [*Pause.*]

KATH: When it's Christmas can I buy him a little gift?

ED: No.

KATH: Send him a card?

ED: Why?

KATH: I'd like to. I'd show you beforehand. [*Pause.*] Can I go to his mamma's grave?

ED: If you want. [*Pause.*] He'll laugh at you.

KATH: He wouldn't, Eddie.

[*Silence.*]

ED: I must go. I'll have a light meal. Take a couple of nembutal and then bed. I shall be out of town tomorrow.

KATH: Where?

ED: In Aylesbury. I shall dress in a quiet suit. Drive up in the motor. The Commissionaire will spring forward. There in that miracle of glass and concrete my colleagues and me will have a quiet drink before the business of the day.

KATH: Are your friends nice?

ED: Mature men.

KATH: No ladies?
   [*Pause.*]

ED: What are you talking about? I live in a world of top decisions. We've no time for ladies.

KATH: Ladies are nice at a gathering.

ED: We don't want a lot of half-witted tarts.

KATH: They add colour and gaiety.

ED: Frightening everyone with their clothes.
   [*Pause.*]

KATH: I hope you have a nice time. Perhaps one day you'll invite me to your hotel.

ED: I might.

KATH: Show me round.

ED: Yes.

KATH: Is it exquisitely furnished? High up?

ED: Very high. I see the river often.
   [*A door slams.*]
Persuade the old man to speak to me.

KEMP [*off*]: Is he gone?

KATH: Speak to him Dadda. He's something to ask you.
   [*Silence.*]

ED [*petulant*]: Isn't it incredible? I'm his only son. He won't see me. [*Goes to the door. Speaks through.*] I want a word with you. [*Pause.*] Is he without human feelings? [*Pause. Brokenly.*] He won't speak to me. Has he no heart?

KATH: Come again.

ED: I'll get my lawyer to send a letter. If it's done legal he'll prove amenable. Give us a kiss. [*Kisses her. Pats her bottom.*] Be a good girl now. [*Exit.*]

KATH: Cheerio. [*Pause.*] I said Cheerio.
   [*Door slams.*]

KATH [*goes to door*]: Why don't you speak to him?
   [*KEMP enters. He does not reply.*]
He invited me to his suite. The luxury takes your breath away. Money is no object. A waitress comes with the tea. [*Pause.*] I'm going to see him there one day. Speak to him Dadda.

١٨٥

KEMP: No.

KATH: Please.

KEMP: Never.

KATH: Let me phone saying you changed your mind.

KEMP: No.

KATH: Let me phone.

KEMP: No.

KATH [*tearfully*]: Oh, Dadda, you are unfair. If you don't speak to him he won't invite me to his suite. It's a condition. I won't be able to go. You found that address?

KEMP: I got lost, though.

KATH: Why didn't you ask? [*Pause.*] You had a tongue in your head. Oh, Dadda, you make me so angry with your silly ways. [*Pause.*] What was the house like?

KEMP: I didn't notice.

KATH: He said it was a hovel. A boy like him shouldn't be expected to live with the rougher elements. Do you know, Dadda, he has skin the like of which I never felt before. And he confesses to being an orphan. His story is so sad. I wept when I heard it. You know how soft-hearted I am.

[*Silence.*]

KEMP: I haven't been feeling well lately.

KATH: Have you seen the optician?

KEMP: My eyes are getting much worse.

KATH: Without a word of a lie you are like a little child.

KEMP: I'm all alone.

KATH: You have me.

KEMP: He may take you away.

KATH: Where to?

KEMP: Edinburgh.

KATH: Too cold.

KEMP: Or Bournemouth. You always said you'd go somewhere with palms.

KATH: I'd always consult you first.

KEMP: You'd put me in a home. [*Pause.*] Would you be tempted? [*Silence.*]

KATH: You ought to consult an oculist. See your oculist at once.

[*Pause.*] Go to bed. I'll bring you a drinkie. In the morning you'll feel different.

KEMP: You don't love me.

KATH: I've never stopped loving you.

KEMP: I'm going to die, Kath ... I'm dying.

KATH [*angrily*]: You've been at that ham haven't you? Half a jar of pickles you've put away. Don't moan to me if you're up half the night with the tummy ache. I've got no sympathy for you.

KEMP: Goodnight then.

KATH [*watches him out of the door. Looks through into the kitchen*]: All right, Mr Sloane? Help yourself ... all right? [*Comes back into the room. Takes lamp from sideboard and puts it on to table beside settee. Goes to record player, puts on record. Pulls curtains across alcove and disappears behind them. The stage is empty. The record plays for a few seconds and then the needle jumps a groove, slides across record. Automatic change switches record off.* KATH *pokes her head from behind curtain, looks at record player, disappears again. Re-appears wearing a transparent négligé. Picks up aerosol spray, sprays room. Calls through door*]: Have you finished, Mr Sloane, dear?

SLOANE [*off*]: Ugh?

KATH: You have? I'm so glad. I don't want to disturb you at your food. [*Sees knitting on sideboard, picks it up.*] Come into the lounge if you wish. I'm just at a quiet bit of knitting before I go to bed. [SLOANE *enters wiping his mouth.*] A lovely piece of ham, wasn't it?

SLOANE: Lovely.

KATH: I'll give you a splendid breakfast in the morning. [*Realizes that there is only one needle in the knitting. Searches in the junk and finds the other. Takes it to the settee.* SLOANE *sits on one end.*] [*Pause.*] Isn't this room gorgeous?

SLOANE: Yes.

KATH: That vase over there come from Bombay. Do you have any interest in that part of the world?

SLOANE: I like Dieppe.

KATH: Ah ... it's all the same. I don't suppose they know the difference themselves. Are you comfortable? Let me plump your cushion. [*Plumps a cushion behind his head. Laughs lightly.*] I really by rights should ask you to change places. This light is showing me up. [*Pause.*] I blame it on the manufacturers. They make garments so thin nowadays you'd think they intended to provoke a rape.

[*Pause.*]

Sure you're comfy? [*Leans over him.*]

[SLOANE *pulls her hand towards him. She laughs, half in panic.*]

SLOANE: You're a teaser ent you?

KATH [*breaks away*]: I hope I'm not. I was trying to find the letter from my little boy's father. I treasure it. But I seem to have mislaid it. I found a lot of photos though.

SLOANE: Yes.

KATH: Are you interested in looking through them? [*Brings the snapshots over.*]

SLOANE: Are they him?

KATH: My lover.

SLOANE: Bit blurred.

KATH: It brings back memories. He reminds me of you. [*Pause.*] He too was handsome and in the prime of manhood. Can you wonder I fell. [*Pause.*] I wish he were here now to love and protect me. [*Leans her arm on his shoulder. Shows him another snap.*] This is me. I was younger then.

SLOANE: Smart.

KATH: Yes my hair was nice.

SLOANE: Yes.

KATH: An' this ... I don't know whether I ought to let you see it.

[SLOANE *attempts to seize it.*]

Now then!

[*He takes it from her.*]

SLOANE: A seat in a wood?

KATH: That seat is erected to the memory of Mrs Gwen Lewis. She was a lady who took a lot of trouble with invalids. [*Pause.*] It was near that seat that my baby was thought of.

SLOANE: On that seat?

KATH [*shyly*]: Not on it exactly. Nearby ...

SLOANE: In the bushes ?...

[*She giggles.*]

KATH: Yes. [*Pause.*] He was rough with me.

SLOANE: Uncomfortable, eh?

KATH: I couldn't describe my feelings. [*Pause.*] I don't think the fastening on this thing I'm wearing will last much longer. [*The snapshots slip from her hand.*] There! you've knocked the photos on the floor.

[*Pause: he attempts to move; she is almost on top of him.*] Mr Sloane … [*Rolls on to him.*] You should wear more clothes, Mr Sloane. I believe you're as naked as me. And there's no excuse for it. [*Silence.*] I'll be your mamma. I need to be loved. Gently. Oh! I shall be so ashamed in the morning. [*Switches off the light.*] What a big heavy baby you are. Such a big heavy baby.

CURTAIN

ACT TWO

Some months later. Morning.

[SLOANE *is lying on the settee wearing boots, leather trousers and a white T-shirt. A newspaper covers his face.* KATH *enters. Looks at the settee.*]

SLOANE: Where you been?

KATH: Shopping, dear. Did you want me?

SLOANE: I couldn't find you.

KATH [*goes to the window. Takes off her headscarf*]: What's Eddie doing?

SLOANE: A bit of serviceing.

KATH: But that's your job.

[SLOANE *removes the newspaper.*]

He shouldn't do your work.

SLOANE: I was on the beer. My guts is playing up.

KATH: Poor boy. [*Pause.*] Go and help him. For mamma's sake.

SLOANE: I may in a bit.

KATH: He's a good employer. Studies your interests. You want to think of his position. He's proud of it. Now you're working for him his position is your position. [*Pause.*] Go and give him a hand.

SLOANE: No.

KATH: Are you too tired?

SLOANE: Yes.

KATH: We must make allowances for you. You're young. [*Pause.*] You're not taking advantage are you?

SLOANE: No.

KATH: I know you aren't. When you've had a drinkie go and help him.

SLOANE: If you want.

[*Pause.*]

KATH: Did mamma hear you were on the razzle?

SLOANE: Yes.

KATH: Did you go up West? You were late coming home. [*Pause.*] Very late.

SLOANE: Three of my mates and me had a night out.

KATH: Are they nice boys?

SLOANE: We have interests in common.

KATH: They aren't roughs are they? Mamma doesn't like you associating with them.

SLOANE: Not on your life. They're gentle. Refined youths. Thorpe, Beck and Doolan. We toured the nighteries in the motor.

KATH: Was Ed with you?

SLOANE: No.

KATH: Did you ask him? He would have come.

SLOANE: He was tired. A hard day yesterday.

KATH: Ask him next time.

[*Pause.*]

SLOANE: We ended up at a fabulous place. Soft music, pink shades, lovely atmosphere.

KATH: I hope you behaved yourself.

SLOANE: One of the hostesses gave me her number. Told me to ring her.

KATH: Take no notice of her. She might not be nice.

SLOANE: Not nice?

KATH: She might be a party girl.

[*Pause.*]

SLOANE: What exactly do you mean?

KATH: Mamma worries for you.

SLOANE: You're attempting to run my life.

KATH: Is baby cross?

SLOANE: You're developing distinctly possessive tendencies.

KATH: You can get into trouble saying that.

SLOANE: A possessive woman.

KATH: A mamma can't be possessive.

SLOANE: Can't she?

KATH: You know she can't. You're being naughty.

SLOANE: Never heard of a possessive mum?

KATH: Stop it. It's rude. Did she teach you to say that?

SLOANE: What?

KATH: What you just said.

[SLOANE *makes no reply.*]

You're spoiling yourself in my eyes, Mr Sloane. You won't ring this girl will you?

SLOANE: I haven't decided.

KATH: Decide now. To please me. I don't know what you see in these girls. You have your friends for company.

SLOANE: They're boys.

KATH: What's wrong with them? You can talk freely. Not like with a lady.

SLOANE: I don't want to talk.

[*Pause.*]

KATH: She might be after your money.

SLOANE: I haven't got any.

KATH: But Eddie has. She might be after his.

SLOANE: Look, you're speaking of a very good class bird.

KATH: I have to protect you, baby, because you're easily led.

SLOANE: I like being led. [*Pause.*] I need to be let out occasionally. Off the lead.

[*Pause.*]

KATH: She'll make you ill.

SLOANE: Shut it. [*Pause.*] Make me ill!

KATH: Girls do.

SLOANE: How dare you. Making filthy insinuations. I won't have it. You disgust me you do. Standing there without your teeth. Why don't you get smartened up? Get a new rig-out.

[*Pause.*]

KATH: Do I disgust you?

SLOANE: Yes.

KATH: Honest?

SLOANE: And truly. You horrify me. [*Pause.*] You think I'm kidding. I'll give up my room if you don't watch out.

KATH: Oh, no!

SLOANE: Clear out.

KATH: Don't think of such drastic action. I'd never forgive myself if I drove you away. [*Pause.*] I won't any more.

[*He attempts to rise.*]

KATH [*takes his hand*]: Don't go, dear. Stay with me while I collect myself. I've been upset and I need comfort. [*Silence.*] Are you still disgusted?

SLOANE: A bit.

KATH [*takes his hand, presses it to her lips*]: Sorry baby. Better?

SLOANE: Mmmm.

[*Silence.*]

KATH: How good you are to me.

[KEMP *enters. He carries a stick. Taps his way to the sideboard.*]

My teeth, since you mentioned the subject, Mr Sloane, are in the kitchen in Stergene. Usually I allow a good soak overnight. But what with one thing and another I forgot. Otherwise I would never be in such a state. [*Pause.*] I hate people who are careless with their dentures.

[KEMP *opens a drawer.*]

KEMP: Seen my tablets?

KATH: If you're bad go to bed.

KEMP: I need one o' my pills.

[*He picks his way through the junk.*]

SLOANE [*goes over to him*]: What you want?

KEMP: Let me alone.

SLOANE: Tell me what you want.

KEMP: I don't want no help. [*Pause.*] I'm managing.

SLOANE: Let me know what you want and I'll look for it.

KEMP: I can manage.

[SLOANE *goes back to the settee. Silence.*]

KATH: What a lot of foreigners there are about lately. I see one to-day. Playing the accordion. They live in a world of their own these people.

KEMP: Coloured?

KATH: No.

KEMP: I expect he was. They do come over here. Raping people. It's a problem. Just come out o' jail had he?

KATH: I really didn't stop long enough to ask. I just commented on the tune he was playing.

KEMP: Oh, they're all for that.

KATH [*leans over Sloane*]: Mamma has something special to say to you.

KEMP: All for that.

SLOANE [*touches her hair*]: What?

KATH [*to* KEMP, *louder*]: I don't think he was dark enough to be coloured, Dadda. Honestly I don't.

KEMP: They should send them back.

SLOANE: What's your news?

KATH: Can't you guess?

SLOANE: No.

KATH: I know you can't.

KEMP: You should've put in a complaint.

KATH: Oh, no Dadda.

KEMP: Playing his bloody music in the street.

KATH: What language! You should be a splendid example to us. Instead of which you carry on like a common workman. Don't swear like that in my presence again.

[Silence. SLOANE *attempts to grab her shopping bag. She rises.* SLOANE *touches her up. She grunts. Smacks his hand.*]

KEMP: What's up?

KATH: Nothing. Aren't the tulips glorious this year by the municipal offices. What a brave showing. They must spend a fortune.

SLOANE: What have you bought me?

KATH: Mamma is going to have a ... [*Makes a rocking motion with her arms.*]

SLOANE: What? [*Pause.*] What?

KATH: A little – [*Looks over to Kemp. Makes the motion of rocking a baby in her arms. Purses her lips. Blows a kiss.*]

[SLOANE *sits up. Points to himself.*]

KATH [*nods her head. Presses her mouth to his ear: whispers*]: A baby brother.

KEMP: What are you having?

KATH: A ... bath, Dadda. You know that woman from the shops? [*Pause.*] You wouldn't believe what a ridiculous spectacle she's making of herself.

KEMP: Oh.

KATH [*to Sloane*]: 'Course it's ever so dangerous at my age. But doctor thinks it'll be all right.

SLOANE: Sure.

KATH: I was worried in case you'd be cross.

SLOANE: We mustn't let anyone know.

KATH: It's our secret. [*Pause.*] I'm excited.

KEMP: Are you having it after tea, Kath?

KATH: Why?

KEMP: I thought of having one as well. Are you there?

KATH: Yes.

KEMP: Have you seen them pills?

KATH: Have I seen his pills. They're where you left them I expect. [*Goes to the sideboard. Finds bottle. Gives it to Kemp.*] How many you had today?

KEMP: Two.

KATH: They're not meant to be eaten like sweets you know.
[*He exits.*]
I been to the Register Office.

SLOANE: What for?

KATH: To inquire about the licence.

SLOANE: Who?

KATH: You.

SLOANE: Who to?

KATH: Me. Don't you want to? You wouldn't abandon me? Leave me to face the music.

SLOANE: What music?

KATH: When Eddie hears.

SLOANE: He mustn't hear.

KATH: Baby, how can we stop him?

SLOANE: He'd kill me. I'd be out of a job.

KATH: I suppose we couldn't rely on him employing you any longer.

SLOANE: Don't say anything. I'll see a man I know.

KATH: What? But I'm looking forward to having a new little brother.

SLOANE: Out of the question.

KATH: Please ...

SLOANE: No. In any case I couldn't marry you. I'm not the type. And all things being equal I may not be living here much longer.

KATH: Aren't you comfy in your bed?

SLOANE: Yes.

KATH [*folds her arms round him. Kisses his head*]: We could marry in secret. Couldn't you give me something, baby? So's I feel in my mind we were married?

SLOANE: What like?

KATH: A ring. Or a bracelet? You got a nice locket. I noticed it. Make me a present of that.

SLOANE: I can't do that.

KATH: As a token of your esteem. So's I feel I belong to you.

SLOANE: It belonged to my mum.

KATH: I'm your mamma now.

SLOANE: No.

KATH: Go on.

SLOANE: But it was left to me.

KATH: You mustn't cling to old memories. I shall begin to think you don't love mamma.

SLOANE: I do.

KATH: Then give me that present. [*Unhooks the chain.*] Ta.

SLOANE: I hate parting with it.

KATH: I'll wear it for ever.

[ED *enters. Stands smoking a cigarette. Turns. Exits. Re-enters with a cardboard box.*]

ED: This yours?

KATH [*goes over. Looks in the box*]: It's my gnome.

ED: They just delivered it.

KATH: The bad weather damaged him. His little hat come off. I sent him to the Gnomes' Hospital to be repaired.

ED: Damaged, was he?

KATH: Yes.

ED: Well, well. [*Pause.*] It's monkey weather out there.

SLOANE: I wasn't cold.

ED: You're young. Healthy. Don't feel the cold, do you?

SLOANE: No.

ED: Not at all?

SLOANE: Sometimes.

ED: Not often. [*Pause.*] I expect it's all that orange juice.

KATH: Mr Sloane was coming out, Eddie. I assure you.

ED: I know that. I can trust him.

KATH: You've a lovely colour. Let me feel your hand. Why it's freezing. You feel his hand Mr Sloane.

ED: He doesn't want to feel my hand. [*Pause.*] When you're ready, boy, we'll go.

SLOANE: Check the oil?

ED: Mmn.

SLOANE: Petrol?

ED: Mmn. [*Pause.*] Down en it?

SLOANE: Down?

ED: From yesterday. We filled her up yesterday.

SLOANE: Did we? Was it yesterday?

ED: Mmn. [*Pause.*] We used a lot since then.

SLOANE: You ought to get yourself a new car. It eats petrol.
[*Pause.*]

ED: Maybe you're right. You didn't use it last night did you?

SLOANE: Me?

ED: I thought you might have.

SLOANE: No.

ED: Funny.
[*Silence.*]

KATH: I see a woolly in Boyce's, Mr Sloane. I'm giving it you as a
birthday present.

ED: What do you want to do that for?

KATH: Mr Sloane won't mind.

ED: Chucking money about.

KATH: Mr Sloane doesn't mind me. He's one of the family.

ED: Hark at it. Shove up, boy.

SLOANE [*moves*]: Sit by me.

ED [*sits next to him*]: You didn't use my motor last night then?

SLOANE: No.

ED: That's all I wanted. As long as you're telling the truth,
boy.
[*He takes Sloane's hand.*]
You've an honest hand. Square. What a grip you got.

SLOANE: I'm improving.

ED: Yes, I can tell that. You've grown bolder since we met. Bigger
and bolder. Don't get too bold will you? Eh? [*Laughs.*] I'm going
to buy you something for your birthday as well.

SLOANE: Can I rely on it?

ED: Aah.

SLOANE: Will it be expensive?

ED: Very. I might consider lashing out a bit and buying you a ... um, er, aahhh ...

SLOANE: Thank you. Thank you.

ED: Don't thank me. Thank yourself. You deserve it.

SLOANE: I think I do.

ED: I think you do. Go and put that box in the kitchen.

KATH: It's no trouble, Eddie.

ED: Let the boy show you politeness.

KATH: But he does. Often. He's often polite to me.

[SLOANE *picks up the box and exits.*]

KATH: I never complain.

[*Pause.*]

ED: Where was he last night?

KATH: He watched the telly. A programme where people guessed each other's names.

ED: What else?

KATH: Nothing else.

ED: He used the car last night.

KATH: No.

[*Pause.*]

ED: If he's not careful he can have his cards.

KATH: He's only young.

ED: Joy-riding in my motor.

KATH: He's a good boy.

ED: Act your age. [*Pause.*] Encouraging him. I've watched you. What you want to keep him in here for all morning?

KATH: I didn't want him here. I told him to go and help you.

ED: You did? And he wouldn't?

KATH: No. Yes.

ED: What do you mean?

KATH: I thought it was his rest period, Eddie. You do give him a rest sometimes. I know 'cause you're a good employer. [*Sits beside him.*]

ED: What do I pay him for?

KATH: To keep him occupied, I suppose.

ED [*makes no reply. At last, irritated*]: You're a pest, you are.

KATH: I'm sorry.

ED [*glances at her*]: Keeping him in when he ought to be at work. How do you expect him to work well with you messing about?

KATH: He was just coming.

ED: Taking him from his duty. Wasting my money.

KATH: I won't any more.

ED: It's too late. I'll pay him off. Not satisfactory.

KATH: No.

ED: Not the type of person that I had expected.

KATH: He likes his work.

ED: He can go elsewhere.

KATH: He's a great help to me. I shall cry if he goes away. [*Pause.*] I shall have to take a sedative.

ED: I'll find someone else for you.

KATH: No.

ED: An older man. With more maturity.

KATH: I want my baby.

ED: Your what?

KATH: I'm his mamma and he appreciates me. [*Pause.*] He told me.

ED: When? When?

KATH: I can't remember.

ED: He loves you?

KATH: No, I didn't say that. But he calls me mamma. I love him 'cause I have no little boy of my own. And if you send him away I shall cry like the time you took my real baby.

ED: You were wicked then.

KATH: I know.

ED: Being rude. Ruining my little matie. Teaching him nasty things. That's why I sent it away. [*Pause.*] You're not doing rude things with this kiddy, are you, like you did with Tommy?

KATH: No.

ED: Sure?

KATH: I love him like a mamma.

ED: I can't trust you.

KATH: I'm a trustworthy lady.

ED: Allowing him to kip here was a mistake.
    [*Silence.*]

KATH: I never wanted to do rude things. Tommy made me.

ED: Liar!

KATH: Insisted. Pestered me he did. All summer.

ED: You're a liar.

KATH: Am I?

ED: He didn't want anything to do with you. He told me that.

KATH: You're making it up.

ED: I'm not.

KATH: He loved me.

ED: He didn't.

KATH: He wanted to marry me.

ED: Marry you? You're a ridiculous figure and no mistake.

KATH: He'd have married me only his folks were against it.

ED: I always imagined you were an intelligent woman. I find you're not.

KATH: He said they was.

ED: Did he? When?

KATH: When the stork was coming.

ED [laughs]: Well, well. Fancy you remembering. You must have a long memory.

KATH: I have.

ED: Let me disillusion you.

KATH: Don't hurt me, Eddie.

ED: You need hurting you do. Mr and Mrs Albion Bolter were quite ready to have you marry Tommy.

KATH: No they wasn't.

ED: Allow me to know.

KATH [Pause]: He wouldn't have lied, Ed. You're telling stories.

ED: I'm not.

KATH: But he said it was 'cause I was poor. [Pause.] I couldn't fit into the social background demanded of him. His duty came between us.

ED: You could have been educated. Gone to beauty salons. Learned to speak well.

KATH: No.

ED: They wanted you to marry him. Tommy and me had our first set-to about it. You should have heard the language he used to me.

KATH: I was loved. How can you say that?

ED: Forget it.

KATH: He sent me the letter I treasure.

ED: I burned it.

[*Pause.*]

KATH: It was his last words to me.

ED: And that kiddy out there. I'm not having him go the same way.

[KATH *goes to the window.*]

KATH: Did you burn my letter?

ED: Yes. [*Pause.*] And that old photo as well. I thought you was taking an unhealthy interest in the past.

KATH: The photo as well?

ED: You forget it.

KATH: I promised to show it to someone. I wondered why I couldn't find it.

ED: You wicked girl.

KATH: I'm not wicked. I think you're wicked. [*Sniffs without dignity.*]

ED [*lights a cigarette. Looks at her*]: While I'm at it I'll get the old man to look at those papers. [*Pause.*] Get my case in will you?

[*She does not reply. He stands up. Exits. Returns with briefcase.*]

I made a mark where he's to sign. On the dotted line. [*Laughs.*] I'll be glad when it's over. To use an expression foreign to my nature – I'll be bloody glad. [*Stares at Kath as she continues to cry. Turns away. Pause.*] Quit bawling will you?

[KATH *blows her nose on the edge of her apron.*]

You should be like me. You'd have something to cry over then, if you got responsibilities like me. [*Silence.*] Haven't you got a hankie? You don't want the boy to see you like that? [*Silence.*]

[SLOANE *enters.*]

Put it away did you?

SLOANE: Yes.

ED: That's a good boy.

[*Pause.*]

KATH: Mr. Sloane.

SLOANE: What?

KATH: Can *I* call you Boy?

SLOANE: I don't think you'd better.

KATH: Why not?

ED: I'm his employer see. He knows that you're only his landlady.
  [SLOANE *smiles*.]

KATH: I don't mean in front of strangers. [*Pause*.] I'd be sparing with
  the use of the name.

ED: No! [*Sharply*.] Haven't you got anything to do? Standing there
  all day.

  [KATH *exits*.]

  Getting fat as a pig she is.

SLOANE: Is she?

ED: Not noticed?

SLOANE: No.

ED: I have.

SLOANE: How old is she?

ED: Forty-one. [*Shrugs*.] Forty-two. She ought to slim. I'd advise that.

SLOANE: She's ...

ED: She's like a sow. Though she is my sister.

SLOANE: She's not bad.

ED: No?

SLOANE: I don't think so.

  [ED *goes to the window. Stands. Lost. Pause*.]

ED: Where was you last night?

SLOANE: I told you –

ED: I know what you told me. A pack of lies. D'you think I'm an
  idiot or something?

SLOANE: No.

ED: I want the truth.

SLOANE: I went for a spin. I had a headache.

ED: Where did you go?

SLOANE: Along the A40.

ED: Who went with you?

SLOANE: Nobody.

ED: Are you being entirely honest?
  [*Pause*.]

SLOANE: Three mates come with me.

ED: They had headaches too?

SLOANE: I never asked.

ED: Cheeky. [*Pause*.] Who are they? Would I want them in my motor?

SLOANE: You'd recognize Harry Thorpe. Small, clear complexioned, infectious good humour.

ED: I might.

SLOANE: Harry Beck I brought up one night. A Wednesday it was. But Doolan no. You wouldn't know him.

ED: Riding round in my motor all night eh?

SLOANE: I'd challenge that.

ED: What type of youth are they?

SLOANE: Impeccable taste. Buy their clothes up West.

ED: Any of them wear lipstick?

SLOANE: Certainly not.

ED: You'd notice would you? [*Throws over a lipstick.*] What's this doing in the back of the motor?
    [*Silence.*]

SLOANE [*laughs*]: Oh ... you jogged my memory ... yes ... Doolan's married ... an' we took his wife along.

ED: Can't you do better than that?

SLOANE: Straight up.

ED [*emotionally*]: Oh, boy ... Taking birds out in my motor.

SLOANE: Would you accept an unconditional apology.

ED: Telling me lies.

SLOANE: It won't happen again.

ED: What are your feelings towards me?

SLOANE: I respect you.

ED: Is that the truth?

SLOANE: Honest.

ED: Then why tell me lies?

SLOANE: That's only your impression.
    [*Pause.*]

ED: Was this an isolated incident?

SLOANE: This is the first time.

ED: Really.

SLOANE: Yes. Can you believe me?
    [*Pause.*]

ED: I believe you. I believe you're regretting the incident already. But don't repeat it. [*Silence.*] Or next time I won't be so lenient. [*Pause.*] I think the time has come for us to make a change.

SLOANE: In what way?

ED: I need you on tap.

SLOANE: Mmmn ...

[Pause.]

ED: At all hours. In case I have to make a journey to a distant place at an unexpected and inconvenient hour of the night. In a manner of speaking it's urgent.

SLOANE: Of course.

ED: I got work to do. [Pause.] I think it would be best if you leave here today.

SLOANE: It might be.

ED: Give it a trial. [Pause.] You see my way of looking at it?

SLOANE: Sure.

ED: And you shouldn't be left with her. She's no good. No good at all. A crafty tart she is. I could tell you things about – the way these women carry on. [Pause.] Especially her. [Opens window. Throws cigarette out.] These women do you no good. I can tell you that. [Feels in his coat pocket. Takes out a packet of mints. Puts one in his mouth. Pause.] One of sixteen come up to me the other day – which is a thing I never expected, come up to me and said she'd been given my address. I don't know whether it was a joke or something. You see that sort of thing ...

SLOANE: Well ... ?

ED: You could check it.

SLOANE: I'd be pleased.

ED: Certainly. I got feelings.

SLOANE: You're sensitive. You can't be bothered.

ED: You got it wrong when you says that. I seen birds all shapes and sizes and I'm most certainly not ... um ... ah ... sensitive.

SLOANE: No?

ED: I just don't give a monkey's fart.

SLOANE: It's a legitimate position.

ED: But I can deal with them same as you.

SLOANE: I'm glad to hear it.

ED: What's your opinion of the way these women carry on?

[Pause.]

SLOANE: I feel ... how would you say?

ED: Don't you think they're crude?

SLOANE: Occasionally. In a way.

ED: You never know where you are with half of them.

SLOANE: All the same it's necessary.

ED: Ah well you're talking of a different subject entirely. It's necessary. Occasionally. But it's got to be kept within bounds.

SLOANE: I'm with you there. All the way.

ED [*laughs.*] I've seen funny things happen and no mistake. The way these birds treat decent fellows. I hope you never get serious with one. What a life. Backache, headache or her mum told her never to when there's an 'R' in the month. [*Pause. Stares from window.*] How do you feel then?

SLOANE: On the main points we agree.

ED: Pack your bags.

SLOANE: Now?

ED: Immediate.

SLOANE: Will I get a rise in pay?

ED: A rise?

SLOANE: My new situation calls for it.

ED: You already had two.

SLOANE: They were tokens. I'd like you to upgrade my salary. How about a little car?

ED: That's a bit [*laughs*] of an unusual request en it?

SLOANE: You could manage it.

ED: It all costs money. I tell you what – I'll promise you one for Christmas.

SLOANE: This year?

ED: Or next year.

SLOANE: It's a date.

ED: You and me. That's the life, boy. Without doubt I'm glad I met you.

SLOANE: Are you?

ED: I see you had possibilities from the start. You had an air. [*Pause.*] A way with you.

SLOANE: Something about me.

ED: That's it. The perfect phrase. Personality.

SLOANE: Really?

ED: That's why I don't want you living here. Wicked waste. I'm going to tell you something. Prepare to raise your eyebrows.

SLOANE: Yes.

ED: She had a kiddy once.

SLOANE: Go on.

ED: That's right. On the wrong side of the blanket.

SLOANE: Your sister?

ED: I had a matie. What times we had. Fished. Swam. Rolled home pissed at two in the morning. We were innocent I tell you. Until she came on the scene. [*Pause.*] Teaching him things he shouldn't 'a done. It was over ... gone ... finished. [*Clears his throat.*] She got him to put her in the family way that's what I always maintain. Nothing was the same after. Not ever. A typical story.

SLOANE: Sad, though.

ED: Yes it is. I should say. Of course in a way of looking at it it laid the foundation of my success. I put him to one side which was difficult because he was alluring. I managed it though. Got a grip on myself. And finally become a success. [*Pause.*] That's no mean achievement, is it?

SLOANE: No.

ED: I'm proud.

SLOANE: Why shouldn't you be?

ED: I'm the possessor of two bank accounts. Respected in my own right. And all because I turned my back on him. Does that impress you?

SLOANE: It impresses me.

ED: I have no hesitation in saying that it was worth it. None.

[*The door opens slowly,* KEMP *stands waiting, staring in, listening.*]

SLOANE: What is it, Pop?

[KEMP *enters the room, listens, backs to the door. Stops.*]

KEMP: Is Ed there with you? [*Pause.*] Ed?

ED [*with emotion*]: Dad ... [*He goes to Kemp, puts an arm round his shoulder.*] What's come over you?

[KEMP *clutches Ed's coat, almost falls to his knees.* ED *supports him.*]

Don't kneel to me. I forgive you. I'm the one to kneel.

KEMP: No, no.

ED: Pat me on the head. Pronounce a blessing. Forgive and forget eh? I'm sorry and so are you.

KEMP: I want a word with you. [*He squints in Sloane's direction.*] Something to tell you.

ED: Words, Dad. A string of words. We're together again.
[*Pause.*]

KEMP: Tell him to go.

ED: Dad, what manners you got. How rude you've become.

KEMP: I got business to discuss.

SLOANE: He can speak in front of me, can't he Ed?

ED: I've no secrets from the boy.

KEMP: It's personal.

SLOANE: I'd like to stay Ed ... in case ...

KEMP: I'm not talking in front of him.

SLOANE: Pop ... [*laughs*] ... Ed will tell me afterwards. See if he doesn't.
[*Pause.*]

KEMP: I want to talk in private.
[ED *nods at the door*, SLOANE *shrugs.*]

SLOANE: Give in to him eh, Ed? [*Laughs.*] You know, Pop ... well ... [*Pause.*] O.K. have it your own way. [*Exits.*]

KEMP: Is he gone?

ED: What's the matter with you?

KEMP: That kid – who is he?

ED: He's lived here six months. Where have you been?

KEMP: What's his background?

ED: He's had a hard life, dad. Struggles. I have his word for it. An orphan deserves our sympathy.

KEMP: You like him?

ED: One of the best.
[*Silence.*]

KEMP: He comes to my room at night.

ED: He's being friendly.

KEMP: I can't get to sleep. He talks all the time.

ED: Give an example of his conversation. What does he talk about?

KEMP: Goes on and on. [*Pause.*] An' he makes things up about me.
[*He rolls up his sleeve, shows a bruise.*] Give me a thumping he did.

ED: When? [*Pause.*] Can't you remember?

KEMP: Before the weekend.

ED: Did you complain?

KEMP: I can't sleep for worry. He comes in and stands by my bed in the dark. In his pyjamas.

    [*Pause.*]

ED: I'll have a word with him.

KEMP [*lifts his trouser leg, pulls down his sock, shows an Elastoplast*]: He kicked me yesterday.

SLOANE [*appears in the doorway*]: There's a man outside wants a word with you, Pop. [*Pause.*] Urgent he says.

KEMP: Tell him to wait.

SLOANE: How long?

KEMP: Tell him to wait will you?

SLOANE: It's urgent.

KEMP: What's his name?

SLOANE: Grove. Or Greeves, I don't know.

KEMP: I don't know nobody called that.

SLOANE: He's on about the ... [*Pause*] ... whether he can dump something. You'd better see him.

KEMP [*swings round, tries to bring Sloane into focus*]: Oh ...

ED [*nods, winks*]: In a minute, boy.

    [SLOANE *closes door, exits.*

    Silence.]

ED: Dad ...

KEMP: He's in bed with her most nights. People talk. The woman from the shop spotted it first. Four months gone, she reckons.

    [*Pause.*]

ED: That's interesting.

KEMP: She's like the side of a house lately. It's not what she eats.

    [*Silence.*] Shall I tell you something else?

ED: Don't.

    [*Pause.*]

KEMP: He's got it in for me.

ED: ... don't – tell me anything –

KEMP: It's because I'm a witness. To his crime.

ED: What crime?

SLOANE [*enters carrying a suitcase. Puts it on the table. Opens it*]: Man en half creating, Pop. You ought to see to him. Jones or Greeves or whatever his name is. He's out the back.

ED: Go and see to him, Dad. [SLOANE *exits.*] See this man, Dad. Go on.

KEMP: There's no man there.

ED: How do you know? You haven't been and looked have you?

KEMP: It's a blind. [*Pause.*] Let me tell you about the boy.

ED: I don't want to hear. [*Pause.*] I'm surprised to find you spreading stories about the kiddy. Shocked. [SLOANE *returns with a pile of clothes.*] That's slander. You'll find yourself in queer street. [SLOANE *begins to pack the case.*] Apologize. [KEMP *shakes his head.*] The old man's got something to say to you, boy.

SLOANE [*smiling*]: Oh, yes?

ED [*to Kemp*]: Haven't you? [*Pause.*] Do you talk to him much? Is he talkative at night?

SLOANE: We have the odd confab sometimes. As I dawdle over my cocoa.

ED: You go and talk to that man, Dad. See if you can't get some sense into him. Dumping their old shit back of the house.

[*They watch* KEMP *exit.*]

[*Silence.*]

ED: He's just been putting in a complaint.

SLOANE: About me?

ED: I can't take it serious. He more or less said you ... well, in so many words he said ...

SLOANE: Really?

ED: Did you ever kick him?

SLOANE: Sometimes. He understands.

ED: An' he said ... Is she pregnant?

[*Pause.*]

SLOANE: Who?

ED: Deny it, boy. Convince me it isn't true.

SLOANE: Why?

ED: So's I – [*Pause.*] Lie to me.

SLOANE: Why should I?

ED: It's true then? Have you been messing with her?

SLOANE: She threw herself at me.
[*Silence.*]

ED: What a little whoreson you are you little whoreson. You are a little whoreson and no mistake. I'm put out my boy. Choked. [*Pause.*] What attracted you? Did she give trading stamps? You're like all these layabouts. Kiddies with no fixed abode.

SLOANE: I put up a fight.

ED: She had your cherry?

SLOANE: No.

ED: Not the first time?

SLOANE: No.

ED: Or the second?

SLOANE: No.

ED: Dare I go on?

SLOANE: It's my upbringing. Lack of training. No proper parental control.

ED: I'm sorry for you.

SLOANE: I'm glad of that. I wouldn't want to upset you.

ED: That does you credit.

SLOANE: You've no idea what I've been through. [*Pause.*] I prayed for guidance.

ED: I'd imagine the prayer for your situation would be hard to come by. [*Pause.*] Did you never think of locking your bedroom door?

SLOANE: She'd think I'd gone mad.

ED: Why didn't you come to me?

SLOANE: It's not the kind of thing I could –

ED: I'd've been your confessor.

SLOANE: You don't understand. It gathered momentum.

ED: You make her sound like a washing machine. When did you stop?

SLOANE: I haven't stopped.

ED: Not stopped yet?

SLOANE: Here, lay off.

ED: What a ruffian.

SLOANE: I got my feelings.

ED: You were stronger than her. Why didn't you put up a struggle?

SLOANE: I was worn out. I was overwrought. Nervous. On edge.
[*Pause.*]

ED: You're a constant source of amazement, boy, a never ending tale
of infamy. I'd hardly credit it. A kid of your age. Joy-riding in an
expensive car, a woman pregnant. My word, you're unforgivable.
[*Pause.*] I don't know whether I'm qualified to pronounce judgement.
[*Pause.*]

SLOANE: I'm easily led. I been dogged by bad luck.

ED: You've got to learn to live a decent life sometime, boy. I blame
the way you are on emotional shock. So perhaps [*Pause*] we ought
to give you another chance.

SLOANE: That's what I says.

ED: Are you confused?

SLOANE: I shouldn't be surprised.

ED: Never went to church? Correct me if I'm wrong.

SLOANE: You got it, Ed. Know me better than I know myself.

ED: Your youth pleads for leniency and, by God, I'm going to give
it. You're pure as the Lamb. Purer.

SLOANE: Am I forgiven?

ED: Will you reform?

SLOANE: I swear it ... Ed, look at me. Speak a few words of forgive-
ness. [*Pause.*] Pity me.

ED: I do.

SLOANE: Oh, Ed, you're a pal.

ED: Am I?

SLOANE: One of my mates.

ED: Is that a fact? How refreshing to hear you say it.

SLOANE: You've a generous nature.

ED: You could say that. I don't condemn out of hand like some. But
do me a favour – avoid the birds in future. That's what's been
your trouble.

SLOANE: It has.

ED: She's to blame.

SLOANE: I've no hesitation in saying that.

ED: Why conform to the standards of the cowshed? [*Pause.*] It's a
thing you grow out of. With me behind you, boy, you'll grow
out of it.

SLOANE: Thanks.

ED: Your hand on it. [SLOANE *holds out his hand.* ED *takes it, holds it for a long time, searches Sloane's face.*] I think you're a good boy. [*Silence.*] I knew there must be some reasonable explanation for your otherwise inexplicable conduct. I'll have a word with the old man.

SLOANE: Gets on my nerves he does.

ED: Has he been tormenting you?

SLOANE: I seriously consider leaving as a result of the way he carries on.

ED: Insults?

SLOANE: Shocking. Took a dislike to me he did the first time he saw me.

ED: Take no notice.

SLOANE: I can't make him out.

ED: Stubborn.

SLOANE: That's why I lose my temper.

ED: I sympathize.
    [*Pause.*]

SLOANE: He deserves a good belting.

ED: You may have something there.

SLOANE: I thought you might be against me for that.

ED: No.

SLOANE: I thought you might have an exaggerated respect for the elderly.

ED: Not me.

SLOANE: I've nothing against him. [*Pause.*] But he's lived so long he's more like an old bird than a bloke. How is it such a father has such a son? A mystery. [*Pause.*] Certainly is. [ED *pats his pockets.*] Out of fags again are you?

ED: Yes.

SLOANE: Give them up. Never be fully fit, Ed.
    [ED *smiles, shakes his head.*]

SLOANE: Are you going to the shop?

ED: Yes.

SLOANE: Good. [*Silence.*] How long will you be?

ED: Five minutes. Maybe ten.

SLOANE: Mmmn. [*Pause.*] Well, while you're gone I'm going to have a word with Pop.

ED: Good idea.

SLOANE: See if we can't find an area of agreement. I'll hold out the hand of friendship an' all that. I'm willing to forget the past. If he is. [*Silence.*] I'd better have a word with him. Call him.

ED: Me?

SLOANE: No good me asking him anything is there?

ED: I don't know whether we're speaking.

SLOANE: Gone funny again has he?

ED [*goes to the window, opens it, looks out. Calls*]: Dad! [*Pause.*] I want a word with you.

KEMP [*off*]: What's that?
    [*Pause.*]

ED: Me – me – I want to see you. [*He closes the window.*] He gets worse. [*Silence.*] Appeal to his better nature. Say you're upset. Wag your finger perhaps. I don't want you to be er, well ... at each other's throats, boy. Let's try ... and ... well be friends. [*Pause.*] I've the fullest confidence in your ability. [*Pause.*] Yes ... well I'm going out now. [*Pause.*] ... it's a funny business en it? ... I mean ... well, it's a ticklish problem. [*Pause.*] Yes ... it is. [*Exit.*]
    [SLOANE *sits, waits. Pause.* KEMP *enters.* SLOANE *rises, steps behind Kemp, bangs door.* KEMP *swings round, backs.*]

KEMP: Ed? [*Pause.*] Where's Ed?

SLOANE [*takes hold of Kemp's stick, pulls it away from him.* KEMP *struggles.* SLOANE *wrenches stick from his hand. Leads Kemp to a chair*]: Sit down, Pop. [KEMP *turns to go.* SLOANE *pushes him into the chair.*] Ed's not here. Gone for a walk. What you been saying about me?

KEMP: Nothing, sonnie.

SLOANE: What have you told him? What were you going to tell him?

KEMP: I – [*Pause.*] Business.

SLOANE: What kind of business? [*Kemp does not reply.*] Told him she's up the stick did you? [*No reply.*] Why did you tell him?

KEMP: He's her brother. He ought to know.

SLOANE: Fair enough.

KEMP: Got to know sometime.

SLOANE: Right. [*Silence.*] What else did you tell him? [KEMP *attempts to rise*, SLOANE *pushes him back.*] Did you say anything else? [KEMP *attempts to rise.*] Eh?

KEMP: No.

SLOANE: Were you going to?

KEMP: Yes.

SLOANE: Why?

KEMP: You're a criminal.

SLOANE: Who says I am?

KEMP: I know you are. You killed my old boss. I know it was you.

SLOANE: Your vision is faulty. You couldn't identify nobody now. So long after. You said so yourself.

KEMP: I got to go. [*Pause.*] I'm expecting delivery of a damson tree.

SLOANE: Sit still! [*Silence.*] How were you going to identify me?

KEMP: I don't have to. They got fingerprints.

SLOANE: Really?

KEMP: All over the shop.

SLOANE: It was an accident, Pop. I'm innocent. You don't know the circumstances ...

KEMP: Oh ... I know ...

SLOANE: But you don't.

KEMP: You murdered him.

SLOANE: Accidental death.

[*Pause.*]

KEMP: No, sonnie ... no.

SLOANE: You're pre-judging my case.

KEMP: You're bad.

SLOANE: I'm an orphan.

KEMP: Get away from me. Let me alone.

SLOANE [*puts the stick into Kemp's hand*]: I trust you, Pop. Listen. Keep quiet.

[*Silence.*]

It's like this see. One day I leave the Home. Stroll along. Sky blue. Fresh air. They'd found me a likeable permanent situation. Canteen facilities. Fortnight's paid holiday. Overtime? Time and a half after midnight. A staff dance each year. What more could one wish to devote one's life to? I certainly loved that place. The air round Twickenham was like wine. Then one day I take a trip to the old man's grave. Hic Jacets in profusion. Ashes to Ashes. Alas the fleeting. The sun was declining. A few press-ups on a tomb belonging to a family name of Cavaneagh, and I left the graveyard. I thumbs a lift from a geyser who promises me a bed. Gives me a bath. And a meal. Very friendly. All you could wish he was, a photographer. He shows me one or two experimental studies. An experience for the retina and no mistake. He wanted to photo me. For certain interesting features I had that he wanted the exclusive right of preserving. You know how it is. I didn't like to refuse. No harm in it I suppose. But then I got to thinking ... I knew a kid once called MacBride that happened to. Oh, yes ... so when I gets to think of this I decide I got to do something about it. And I gets up in the middle of the night looking for the film see. He has a lot of expensive equipment about in his studio see. Well it appears that he gets the wrong idea. Runs in. Gives a shout. And the long and the short of it is I loses my head which is a thing I never ought to a done with the worry of them photos an all. And I hits him. I hits him.

[*Pause.*]

He must have had a weak heart. Something like that I should imagine. Definitely should have seen his doctor before that. I wasn't to know was I? I'm not to blame.

[*Silence.*]

KEMP: He was healthy. Sound as a bell.

SLOANE: How do you know?

KEMP: He won cups for it. Looked after himself.

SLOANE: A weak heart.

KEMP: Weak heart my arse. You murdered him.

SLOANE: He fell.

KEMP: He was hit from behind.

SLOANE: I had no motive.

KEMP: The equipment.

SLOANE: I never touched it.

KEMP: You meant to.

SLOANE: Not me, Pop. [*Laughs.*] Oh, no.

KEMP: Liar ... lying little bugger. I knew what you was from the start.

[*Pause.*]

SLOANE: What are you going to do? Are you going to tell Ed? [*Kemp makes no reply.*] He won't believe you. [*Kemp makes no reply.*] He'll think you're raving.

KEMP: No ... you're finished. [*Attempts to rise.* SLOANE *pushes him back.* KEMP *raises his stick,* SLOANE *takes it from him.*]

SLOANE: You can't be trusted I see. I've lost faith in you. [*Throws the stick out of reach.*] Irresponsible. Can't give you offensive weapons.

KEMP: Ed will be back soon. [*Rises to go.*]

SLOANE: He will.

KEMP: I'm seeing him then.

SLOANE: Are you threatening me? Do you feel confident? Is that it? [*Stops. Clicks his tongue. Pause. Leans over and straightens Kemp's tie.*] Ed and me are going away. Let's have your word you'll forget it. [*Kemp does not reply.*] Pretend you never knew. Who was he? No relation. Hardly a friend. An employer. You won't bring him back by hanging me. [*Kemp does not reply.*] Where's your logic? Can I have a promise you'll keep your mouth shut?

KEMP: No.

[SLOANE *twists Kemp's ear.*]

KEMP: Ugh! aaah ...

SLOANE: You make me desperate. I've nothing to lose you see. One more chance, Pop. Are you going to give me away?

KEMP: I'll see the police.

SLOANE: You don't know what's good for you. [*He knocks Kemp behind the settee. Kicks him.*] You bring this on yourself. [*He kicks him again.*] All this could've been avoided. [KEMP *half-rises, collapses again. Pause.* SLOANE *kicks him gently with the toe of his boot.*] Eh then. Wake up. [*Pause.*] Wakey, wakey. [*Silence. He goes to the door and calls.*] Ed! [*Pause.*] Ed!

[KATH *comes to the door. He pushes her back.*]

KATH [*off*]: What's happened?

SLOANE: Where's Ed? Not you! I want Ed!

CURTAIN

[*Door slams off.*]

ED [*entering*]: What is it? [*Sees* KEMP *lying on the floor. Kneels.* SLOANE *enters, stands in the doorway.* KATH *tries to push past. Struggle.* SLOANE *gives up. She enters.*]

SLOANE: Some kind of attack.

ED: What did you do?

KATH: If only there were some spirits in the house. Unfortunately I don't drink myself. [*She loosens Kemp's collar.*] Somebody fetch his tablets.
 [*Nobody moves.*]

ED: He's reviving.

KATH: Speak to me, Dadda. [*Pause.*] He's been off his food for some time. [*Pause.*] He's cut his lip.

ED [*lifts Kemp*]: Can you walk?

KEMP [*muttering*]: Go away ...

ED: I'll carry you upstairs. [KATH *opens the door, stands in the passage.*] He'll be better in a bit. Is his bed made?

KATH: Yes. Let him lie still and he'll get his feelings back. [ED *exits with* KEMP. *Slowly.*] Mr Sloane, did you strike the Dadda?

SLOANE: Yes.

KATH: You admit it? Did he provoke you?

SLOANE: In a way.

KATH: What a thing to do. Hit an old man. It's not like you. You're usually so gentle.

SLOANE: He upset me.

KATH: He can be aggravating I know, but you shouldn't resort to violence, dear. [*Pause.*] Did he insult you? [*Pause.*] Was it a bad word? [*Pause.*] I don't expect you can tell me what it was. I'd blush.

SLOANE: I hit him several times.

KATH: You're exaggerating. You're not that type of young man. [*Pause.*] But don't do it again. Mamma wouldn't like it. [ED *enters.*] Is he all right?

ED: Yes.

KATH: I'll go up to him.

ED: He's asleep.

KATH: Sleeping off the excitement, is he? [*Exit.*]

ED [*taking Sloane aside*]: How hard did you hit him?

SLOANE: Not hard.

ED: You don't know your own strength, boy. Using him like a punchbag.

SLOANE: I've told you –

ED: He's dead.

SLOANE: Dead? His heart.

ED: Whatever it was it's murder, boy. You'll have some explaining to do. [*Lights a cigarette.* KATH *enters with a carpet sweeper, begins to sweep.*]

KATH: I'd take up a toffee, but he only gets them stuck round his teeth.

ED: You're not usually at a loss, surely? You can conjure up an idea or two.

KATH: Let Mr Sloane regain his composure, Ed. Let him collect his thoughts. Forget the incident. [*She goes upstage, begins to hum 'The Indian Love Call'.*]

[SLOANE *looks at Ed.* ED *smiles, shakes his head.*]

ED: That isn't possible, I'm afraid.

KATH: He meant no harm.

ED: What are you doing?

KATH: My housework. I mustn't neglect my chores.

ED: Can't you find a better time than this?

KATH: It's my usual time. Guess what's for dinner, Mr Sloane.

SLOANE: I'm not hungry.

ED: He doesn't want any.

KATH: Guess what mamma's prepared?

ED: Let him alone! All you think of is food. He'll be out of condition before long. As gross as you are.

KATH: Is he upset?

ED: Tell her.

SLOANE: I'm really upset.

ED: Turned your stomach, has it?

KATH: Will you feel better by this afternoon?

SLOANE: I don't know.

ED: He's worried.

KATH: The Dadda won't say anything, dear, if that's what's on your mind. He'll keep quiet. [*Pause.*] That new stove cooks excellent, Eddie.

ED: Does it?

KATH: Yes. I cooked a lovely egg yesterday. Mr Sloane had it. I think they ought to have put the grill different, though. I burned my hand.

ED: You want to look what you're doing.

KATH: It's awkwardly placed.

ED: Cooking with your eyes shut.

KATH [*Pause*]: You haven't guessed yet what's for dinner. Three guesses. Go on.

SLOANE: I don't know!

KATH: Chips.

SLOANE: Really?

KATH: And peas. And two eggs.

SLOANE: I don't give a sod what's for dinner!

ED: Don't use those tones to my relations, Sloane. Behave yourself for a change. [*Lights a cigarette.*]

SLOANE: Can I see you outside?

ED: What do you want to see me outside for?

SLOANE: To explain.

ED: There's nothing to explain.

SLOANE: How I came to be involved in this situation.

[KATH *puts the Ewbank away.*]

ED: I don't think that would be advisable. Some things will have to be sorted out. A check on your excesses is needed.

SLOANE: Are you sure he's –

ED: As forty dodos. I tried the usual methods of ascertaining; no heartbeats, no misting on my cigarette case. The finest legal brains in the country can't save you now.

[KATH *re-enters.*]

SLOANE: I feel sick.

KATH: It's the weather.

SLOANE: No.

KATH: Take a pill or something. I had some recommended me the other day. [*Opens a drawer, searches. She finds the tablets, shakes out two into her hand. Offers them to Sloane.*] Take them with a glass of water. Swallow them quick. They'll relieve the symptoms.

SLOANE: I don't want them! [*He knocks them from her hand.*] I don't want pills! [*Exits.*]

KATH: He's bad, isn't he?

ED: A very bad boy.

KATH [*picks up one tablet, searches for the others, gives up*]: Somebody will tread on them. That's the reason for these stains. Things get into the pile. The Dadda dropped a pickled walnut and trod it into the rug yesterday. If only we had a dog we wouldn't have so much bother.

ED: You're not having a dog.

KATH: Eddie, is Mr Sloane ill?

ED: He may be.

KATH: He looks pale. I wonder if he isn't sickening for something.

ED: He might have to go away. Something has happened which makes his presence required elsewhere.

KATH: Where?

ED: I'm not sure. Not for certain.

KATH: Is he in trouble?

ED: Dead trouble.

KATH: It was an accident surely?

ED: You know then?

KATH: The Dadda told me about it. Mr Sloane was unfortunate. He was joking, I expect.

ED: He never jokes.

KATH: No, he's remarkably devoid of a sense of fun. Dadda was full of it.

ED: I don't understand you.

KATH: Oh, I said he had no proof. I didn't waste my energy listening to him. Sometimes I think he makes up these things to frighten me. He ought to curb his imagination. [*Exits.*]

ED: I should have asked for references. I can see that now. The usual credentials would have avoided this. An attractive kid, so disarming, to – to tell me lies and –

KATH [*enters carrying a china figure*]: This shepherdess is a lovely piece of chinawork. She comes up like new when I give her a wash.

ED: Now?

KATH: The crack spoils it, though. I should have it mended professionally. [*Exit. Re-enters carrying large vase.*] Dadda gets up to some horrible pranks lately. Throwing things into my best vase now. The habits of the elderly are beyond the pale. [*She exits.* ED *sits on the settee.*]

ED: I must sort out my affairs and quick.

SLOANE [*enters, glances at Ed.* ED *does not look up.*]: Accept my apology, Ed. Sorry I was rude, but my nerves won't stand much more, I can tell you. [*He opens the suitcase. Begins to pack.*] She's got two of my shirts in the wash. Good ones. [*Opens sideboard, takes out cardigan.*] Can't risk asking her for them. [*Looks under sideboard, finds canvas shoes.*] She's been using this razor again. [*Holding up razor.*] I can tell. That's not hygienic, is it?

ED: What are you doing?

SLOANE: Packing.

ED: Why?

SLOANE: I'm going away.

ED: Where?

SLOANE: With you.

ED: No, boy. Not with me.

SLOANE: It was settled.

ED: I can't allow you to take up abode in Dulverton Mansions now.

SLOANE: Why not?

ED: What a fantastic person you are. You've committed a murder!

SLOANE: An accident.

ED: Murder.

SLOANE: Those pills were undermining his constitution. Ruining his health. He couldn't have lasted much longer.

ED: Attacking a defenceless old man!

SLOANE: He had his stick.

ED: He wasn't strong enough to use it.

SLOANE: I blame that on the pills. Who prescribed them?

ED: His doctor.

SLOANE: Reputable is he?

ED: He's on the register. What more do you want?

SLOANE: You'll find medical evidence agrees with my theory.

ED: The pills had nothing to do with it. You've no excuse. None.

SLOANE: What kind of life is it at his age?

ED: You've abused my trust.

SLOANE: I did him a service in a manner of speaking.

ED: You'll have to face the authorities.

SLOANE: Look, I'm facing no one.

ED: You've no choice.

SLOANE: I'll decide what choice I have.

ED: Get on the blower and call the law. We're finished.

SLOANE: You wouldn't put me away, would you?

ED: Without a qualm.

SLOANE: You're my friend.

ED: No friend of thugs.

SLOANE: He died of heart failure. You can't ruin my life. I'm impressionable. Think what the nick would do to me. I'd pick up criminal connexions.

ED: You already got criminal connexions.

SLOANE: Not as many as I would have.

ED: That's a point in your favour.

SLOANE: Give me a chance.

ED: You've had several.

SLOANE: One more.

ED: I've given you chances. Expected you to behave like a civilized human being.

SLOANE: Say he fell downstairs.

ED: What kind of a person does that make me?

SLOANE: A loyal friend.

ED: You'll get me six months. More than that. Depends on the judge.

SLOANE: What a legal system. Say he fell.

ED: Aiding and abetting.

SLOANE: Fake the evidence.

ED: You're completely without morals, boy. I hadn't realized how depraved you were. You murder my father. Now you ask me to help you evade Justice. Is that where my liberal principles have brought me?

SLOANE: You've got no principles.

ED: No principles? Oh, you really have upset me now. Why am I interested in your welfare? Why did I give you a job? Why do thinking men everywhere show young boys the strait and narrow? Flash cheque-books when delinquency is mentioned? Support the Scout-movement? Principles, boy, bleeding principles. And don't you dare say otherwise or you'll land in serious trouble.

SLOANE: Are you going to help me?

ED: No.

SLOANE: We must find a basis for agreement.

ED: There can be no agreement. I'm a citizen of this country. My duty is clear. You must accept responsibility for your actions.

SLOANE [sits beside Ed. Lays a hand on his knee]: I accept responsibility.

ED: Do you?

SLOANE: Fully.

ED: Good. Remove that hand will you?

SLOANE: Certainly.

ED: What you just said about no principles – That's really upset me. Straight. Really upset me.

SLOANE: Sorry, Eddie, sorry.

ED: One thing I wanted to give you – my principles. Oh, I'm disillusioned. I feel I'm doing no good at all.

SLOANE: I'm very bad. Only you can help me on the road to a useful life. [Pause.] A couple of years ago I met a man similar to yourself. Same outlook on life. A dead ringer for you as far as physique went. He was an expert on the adolescent male body. He'd completed an exhaustive study of his subject before I met him. During the course of one magical night he talked to me of his principles – offered me a job if I would accept them. Like a fool I turned him down. What an opportunity I lost, Ed. If you were to make the same demands I'd answer loudly in the affirmative.

   [Pause.]

ED: You mean that?

SLOANE: In future you'd have nothing to complain of.

ED: You really mean what you say?

SLOANE: Let me live with you. I'd wear my jeans out in your service. Cook for you.

ED: I eat out.

SLOANE: Bring you your tea in bed.

ED: Only women drink tea in bed.

SLOANE: You bring me my tea in bed then. Any arrangement you fancy.

[KATH *screams loudly offstage. Pause. Screams again nearer. She enters.*]

KATH: Ed!

ED: Come here.

KATH: Ed, I must – [ED *takes her arm, she pulls back.*] It's Dadda – he's dead. Come quick.

ED: Sit down. [*To Sloane.*] Bring the car round. We'll fetch the doctor.

KATH: Eddie, he's dead.

ED: I know. We know. Didn't want to upset you.

[SLOANE *exits.*]

KATH: I can't believe he's dead. He was in perfect health.

ED: He was ill.

KATH: Was he?

ED: You told me he was.

KATH: I didn't believe it. I only took his word for it.

ED: Didn't he say he was ill?

KATH: Often. I took no notice. You know how he is. I thought he was having me on.

ED: He was telling the truth.

KATH [*begins to sniff*]: Poor Dadda. How he must have suffered. I'm truly ashamed of myself. [*She wipes her eyes on her apron.*] It's all the health scheme's fault. Will I have to send his pension book in?

ED: Yes.

KATH: I thought I would.

ED: Now listen –

KATH: Eddie.

ED: – carefully to what I say. [*He passes a hand across his mouth.*] When the doctor comes what are you going to tell him?

KATH: Me?

ED: He'll want to know.

KATH: I'll say Dadda had an attack. He passed away sudden.

224

ED: What about the cuts on his face?

KATH: He was rude to Mr Sloane, Eddie. Provoked him.

ED: They won't wear that.

KATH: Won't they? [*Pause.*] I shall never get in my black. I've put on weight since we buried mamma.

ED: They'll get the boy for murder.

KATH: They'd never do that would they?

ED: They'll hang him.

[*Pause.*]

KATH: Hang him?

ED: They might. I'm not sure. I get confused by the changes in the law.

KATH: Is it bad?

ED: Awful. You wouldn't see him again. You understand?

KATH: The Dadda was rude. He said a rude word about me.

ED: That's no excuse in the eyes of the law. You must say he fell downstairs.

KATH: I couldn't.

ED: I would never suggest deceiving the authorities under normal circumstances. But we have ourselves to think of. I'm in a funny position. I pay his wages. That's a tricky situation.

KATH: Is it?

ED: I'm compromised. My hands are tied. If the situation was different I might say something. Depend on it.

KATH: Wouldn't they make an exception? If we gave him a good character?

ED: He hasn't got a good character.

KATH: We could say he had.

ED: That would be perjury.

KATH: He has nice manners when he wants. I've seen them.

ED: I feel bad doing this. You see the position? He went too far. But he did it out of respect for you. That's some consideration.

KATH: He did it out of love for me?

ED: You should be grateful. No doubt of that. [*Pause.*] Do you polish that lino?

KATH: Eh?

ED: On the stairs?

KATH: No, never. I have to think of the Dadda.

ED: Go and polish them.

KATH: Doctor will be cross.

ED: Let him be.

KATH: He'll think I'm silly. He'll think I caused Dadda's fall.

ED: It doesn't matter as long as he thinks it was an accident.

KATH [*bites her lip, considers*]: Shall I put Dadda's new shoes on him?

ED: Now you're using your initiative. Slippy are they?

KATH: He only wore them once.

ED: Good girl.

[SLOANE *enters.*]

SLOANE: Ready? Come on then.

[ED *nods to Kath, waiting. She looks from one to the other. Notices the case.*]

KATH: Why is he taking his case?

ED: He's coming with me. He can't stay here.

KATH: Why not?

ED: They'll suspect.

[*Pause.*]

KATH: When is he coming back?

ED: Day after next.

KATH: He doesn't need that big case. [*She exits.*]

ED: Get in the car, boy.

SLOANE: How about my shirts?

ED: I'll see about buying a couple.

KATH [*off*]: Why is he taking his clothes?

ED: What are you on about?

[KATH *returns.*]

KATH: I've just checked. They aren't in the laundry basket.

ED: Snooping around. Don't you trust me?

KATH: You're taking him away.

SLOANE: We thought I ought to live in.

KATH: Do you want to leave?

SLOANE: I'll be back when this has blown over.

KATH: Why are you leaving your mamma? There's no need for him to go away, Eddie. Doctor knows he lives here.

ED: He'll instigate proceedings.

KATH: Doctors don't do that. He wants to stay.

ED: Ask him. [*To Sloane.*] Do you want to stay?

SLOANE: No.

ED: The question is answered.

KATH: Ed –

ED: Send a wire –

KATH: I've something to tell you.

[*She lifts her apron. Shyly.*]

I've a bun in the oven.

ED: You've a whole bloody baker's shop in the oven from the look of that.

KATH: Mr Sloane was nice to me. Aren't you shocked?

ED: No, it's what I expect of you.

KATH: Aren't you angry with Mr Sloane?

ED: I'm angry with you.

KATH: Are you?

ED: Mr Sloane's already explained.

KATH: What did he explain?

ED: How you carried on.

KATH: I didn't carry on! What a wicked thing to say.

ED: Seducing him.

KATH: Did he say that?

ED: Told me the grisly details.

[*Silence.*]

KATH: Mr Sloane, dear, take back your locket.

ED: What locket?

KATH: He gave me a locket. [*She takes off the locket.* SLOANE *attempts to take it.*] I don't believe he'd take it if you weren't here, Ed. [*She puts the locket back. To Sloane.*] How could you behave so bad. Accusing me of seducing you.

SLOANE: But you did!

KATH: That's neither here nor there. Using expressions like that. Making yourself cheap. [SLOANE *turns to the suitcase.*] I see the truth of the matter. He's been at you. Isn't that like him?

ED: He wants to come with me.

KATH: Let him decide for himself.

ED: He's got problems. Needs a man's hand on his shoulder.

KATH: I'm afraid you're unduly influencing him.

ED: You've been found out.

KATH: Found out?

ED: Exposed.

KATH: Rubbish!

ED: Making a spectacle of yourself. Corrupting a kid young enough to be your son.

KATH: He loves me.

ED: Prove it.

KATH: A woman knows when she's loved.

ED: I blame myself for letting him stay. Knowing your character.

KATH: My character will stand analysis.

ED: You're older than him.

KATH: I'm a benign influence. A source of good.

ED: You spoil him.

KATH: Who tucks him up at night? And he likes my cooking. He won't deny that.

ED: No.

KATH: See I'm right.

ED: I can't argue with you.

KATH: You can't.

ED: You don't make sense.

KATH: I do.

ED: You have no logical train of thought.

KATH: What is that?

ED: No power of argument.

KATH: I keep his trousers pressed nice. He's been smarter since I knew him.

ED: He's lost with you.

KATH: I gave him everything.

ED: No backbone. Spineless.

KATH: He's lovely with me. Charming little baby he is.

ED: No, he's soft. You softened him up.

KATH: I gave him three meals a day. Porridge for breakfast. Meat and two veg for dinner. A fry for tea. And cheese for supper. What more could he want?

ED: Freedom.

KATH: He's free with me.

ED: You're immoral.

KATH: It's natural.

ED: He's clean-living by nature; that's every man's right.

KATH: What are you going to give him?

ED: The world.

KATH [*comes round the case, looks in*]: The state of this case. Mr Sloane, dear, you can't even pack. See how he needs me in the smallest things? Can't manage without a woman.

ED: Let him try.

KATH: Women are necessary.

ED: Granted.

KATH: Where's your argument?

ED: In limited doses.

KATH: You're silly, Eddie, silly ...

ED: Let him choose. Let's have it in black and white, boy.

SLOANE: I'm going with Ed.

[ED *nods, smacks Sloane's shoulder, laughs.*]

KATH: Is it the colour of the curtains in your room?

SLOANE: No.

KATH: Is it because I'm pregnant?

SLOANE: No. Better opportunities. A new life.

KATH: You vowed you loved me.

SLOANE: Never for a second.

KATH: I was kind to you.

SLOANE: Yes.

KATH: Are you grateful?

SLOANE: I paid.

KATH: I paid too. Baby on the way. Reputation ruined.

SLOANE: You had no reputation.

KATH: Is that what he's taught you?

ED: I taught him nothing. He was innocent until you got your maulers on to him.

KATH: He'd packed the experience of a lifetime into a few short years.

ED: Pure in heart he was. He wouldn't know where to put it.

KATH: I attracted him instantly.

ED: You couldn't attract a blind man.

229

KATH: He wanted to marry me.

ED: What a bride!

KATH: We were to ask your consent.

ED: Look in the glass, lady. Let's enjoy a laugh. [*He takes her to the mirror.*] What do you see?

KATH: Me.

ED: What are you?

KATH: My hair is nice. Natural. I'm mature, but still able to command a certain appeal.

ED: You look like death!

[*She shakes him off. He drags her back to the mirror.*]

ED: Flabby mouth. Wrinkled neck. Puffy hands.

KATH: It's baby coming.

ED: Sagging tits. You cradle-snatcher.

KATH: He said I was a Venus. I held him in my arms.

ED: What a martyrdom!

KATH: He wanted for nothing. I loved him sincerely.

ED: Your appetite appalled him.

KATH: I loved him.

ED: Insatiable.

KATH [*to Sloane*]: Baby, my little boy ...

ED: He aches at every organ.

KATH: ... mamma forgives you.

ED: What have you to offer? You're fat and the crows-feet under your eyes would make you an object of terror. Pack it in, I tell you. Sawdust up to the navel! You've nothing to lure any man.

KATH: Is that the truth, Mr Sloane?

SLOANE: More or less.

KATH: Why didn't you tell me?

ED: How could he tell you? You showed him the gate of Hell every night. He abandoned Hope when he entered there.

KATH [*snaps the suitcase shut*]: Mr Sloane, I believed you were a good boy. I find you've deceived me.

SLOANE: You deceived yourself.

KATH: Perhaps. [*She holds out her hand.*] Kiss my hand, dear, in the manner of the theatre. [*He kisses her hand.*] I shall cry. [*She feels for a handkerchief.*]

ED: On with the waterworks.

KATH: I'm losing you for ever.

SLOANE: I'll pop round.

KATH: I'll not be able to bear it.

SLOANE: You'll have the baby.

KATH: I shall die of it, I'm sure.

ED: What a cruel performance you're giving. Like an old tart grinding to her climax.

[SLOANE *kisses Kath's cheek.*]

KATH: Baby ... [*She holds him close. Looks at Ed over Sloane's shoulder.*] Before you go, Mr Sloane, we must straighten things out. The Dadda's death was a blow to me.

SLOANE [*releases her*]: Ed can vouch for me. You can support his story.

KATH: What story?

SLOANE: The old man fell downstairs.

KATH: I shall never under any circumstances allow anyone to perjure me. It was murder.

[*Pause.* SLOANE *releases her. Pause.*]

SLOANE: He was ill.

KATH: Ah, you know as well as I he was perfectly healthy this morning.

SLOANE: Ed will give me an alibi.

KATH: He wasn't there, dear. Respect the truth always. It's the least you can do under the circumstances.

SLOANE: He'll say he was a witness.

KATH: It's not in accordance with my ideas of morality.

SLOANE: Look – mamma ... see –

KATH: When doctor comes he'll want to know things. Are you asking me to deceive our G.P.? He's an extremely able man. He'll notice discrepancies. And then where will we be? He'd make his report and mamma would be behind bars. I'm sure that isn't your idea. Is it?

SLOANE: Ed is supporting me.

KATH: He must decide for himself. I won't practise a falsehood.

SLOANE: You're not going back on your word?

KATH: You know how I go to pieces under cross-examination.

SLOANE: Make an effort.

KATH: Who for?

SLOANE: Me.

KATH: You won't be here.

SLOANE: I'll come and see you.

KATH: No. Call me names if you wish, but I won't tell stories. I'm a firm believer in truth.

ED: Look ... Kathy – Say you were out when the accident occurred.

KATH: No.

ED: Down the shops.

KATH: But I wasn't.

ED: You didn't see him fall.

KATH: I would have heard him.

ED: Say you were out of range.

KATH: No.

ED: Forget the whole business.

KATH: No.

ED: Go to the police then. What will you achieve? Nothing. This boy was carried away by the exuberance of youth. He's under age.

KATH [hands the suitcase to Ed]: You struck the Dadda down in cold blood, Mr Sloane. In the course of conversations before his death he told me one or two things of interest.

SLOANE: Concerning whom?

KATH: We talked only of you. I could hardly give credence to the report of your crimes. I didn't believe the old man. I'm paid for it now.

ED: The last word, eh? Using your whore's prerogative?

KATH: Stay with me.

SLOANE: No.

KATH: Hold me tight again.

SLOANE: No.

KATH: There's no need to go away, dear. Don't make me unhappy.

SLOANE: I'm going with Ed.

KATH: I was never subtle, Mr Sloane ... If you go with Eddie I'll tell the police.

SLOANE: If I stay here he'll do the same.

ED: It's what is called a dilemma, boy. You are on the horns of it.
   [Silence.]

232

KATH: You see how things are, Mr Sloane?
  [SLOANE *smacks her face, she screams.*]
ED: What are you doing?
SLOANE: Leave her to me.
KATH: Don't attempt to threaten me.
ED: There's no suggestion of threats.
KATH: What's he doing then?
ED: Let her alone, boy.
SLOANE: Keep out of this! [ED *lays a hand on Sloane's shoulder, tries to pull him away from Kath.* SLOANE *turns, shoves Ed from him.*] Did you hear what I said? Keep out of it!
ED: Don't be violent. No violence at any cost. [SLOANE *gets Kath into a corner; struggles with her.*] What's this exhibition for? This is gratuitous violence. Give over both of you!
SLOANE [*shakes Kath*]: Support me, you mare! Support me!
KATH: Make him stop! I shall be sick. He's upsetting my insides.
ED [*runs round*]: What did you want to provoke him for?
  [SLOANE *shakes Kath harder. She screams.*]
KATH: My teeth! [*She claps a hand over her mouth.*] My teeth. [SLOANE *flings her from him. She crawls round the floor searching.*] He's broke my teeth! Where are they?
ED: Expensive equipment gone west now see? I'm annoyed with you, boy. Seriously annoyed. Giving us the benefit of your pauperism. Is this what we listen to the Week's Good Cause for? A lot of vicars and actresses making appeals for cash gifts to raise hooligans who can't control themselves? I'd've given my cheque to the anti-Jewish League if I'd known.
KATH [*reaching under the settee*]: I'll still forgive and forget.
ED: Coming in here as a lodger. Raised in a charity home. The lack of common courtesy in some people is appalling.
SLOANE: She's won! The bitch has won!
  [*He grips Ed's arm.* ED *shrugs him away.*]
ED: We'll discuss the matter.
SLOANE: We need action not discussion. Persuade her. Cut her throat, but persuade her!
ED: Don't use that tone of voice to me, boy. I won't be dictated to. [*Pause.*] Perhaps we can share you.

SLOANE: Deal with her.

ED: We'll think of something.

SLOANE: She must be primed. Get her evidence correct.

ED: Don't worry. I'm in perfect control of the situation.

SLOANE: You're in control of nothing! Where are your influential friends? Ring them, we need protection.

KATH: It's his nerves. He doesn't know what he's doing.

ED: Put your teeth in will you? Sitting there with them in your hand.

KATH: He's broke them.

ED: They're only chipped. Go on, turn your back.

KATH [*puts her teeth in*]: What are we going to do, Eddie?

ED: Stand up. We can't conduct a serious discussion from that position.

KATH: Help me up, Mr Sloane. Thank you, baby. See, Ed, he hasn't lost respect for me.

ED: An arrangement to suit all tastes. That is what's needed.

KATH: I don't want to lose my baby.

ED: You won't lose him.

KATH: But –

ED [*holds up a hand*]: What are your main requirements? I take it there's no question of making an honest woman of you? You don't demand the supreme sacrifice?

SLOANE: I'm not marrying her!

ED: Calm down will you?

SLOANE: Remember our agreement.

ED: I'm keeping it in mind, boy.

SLOANE: Don't saddle me with her for life.

KATH: He's close to tears. Isn't he sweet?

ED: Yes, he's definitely attractive in adversity. Really, boy, what with one thing and another ... I warned you against women, didn't I? They land you in impossible predicaments of this nature.

SLOANE: You can solve it, Ed.

ED: You believe that, do you? I hope so. Marriage is a non-starter then?

KATH: He's led me on.

ED: Are you repentant now? Truly ashamed of yourself?

SLOANE: I am.

ED: You aren't going to press your claims are you? Even if he thee worshipped with his body, his mind would be elsewhere. And a wife cannot testify against her husband.

KATH: Can't she?

ED: No, a minor point.

KATH: I don't mind about marriage as long as he doesn't leave me.

ED: Fine. [*Pause.*] I think, boy, you'd better go and wait in the car. Keep the engine running. I won't be long. I want a private talk with my sister.

SLOANE: Is it going to be O.K.?

ED: Well ... perhaps.

SLOANE: I'll be grateful.

ED: Will you?

SLOANE: Eternally.

ED: Not eternally, boy. Just a few years. [*He pats Sloane on the shoulder.* SLOANE *exits.*] What will the story be?

KATH: Like you said – he fell downstairs.

ED: That will explain the cuts and bruises. You'd better say you were out. Stick to that. You know nothing. I'll manage the doctor.

KATH: Yes, Ed.

ED: Can I trust you?

KATH: Yes.

ED: Then let's have no more threats. You'll support him?

KATH: As long as he stays here.

ED: You've had him six months; I'll have him the next six. I'm not robbing you of him permanently.

KATH: Aren't you?

ED: No question of it. [*Pause.*] As long as you're prepared to accept the idea of partnership.

KATH: For how long?

ED: As long as the agreement lasts.

KATH: How long is that?

ED: By the half-year.

KATH: That's too long, dear. I get so lonely.

ED: I've got no objections if he visits you from time to time. Briefly. We could put it in the contract. Fair enough?

KATH: Yes.

ED: I'd bring him over myself in the car. Now, you'll be more or less out of action for the next three months. So shall we say till next August? Agreed?

KATH: Perfect, Eddie. It's very clever of you to have thought of such a lovely idea!

ED: Put it down to my experience at the conference table.
    [*Car sounds off.*]

KATH: Can he be present at the birth of his child?

ED: You're not turning him into a mid-wife.

KATH: It deepens the relationship if the father is there.

ED: It's all any reasonable child can expect if the dad is present at the conception. Let's hear no more of it. Give me that locket.

KATH: It was his present to me.

ED: You'll get it back in March. [*She hands him the locket. He puts it on.*] And behave yourself in future. I'm not having you pregnant every year. I'll have a word with him about it. [*He kisses her cheek, pats her bottom.*] Be a good girl.

KATH: Yes, Ed.

ED: Well, it's been a pleasant morning. See you later. [*He exits. The front door slams. KATH goes to the sideboard and rummages in drawer; takes out a sweet, unwraps it and puts it into her mouth. Sits on settee.*]

CURTAIN

*Two other volumes in Penguin Plays
are described on the
following pages*

RHINOCEROS · THE CHAIRS
THE LESSON

Eugène Ionesco

Twelve years ago the plays of Ionesco, a Rumanian by origin, were being acted in Left Bank theatres in Paris and very poorly attended. Now regarded as one of the most important writers of the *avant-garde*, he has a world-wide reputation and his plays are translated into many languages.

Sir Laurence Olivier took the leading part in *Rhinoceros* when it was produced in London in 1960 at the Royal Court Theatre, where *The Chairs* had already been performed in 1957. *The Lesson* was produced at the London's Arts Theatre Club in 1955.

Ionesco himself is hesitant to theorize about his work or assess its importance. His plays represent, he says, 'a mood and not an ideology, an impulse not a programme'. The substance of the world seems to vary, for him, between solidity and illusory unreality, and he projects on to the stage, with a strangely universal effect of comedy, his own internal conflict.

His influence can be traced among the youngest generation of English playwrights.

Now in one volume

EPITAPH FOR GEORGE DILLON

John Osborne and Anthony Creighton

Epitaph for George Dillon was written by John Osborne in collaboration with Anthony Creighton before *Look Back in Anger*, the play which brought him to fame. Dillon himself is an earlier, more complex Jimmy Porter, viewed perhaps with a more critical eye than his successor. The play has been called 'the most wholly satisfactory of the plays Osborne has worked on'.

THE KITCHEN

Arnold Wesker

In *The Kitchen* Arnold Wesker presents, as a microcosm of the world, the stifling hell of an overcrowded restaurant kitchen. The bustle of the waitresses, the frenzy of the cook, lead tensely to an unexpected climax of horror and violence. *The Kitchen* was first presented at the Royal Court in 1959 and later filmed.

THE HAMLET OF STEPNEY GREEN

Bernard Kops

The Hamlet of Stepney Green was Bernard Kops's first play and one of the most highly praised of the dramas which followed on *Look Back in Anger*. The story of a twentieth-century Hamlet, a dreamer with ambitions as a crooner, it draws on Jewish traditions to produce an unaffected poetic folk-drama.

For a complete list of books available please write to Penguin Books whose address can be found on the back of the title page